Selections from the *Alpine Journal*
compiled and introduced
by Walt Unsworth

AND GLACIERS

The Mountaineers
Seattle

THE MOUNTAINEERS: Organized 1906
".... to explore, study, preserve, and enjoy
the natural beauty of the Northwest."

Published by The Mountaineers
715 Pike Street, Seattle, Washington 98101
ISBN 0-89886-044-X
Library of Congress Catalog Card No. 81-83778

Published simultaneously:
    In Canada, by Douglas & McIntyre Ltd.,
        1615 Venables Street, Vancouver, British Columbia V5L 2H1
    In United Kingdom, by Allen Lane, Penguin Books Ltd.,
        536 King's Road, London SW10 OUH

Manufactured in the United States of America

PEAKS, PASSES

 *Contents*

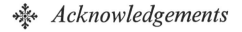 *Acknowledgements*

My thanks are due to the President and Committee of the Alpine Club for their permission to use material from the *Journal*. In particular I would like to acknowledge the advice and encouragement received from Peter Lloyd, Harry Archer, Edward Pyatt and Robin McCall when the project was first mooted.

I would also like to thank the various authors and copyright holders who have allowed me to reprint their work and I apologize to those whom I have been unable to trace.

Finally, my thanks are due to the photographers whose names appear in the List of Plates.

Walt Unsworth
Milnthorpe, Cumbria
1980

❄ *List of Plates*

 *Introduction*

The idea of a Club composed of amiable eccentrics who spent their holidays trying to climb the most dangerous peaks in the Alps could only have been conceived in Victorian Britain. Even in that most clubbable of societies, the infant Alpine Club had an uncertain birth for, when the first meeting was called in December 1857, only eleven people turned up. Things got better from then on, though; it quickly became a lusty infant and rapidly achieved maturity.

There was no Tradesmen's Entrance in those early days, nor for many years after. The Club was founded by the affluent, highly literate middle-classes. These were the sort of people who not only read books but wrote them too, so it was natural that they should want to put their adventures and experiences into print – and, indeed, it must be said that the sharing of information about the largely unknown mountain regions of the world was one of the aims of the Club's founders.

Consequently, a year after the Club was formed William Longman, publisher and member, brought out a collection of writings under the title *Peaks, Passes and Glaciers*. It was edited by John Ball, the Club President, who suggested in his Preface that the volume might find a wider readership than the Club itself – a statement amply justified by the need for a second edition six weeks later. Third, fourth and fifth editions followed during the next few months.

Popular though the first book had proved, the experiment wasn't repeated until 1862 when a two-volume Second Series, again called *Peaks, Passes and Glaciers*, was published. In a way it was a stop-gap, catching up on important unpublished papers. What was really required was a regular journal and so in the following year, 1863, the first volume of the *Alpine Journal* appeared. It has appeared regularly ever since, though 'regularly' has had a flexible interpretation over the years.

There are now over eighty substantial volumes, and since it has always concerned itself with the whole spectrum of world mountaineering, the collection forms a unique history of the sport. In the *AJ*, as it is affectionately known, one can find first-hand accounts of most of the major mountaineering adventures, not to mention more literary pieces, biographies – and some pungent editorial criticism from time to time! So, historical considerations apart, the collection is a repository of some very fine mountaineering stories.

It seemed to me a pity that so many good stories should remain hidden away in old volumes, often quoted but never reproduced, when the interest in mountains and climbing has never been greater than it is today. The reasons are understandable, of course – complete sets of the *AJ* are not all that common and, quite apart from the expense, those eighty-odd volumes take up a lot of shelf space. Furthermore, I doubt whether there are many public libraries outside the major cities which have a set available. Hence the present anthology, unashamedly issued under the old title of *Peaks, Passes and Glaciers*.

Naturally, the extracts I have chosen represent only a tiny fraction of the whole; and though I have divided them roughly into three periods: Early Days, Middle Years and Maturity, they are not meant to be a history of mountaineering. They are simply some of the highlights along the way, chosen because they have a good tale to tell or because they are intrinsically interesting.

Some of the articles are reproduced in their entirety, but others are taken from longer pieces. In every case, however, the material is substantially as the author wrote it – editing has been kept to a minimum so as not to detract from the original flavour. For the benefit of those readers who would like to know more about the various authors and the background to the articles, I have added a list of notes at the back of the book.

PART ONE
EARLY DAYS

Edward Whymper

1 ❄ *The Ascent of Mont Pelvoux*

So far as I have been able to learn, attempts to ascend the Mont Pelvoux have not been numerous. The first on record is that of the party of French engineers headed by Captain (now General) Durand, who made it to take some observations for the great French map. They mounted from the side of the Val Sapenière, got to the top of the second peak in height and remained somewhere on it, lodged in a tent, for several days, at a height of 3,933 mètres. They took numerous porters to carry wood for fires, and erected a large cairn of stones on the summit, which has caused this peak to take the name of Pic de la Pyramide.

In 1859, M. Senon essayed to reach the highest summit, but only got to the edge of the plateau of snow, at the point from which the small glacier commences to stream; he was, I believe, compelled to return by bad weather. And, in the middle of August, 1860, Messrs. Bonney and William Matthews tried it from the same side, but were likewise defeated by the weather. They passed two nights under a fallen rock which bears the imposing name of 'Cabane des Bergers de Provence', but is only a boulder with a hole under it, and on the third day they were tempted upwards by an appearance of fine weather. It again changed when they got up to 10,430 feet; clouds surrounded the party, and their local guide refused to advance, so they were reluctantly compelled to return, and shortly afterwards left the district.

I started for this unknown region early in July 1861, and, with knapsack on back and ice-axe in hand, landed at Havre, where my appearance on the quay created a slight sensation. *'Sacre!'* muttered a bloated gendarme, nudging his comrade, *'voici un grand militaire.'* *'Ah, oui!'* replied he, thinking himself wiser than his neighbour, *'un sapeur sans doute.'* Here I got my mountain gear passed the custom-house, and sent it direct to La Bessée, whilst I started to make a complete circuit of the French coast. Four weeks later, at Nismes, I found myself completely collapsed by the heat, which was 94° in the shade, and thought it was more prudent to break than to continue my programme; so I took the night train to Grenoble.

I arrived at Grenoble early in the morning, and found that all the places in the courrier to Briançon were, as usual, engaged two days beforehand; but this was of little consequence, as I got a place in the diligence to Bourg d'Oysans. Here I found my friend Macdonald, and learnt that he was going to try the Pelvoux in about ten days. As I was at that moment *en route* for the mountain, I informed him of my intention, and we agreed to meet at La Bessée on the 3rd of August. In five minutes more I was perched in the banquette, and had another dreary night on the road: we took nearly eight hours to accomplish less than thirty miles.

At five minutes to 5 I started from Bourg d'Oysans and got into Briançon at 6; deducting stoppages, it was ten hours' walking [about 38½ miles – *Editor*].

The next day I walked over to La Bessée and sought Jean Reynaud, the worthy *agent voyer* of the district, whose acquaintance I had formed in the previous autumn. He had received the packet in which were the necessaries for our expedition, and nothing prevented our starting at once but the absence of Macdonald and the want of a bâton. Reynaud suggested a visit to the postmaster, who possessed a bâton of local celebrity. Down we went, but the bureau was closed; we hallooed through the slits, but no answer. At last this official was discovered endeavouring (and with very fair success) to make himself intoxicated. He was just able to ejaculate, 'La France, c'est la première nation du monde,' a phrase used by a Frenchman when in a state that a Briton begins to shout, 'We won't go home till morning' – national glory being uppermost in the thoughts of one, and home in those of the other. The bâton was produced, but when I saw it my heart sank within me. Imagine a branch of a young oak, about five feet long and three inches thick, gnarled, and twisted in several directions, terminated by a point more like the end of Goliath's spear than a rational bâton – it was, in fact, ten inches long. 'Monsieur,' said the *chef de bureau*, as he presented it, '*la France, c'est la première nation du monde, par ses'* – he stuck. '*Bâtons?*' I suggested. '*Oui, oui, Monsieur, par ses bâtons, par ses – ses,*' and here he couldn't get on at all. But as I looked at this young limb, I thought of my own, and asked if there really was not a lighter weapon in the village. Reynaud, who knew everything about everybody, said there was not; so there was no help for it, and off we went, leaving the official staggering in the road, muttering, '*La France, c'est la première nation du monde.*'

The morning of the 3rd of August dawned, but no Macdonald appeared, so we were obliged to start without him. We left La Bessée at twenty minutes to 11, the party consisting of Jean Reynaud, myself, and a porter – Jean Casimir Giraud, *dit* Petits Clous, the shoemaker of the place. An hour and a half's smart walking took us to La Ville de Val Louise, our hearts being gladdened on the way by the glorious peaks of Pelvoux shining out without a cloud around them. We entered La Ville, where we provisioned ourselves. Reynaud kindly volunteered to look after the commissariat, and I found to my annoyance, when we were about to start, that I had given tacit consent to a young wine-cask being carried with us, which was a great nuisance from the commencement. One man tried to carry it, and then another, but it was excessively awkward to handle; so at last it was slung on one of our bâtons, and carried between two, which gave our party the appearance of a mechanical diagram to illustrate the uses of levers.

At 'La Ville' the Val Louise splits into two branches, the Val d'Entraigues on the left, and the Vallon d'Alefred on the right; our route was up the latter, and we moved steadily forwards to the village of La Pisse, where I was told lived Pierre Sémiond, who was reputed to know more about the Pelvoux than any other man. He looked an honest fellow, but unfortunately he could not come, and recommended his brother instead. I asked to see him, and an aged creature appeared, whose furrowed and wrinkled face hardly seemed to announce the man we wanted; but having no choice, we were obliged to engage him, and we again set forth.

The mountain could not be seen at La Ville, owing to a high ridge which intervened; we were now moving along the foot of this to get to the chalets of Alefred, or, as they are sometimes called, Aléfroide, where the actual mountain commences. From La Pisse and upwards, the view of it was very grand. The whole height of that peak, which in these valleys goes under the name of the 'Grand Pelvoux', was seen at one glance from its summit to the base, at least 7,500 feet of apparently perpendicular cliffs. Walnut and other trees in great variety gave shadow to our path, and fresh vigour to our limbs, while below, in a sublime gorge, thundered the torrent, whose waters took their rise from the snows we hoped to tread on the morrow.

From this point the subordinate but more proximate peaks appear considerably higher than the loftier ones behind.

The chalets of Alefred are a cluster of miserable wooden huts at the foot of the Grand Pelvoux, and are close to the junction of the streams which descend from the glacier de Sapenière on the left, and the glaciers Blanc and Noir on the right. We only rested a minute to purchase some butter and milk, but Sémiond picked up a disreputable-looking lad (who, I fancy, called him 'father') to assist to carry, push, haul, and otherwise move the wine-cask.

Our route now turned sharply to the left, and all were thankful that the day was drawing to a close, so that we had the shadows from the mountains. A more frightful and desolate valley it is impossible to imagine: miles and miles of boulders, débris, stones, sand, and even mud; – few trees, and they placed so high as to be almost out of sight; – no vegetation; not a soul inhabits it, no birds are in the air, no fish in its waters; the mountain is too steep for the chamois, the slopes too inhospitable for the marmot, the whole too repulsive for the eagle; not a living thing did we see in this sterile and savage valley for four days, barring some few poor goats which had been driven there against their will.

It was truly a scene in keeping with the diabolical deed perpetrated here about four hundred years ago – the murder of the Vaudois of Val Louise in the caverns which were now in sight, though high above us. Their story is very sad. For more than three hundred years they had inhabited these retired valleys in tranquil obscurity; they were peaceful and industrious – troubadours sang their praises – and, had they been but known, they would have been beloved by all, save those to whom innocence is nauseous, and goodness ever hateful.

The Archbishop of Embrun endeavoured, but with little success, to get them within the pale of his church; his efforts were aided by many others, who, commencing by imprisonments and tortures, at last adopted the more natural method of burning them by hundreds at the stake. The wretched inhabitants fled at last to the caverns in this valley, where, having collected sufficient provisions for two years, they took up their abode. But intolerance is ever painstaking, and their retreat was soon discovered. Historians differ as to the mode of attack, but they agree as to the final result, – they were relentlessly exterminated without distinction of age or sex. More than 3,000 persons, it is said, perished in this frightful massacre; the growth of three hundred and fifty years was destroyed at one blow, and the valley was completely depopulated. Louis XII caused it to be repeopled, and after three hundred and fifty years have once more passed away, behold the result, – a race of monkeys. Of one thing I am certain, – they must have been taken by surprise when attacked, or else there was treachery. The position of the caverns is such, that a handful of resolute men could defy an army. Steep slopes and precipitous rocks lead up to them for several hundred feet, while above, it is all inaccessible cliff.

There is but little water in this valley, and when you get any it is usually muddy and bad; but we arrived at a splendid little spring about half an hour after we passed the Baume. The situation of this is worth noticing; it is about forty yards higher up the valley, and nearer the Pelvoux than the outermost of a small patch of pines: it is very small, but the quality of the water is excellent. We rested a little and hastened upwards, till we nearly arrived at the foot of the Sapenière glacier, when Sémiond said we must turn to the right up the slopes. This we did, and clambered for half an hour through scattered pines and fallen boulders, when evening began to close in so rapidly that it was time to look for a resting-place. There was no difficulty in getting one, for all round was a chaotic assemblage of rocks. We selected the under side of one, which was more than fifty feet long by twenty high, cleared it of rubbish, and set about collecting wood for a fire, which was soon blazing right merrily.

That camp-fire is a pleasant reminiscence. The wine-cask had got through all its troubles; – was tapped, and the Frenchmen pretended to derive some consolation from its execrable contents. Reynaud ever and anon chanted some scrap of French song, and each contributed his share of joke, story, and verse; the weather was perfect, and our prospects for the morrow were good. My companions' joy culminated when I threw a packet of red fire into the flames: it hissed and bubbled for a moment or two, and then broke out into a grand flare. The effect of the momentary light was magnificent; all around, the mountains were illuminated for a second, and then relapsed into their solemn gloom. One by one our party dropped off to sleep, and at last I got into my blanket-bag; it was hardly necessary, for although we were at a height of at least 7,000 feet, the minimum temperature was above 40° Fahrenheit.

We roused at three, but did not start till half-past four. Giraud had been engaged as far as this rock only, but as he pressed anxiously to be allowed to go on as a volunteer, we allowed him to accompany us. We mounted the slopes quickly, and in a few minutes got above the trees, then had a couple of hours' clambering over bits of precipitous rock and banks of débris, and at a quarter to 7 got to the narrow glacier, Clos de l'Homme, which streams from the plateau and nearly reaches the Glacier de Sapenière. We had been working as much as possible to the right, in hopes that we should not have to cross it, but were continually driven back, till at last we found it was absolutely necessary. Old Sémiond had a strong objection to the ice, and made explorations on his own account to endeavour to avoid it, but Reynaud and I preferred crossing it, and Giraud stuck to us. It was exceedingly narrow – in fact, one could throw a stone across it. At the point we wished to cross, it overlapped the rock, and was easily mounted on the side, but in the centre swelled into a steep dome, up which we were obliged to cut. The inclination was, perhaps, as much as 40°, and the slope not more than ninety feet in length. I commenced a few steps, but Giraud stepped forward, and said he should like to try his hand. When once he got the axe he would not give it up, and here as well as afterwards, when it was necessary to cross the couloirs which abound on the higher part of the mountain, he did all the work, and did it admirably. Chop, chop, chop, and one step was cut (two blows down and one sideways always sufficed), and in an incredibly short time he was at the top of the dome ready to pull us up. While he was at work an absurd accident, but which might have proved serious, happened to me. I was standing at the foot of the steep incline already mentioned, but was so immediately under Giraud that I had the benefit of his shower of ice-chips. I, therefore, moved my position, and, in doing so, somehow managed to slip, and commenced sliding straight in the

direction of a large crevasse. Fortunately a deep step we had cut was within
reach of one arm; – I caught at it, and brought myself to anchor, but
remained at full length on the slope without the power of getting on my
feet. I held on for a few seconds, when Reynaud threw me the end of the
rope and pulled me up.

When we were at length across, old Sémiond, of course, came after us.
We zigzagged up some snow-slopes, and then commenced the interminable array of buttresses which are the great peculiarity of the Pelvoux.
They were in many parts very steep, but, on the whole, afforded good hold,
and no climbing should be called difficult that does that. They abounded in
gullies, sometimes of great length and depth – 70° was no uncommon inclination. They were frequently very rotten, and would have been difficult
for a single man to pass – with two they are sufficiently awkward: if you
are top man, you find yourself being continually abused by the man beneath
for the half-hundredweights of stones you send down on his head; and if
you are the lower man, you find that there are pleasanter things in the
world than being harpooned by your friend's bâton, or having his heavy-
nailed boots leave their impression on your fingers. But, after all, climbing
without these incidents would be very slow – they help to break the
monotony.

We went up chimneys and gullies by the hour together, and always
seemed to be coming to something, although we never got to it. We
stand at the foot of a great buttress, about 200 feet high, and look up. It
does not go to a point, because we cannot see the top, although we feel
convinced that, behind the edge of the fringe of pinnacles we do see, there
is a top, and that that is the edge of the plateau we so much desire to
attain. Up we mount and reach the pinnacles, but lo! another set is
seen, and another, and yet more, till at last we reach the top to find
that it is only a buttress, and that we have to descend forty or fifty feet
before we can commence to mount again. When this operation had been
performed a few dozen times, it began to be wearisome, especially as we
were thoroughly in the dark as to our whereabouts. Sémiond, however,
encouraged us, said he knew we were on the right route, and away we went
once more.

The unavoidable risk we ran from falling stones when we followed each
other, had now driven us to act in the most independent manner – each
selected the route which was in his eyes the best; so, by-and-by, I found
myself alone with Giraud, having completely lost sight of the others. A
shout from above presently announced they had met an obstacle; a bit of
cliff went straight up which could not be climbed, and it seemed necessary
to descend 200 feet to get on to another arête. In a few minutes we came to
it, a perpendicular wall of no great height, but quite impracticable. A small
cascade came bounding over the top from the end of a long couloir, and

had worn itself a route down the face. Giraud was for descending to join the others who had gone away to the right; but I did not like the loss of time, so stopped to consider. On the cliff there was not hold for a cat, but up the cascade there seemed a chance. By getting on that knob I calculated that a long stretch would bring that ledge just within reach; then, by leaning across on my bâton, I should just get to that bit in the middle. 'Giraud,' said I, breaking off in my calculation, 'suppose we go up the cascade.' He looked at me with a comical air, to see if I was joking, then at the cascade, then back at me, saying, *'Il n'est pas possible, Monsieur Edward.'* 'Giraud, my boy, if I go up, will you follow?' He scratched his head, gave one more look, and stared vacantly into the sky. 'Jean Casimir Giraud, will you come up after me?' 'Y–e–s.' So I buttoned my jacket, turned up the collar, looked to my knapsack, commenced the climbing, and succeeded in getting up. Giraud hesitated, and looked up with an expression of blank astonishment; but he kept his word and joined me on the top. This manoeuvre was of double service; we saved half an hour, and had all the advantages of a shower-bath without the trouble of stopping.

It was now nearly midday, and we seemed no nearer the summit of the Pelvoux than when we started. The buttresses commenced again, and the gullies were varied by steep couloirs of hard snow. At last we all joined together and held a council. 'Sémiond, my antique friend, do you know where we are now?' 'Oh, yes, perfectly, to a yard and a half.' 'Well, then, how much are we below this plateau?' He affirmed we were not half an hour from the edge of the snow. 'Very good; let us proceed.' Half an hour passed, and then another, but we were still in the same state – pinnacles, buttresses, and couloirs in profusion, but no plateau. So I called him again, for I had noticed he had been staring about latterly as if in doubt. I repeated the question, 'How far below are we now?' Well, he thought it might be half an hour more. 'But you said that just now; are you sure we are going right?' 'Yes; he believed we were.' Believed! that wouldn't do. 'Are you sure we are going right for the Pic des Arcines?' 'Pic des Arcines!' he ejaculated in astonishment, as if he had heard the word for the first time, 'Pic des Arcines; no! but for the pyramide, the celebrated pyramide he had helped the great Capitaine Durand, &c.'

Here was a fix, – we had been talking about it to him for a whole day, and now he coolly confessed he knew nothing about it. I turned to Reynaud, who seemed thunderstruck. 'What did he suggest?' He shrugged his shoulders. 'Well,' said I, after explaining my mind to Sémiond, pretty freely, 'the sooner we turn back the better, for I have no wish to see your pyramide.'

We halted for an hour, enjoyed the prospect as well as we were able, and then commenced the descent. I know it took us nearly seven hours to come down to our rock; but I paid no heed to the distance, and do not remember anything about it. When we got down, we made a discovery – a blue silk veil lay by our fireside. As these articles are not indigenous, there was to my mind but one solution – Macdonald had arrived; but where was he, and why had he gone? We soon packed our baggage, and tramped in the dusk through the stony desert to Alefred, where we arrived about half-past nine. 'Where is the Englishman?' was my first question. He was gone to sleep at La Ville. 'What was he like?' – I found that I was not mistaken.

We passed that night in a hay-loft, and slept soundly in spite of our woes; and in the morning, after settling with Sémiond, who professed himself *très content*, I posted down in advance of the others to catch Macdonald. I had already determined on my plan of operation, which was to get him to join me, return, and be independent of all guides, simply taking the best man I could get as a porter. I set my heart on Giraud, for he was a right good fellow, with no pretence, although in every respect up to the work; but I was disappointed – he was obliged to go to Briançon.

My walk soon became exciting. No end of peasants inquired the result of our expedition, and common civility obliged me to stop. But I was afraid of losing my man, for I had been told he would wait only till 10 o'clock, and that time was close at hand. At last I dashed over the bridge, – time from Alefred an hour and a quarter, – but a cantonnier stopped me, saying that *Monsieur l'Anglais* had just started for La Bessée. I rushed after him, turned angle after angle of the road, but could not see him; at last, as I came round a corner, he was also just turning another, going very fast. I shouted with the voice I learnt in Switzerland, and, luckily, he heard me. We returned, re-provisioned ourselves at La Ville, and the same evening saw us passing our first rock *en route* for another. Our party consisted of Reynaud, Sémiond, an apprentice of Giraud's, and our two selves. I have said we determined to take no guide, but on passing La Pisse old Sémiond turned out and offered his services. He went well in spite of his years and disregard of truth. 'Why not take him?' said Macdonald. So we offered him a fifth of his previous pay, and in a few seconds he closed with the offer, but this time came in an inferior position: we were to lead, he to follow.

Our second follower was a remarkable youth of twenty-seven years. Want of space forbids any detailed account of his pranks; how he drank Reynaud's wine, smoked our cigars, and quietly secreted the provisions when we were nearly starving. For coolness he beat any person I have met. Discovery of his proceedings did not at all flurry him, and he finished up by getting several items on his own account added to our bill, which, not a little to his disgust, we disallowed.

This night we fixed our camp high above the tree line, and indulged ourselves in the healthy employment of carrying all our fuel up to it. The present rock was not so comfortable as the first, and before we could settle, we were obliged to turn out a large mass which was in our way. It was very obstinate, but moved at length; slowly and gently at first, but faster and faster it went, at last taking great bounds in the air, striking a stream of fire at every touch, which shone brightly out as it entered the gloomy valley below, and long after it was out of sight, we heard it jumping downwards and then settle with a subdued crash on the glacier beneath. As we turned back from this curious sight, Reynaud asked if we had ever seen a torrent on fire. I thought he was joking, but he was in sober earnest. 'Every spring,' said he, 'when the snows begin to melt, many rocks are brought down by the streams, and this is particularly the case in that most turbulent of French rivers, the Durance. At the point where it comes through that narrow gorge at La Bessée, I have seen it frequently so choked with boulders, that no water whatever could be seen, but only rocks rolling over and over, grinding each other into powder, and being dashed into fragments, while the sparks and flashes which they emitted gave it quite the appearance of being on fire.'

We had another merry evening with nothing to mar it. The weather was perfection, and all Alpine men will imagine, better than I can describe, the treat we had at sunset and sunrise. Macdonald related his experiences over the *café noir*. 'I arrived,' he said, 'at La Ville, shortly after you had left, and, hastening up to La Pisse, learnt that you were going to sleep in a cavern on the mountain side. The thoughts of losing even a chance of an ascent were maddening, so I procured a man to carry my luggage, and started up the valley. I was in bad training, and as tired and sleepy as nothing but thirty consecutive hours in a diligence can make one, so I was not sorry we were obliged to slacken our pace in consequence of the roughness of the ground. We stumbled wearily upwards, till at nine o'clock my guide announced that he thought we were near our destination, but being pitch-dark he would not proceed, as he knew not whether we were above or below the cavern. I was much too tired to dispute his resolution; we therefore chose a big rock as a resting-place, crawled under its lee, and divided our provisions. I soon fell asleep, but rose at the first sign of daybreak. The guide stood at my side, and pointed out the cavern for which we had searched, not twenty yards below; but of course nobody had slept there, and he confessed he knew nothing about you. I asked him if there were no other in which you might have slept. Yes, there was one *tout là bas* and close to the glacier; so off we went on the chance of finding you. But long before we got to it, I discerned your party making its way along a rocky arête 2,000 feet above us, and at a great distance. It was perfectly useless to try to overtake you, so I lay down and watched you with a heavy heart until you turned the corner of a buttress and vanished out of sight.'

We lay backwards in luxurious repose, looking at the spangled sky with its ten thousand brilliant lights, smoking our pipes, and talking over the prospects of the coming day. Nought broke the solemn stillness of the night but the heavy breathing of our already sound asleep comrades. Nothing: it was a silence to be felt. We were alone. Alone? Hark, what is that dull booming sound above us? Is that nothing? There it is again, plainer – on it comes, nearer, clearer – what a fearful crash! – 'tis a crag escaped from the heights above. We jump to our feet. Down it comes with awful fury; what power can withstand its violence? Dancing, leaping, flying, dashing against others, roaring as it descends. Ah, it has passed! No; there it is again, and we hold our breath as, with resistless power and explosions like artillery, it darts past, with an avalanche of shattered fragments trailing in its rear! 'Tis gone, and we breathe more freely as we hear the finale on the glacier below. It was an awful moment, and we felt it.

We retired at last, but I was too excited to sleep, and at a quarter past 4 every man once more shouldered his pack and started up. This time we agreed to keep more to the right, and see if it were not possible to get to the plateau without losing any time by crossing the glacier. To describe our route would be to repeat what has been said before. We mounted steadily upwards for an hour and a half, sometimes walking, but more frequently climbing, when we found, after all, that it was necessary to cross the glacier. The part on which we struck came down a very steep slope and was much crevassed. But the word crevassed hardly expresses the writhed and twisted look it presented; it was a mass of séracs of most formidable appearance. We found, however, more difficulty in getting on than across it; but, thanks to the rope, we passed it somehow, and the interminable buttresses began again. Hour after hour we pounded upwards, frequently at fault and obliged to descend, but the progress was sure and steady. The ridge behind us had long ago sunk, and we looked over it, and all others, till our eyes rested nearly forty miles away on the majestic Viso. Hour after hour passed, and monotony was the order of the day: when 12 o'clock came we lunched, and contemplated the scene with satisfaction; all the summits in sight, with the single exception of the Viso, had given in, and we looked over an immense expanse – a perfect sea of peaks and snow-fields. Still the pinnacles rose above us, and opinions were freely uttered that we should see no summit of Pelvoux that day. Old Sémiond had become a perfect bore to all; whenever one rested for a moment to look about, he would say with a complacent chuckle, '*N'ayez pas peur, suivez-moi.*' We came at last to a very bad piece, rotten and steep, and no hold. Here Reynaud and Macdonald confessed themselves tired, and talked of going to sleep. A way was discovered out of the difficulty, and I took the opportunity to make an outline of a neighbouring buttress, while sitting on the top of another. While so employed, some one called out, 'Look at the Viso,' and we saw that we almost looked over it. We worked away with redoubled energy, hauling one, shoving another, till at length we caught sight of the head of the glacier as it streamed out of the plateau. This gave us fresh hopes; we were not deceived; and with a simultaneous shout we greeted the appearance of our long-wished-for snows. A large bergschrund separated us from them; but a bridge was found. We tied ourselves in line and moved safely over it. Directly we got across to the top of the snow, there rose before us a fine snow-capped peak. Old Sémiond cried: 'The pyramide! I see the pyramide!' 'Where, Sémiond, where?' 'There, Monsieur, on the top of that peak.'

And there, sure enough, was the very cairn he had helped to erect thirty years before. But where was the Pic des Arcines we were to see? – it was nowhere visible, but only an immense expanse of snow bordered by three lower peaks. Somewhat sadly we moved towards the pyramid, sighing that there was no other to conquer, but hardly had we gone two hundred paces, before there rose a superb white cone on the left, which had been hidden before by a slope of snow. At the same moment Macdonald and I shouted, 'The Pic des Arcines!' and inquired in a breath of Sémiond, if he knew whether that peak had been ascended by any one. As for him he knew nothing, except that the peak before us was called the pyramid, from the cairn he had, &c. &c.; and that it had not been ascended since. 'All right, then, face about;' and we immediately turned at right angles for the cone, the porter making faint struggles for his beloved pyramide. Our progress was in the sixth of a mile stopped by the edge of the ridge connecting the two peaks, and being in the centre of a curve we perceived that it curled over in a lovely volute, on which we were now standing. We involuntarily retreated. The porter, who was last in the line, took the opportunity to untie himself, and refused to come on; said we were running dangerous risks; and talked vaguely of crevasses. Such childish folly we opposed, tied him up again, and proceeded. The snow was very soft; we were always knee-deep, and as with my knapsack I was the heaviest, I was frequently floundering helplessly up to my middle; but a simultaneous jerk before and behind always released me. By this time we had arrived at the foot of the final peak. The left-hand arête seemed easier than that on which we stood, so we curved round to get there. Some rocks peeped out 150 feet below the summit, and up these we crawled, leaving our porter behind, as he said he was afraid. I could not resist the temptation, as we went off, to turn and beckon him onwards, saying, '*N'ayez pas peur, suivez-moi;* but he did not answer to the appeal, and never went to the top. The rocks led to a short arête of ice – our plateau on one side and a precipice nearly vertical on the other. We cut up the arête, and at a quarter to 2, three happy individuals stood shaking hands on the loftiest summit on the conquered Pelvoux – the true Pic des Arcines.

The day still continued everything that could be desired, and far and near countless peaks burst into sight without a cloud to hide them. The mighty Mont Blanc, full seventy miles away, first caught our eyes, and then, still farther off, the Monte Rosa group, while, rolling away to the east, one unknown range after another succeeded in unveiled splendour, fainter and fainter in tone, but still perfectly defined, till at last the eye was unable to distinguish sky from mountain, and they died away in the far-off horizon. Monte Viso rose grandly up, but it was only forty miles away, and we looked clean over it to a hazy mass we knew must be the plains of Piedmont. Southwards a blue mist seemed to indicate the existence of the distant Mediterranean; to the west we looked over to the mountains of Auvergne. Such was the panorama, a view extending in nearly every direction for more than one hundred miles. It was with some difficulty we wrenched our eyes from the more distant objects to contemplate the nearer. Mont Dauphin was very conspicuous; but though I knew its situation I looked a long time for La Bessée. Besides these, not a human habitation can be seen; all is rock, snow, and ice, and large as we knew were the snow-fields of Dauphiné, we were surprised to find they very far surpassed our most ardent imagination. Nearly in a line between us and the Viso, was a splendid group of mountains, of whose existence I was unaware. They are immediately to the south of Chat. Queyras, are not laid down on any map, neither do I think they have been mentioned by any author. They are decidedly loftier than the Viso, and their highest summits (for there are several) probably attain to nearly 13,000 feet. More south an unknown peak was even higher, while close to us we were astonished to discover that the mountain to which Elie de Beaumont frequently refers seemed even higher than the peak on which we stood. At least this was my opinion, and I formed a minority, as Macdonald thought it not so high, and Reynaud much about the same. As I had not read Elie de Beaumont's book at that time, I deferred to the majority. But after reading it I think it is evident, for two good reasons, that this mountain is that to which the French engineers assigned 4,105 mètres: – first, our peak was not nearly so much as 450 feet above that of the pyramid – it might, perhaps, be 150 to 200; secondly, our peak was not at the distance of 3,000 mètres from the pyramid, but was probably 800 yards. The great black mountain complied, however, with these conditions, as it was certainly three or four times our distance, and also appeared to me to rise at least 200 feet above us. But, for all this, we unquestionably reached the highest point of Pelvoux, and in saying this we are not at variance with Elie de Beaumont, who, as I have shown, refers to the black mountain as one separate and distinct. The testimony of our eyes was quite sufficient to show this, for, after a few steps had gently curved away, they shot down into a tremendous abyss, of which we could not see the bottom, whose depth we guessed at least 2,500 feet. After our eyes left the snow on which we stood, they rested on nothing until this mighty wall-sided mountain was seen rising on the other side, black as night, too steep for snow, with arêtes like knife-edges, and a summit sharp as a needle. We were in complete ignorance of its whereabouts, for none of us had been on the other side; we imagined that La Bérarde was in the abyss at our feet, but it was in reality beyond the mountain.

We left the summit at last, and descended to the rocks and to our porter. I melted some snow, and found that, with the air at 9·75° Centigrade, it boiled at 87·75° Cent.; and after we had fed, and smoked our cigars (lighted, be it remarked, from a common match), we found that it was 10 minutes past 3 o'clock, and high time to be off. We dashed, waded, and tumbled through the snow, and in twenty-five minutes began the long descent of the rocks. We had taken eight hours to come up them, but now it was getting on to 4 o'clock, and as it would be dark at 8 o'clock, it was evident that there was no time to be lost, and we pushed on to the utmost. Nothing remarkable occurred going down; we kept rather closer to the glacier, and crossed at the same point as in the morning. Getting *off* it was like getting *on* it, rather awkward. Old Sémiond had got over, so had Reynaud; Macdonald came next, but as he made a long stretch to get on to a higher mass, he slipped, and in a moment would have been in the bowels of a crevasse had he not been tied. Thanks to the rope, he was safely landed.

By the time we had crossed, it was rapidly becoming dark, but I still hoped that we should get to our rock in safety. Macdonald was not so sanguine, and he was right; for at last we found ourselves quite at fault, and wandered helplessly up and down for nearly an hour, while Reynaud and the porter indulged in a little mutual abuse. But the dreary fact was now quite apparent, that, as we could not get down, we must stay where we were.

A more detestable locality for a night out of doors, it is difficult to imagine. There were no large rocks nor shelter of any kind; it was too steep to promenade, and perfectly exposed to the chilling wind which began to rise. Loose rubbly stones covered the ground, and had to be removed before we could sit with any comfort. This was an advantage, though we hardly thought so at the time, as it gave us some employment, and after an hour's active exercise of that interesting kind, I obtained a small strip of about nine feet long, on which I could walk. Reynaud was at first furious, and soundly abused the porter, whose opinion as to the route had been followed rather than that of our friend, but at last settled down to a deep dramatic despair, and wrung his hands with frantic gesture, as he exclaimed, *'Oh malheur, malheur! Oh misérables!'* We were certainly in a predicament; we were at least 10,500 feet high, and if it commenced to rain or snow, as the gathering clouds and rising wind seemed to threaten, we might be in a sore plight; but fortunately matters did not get so bad as that. We were hungry, having eaten little since 3 A.M., and a torrent we heard close at hand, but could not discover, aggravated our thirst. Sémiond endeavoured to get some water from it; and it will give an idea of the difficulty of moving, when I say, that although he got to it, and it was not a hundred feet off, he was wholly unable to return, and we had to solace him by shouting at intervals through the night.

Thunder commenced to growl and lightning play among the peaks above, and the wind, which had brought the temperature down to nearly 32° Fahrenheit, began to chill us to the bones. We examined our resources. They were six and a half cigars, two boxes of Vesuvians, one third of a pint of brandy-and-water, and half a pint of spirits of wine; rather scant for three fellows who had to get through seven hours before daylight. I lighted my spirit lamp, and mixing the remaining spirits of wine, brandy, and some snow together, heated them by it. It made a strong liquor, but we only wished for more of it. When that was done, Macdonald endeavoured to dry his socks by the lamp, and then the three lay down under my plaid to pretend to sleep. And it was a pretence! Reynaud's woes were aggravated by toothache; Macdonald somehow managed to close his eyes. After lying still, but badly cramped up, for two hours, I couldn't stand it any longer, and promenaded my limited platform for the rest of the night, varying my walk by dancing, like a bear on hot plates, to keep my feet alive, and smoked the cigars the others would not touch. Never before, nor since, have I found a weed so grateful.

The longest night must end, and ours did at last. Sémiond came and shook us up at early dawn. I believe I was getting very fast into a state of torpor, walking up and down mechanically, without the slightest notion of what was going on; the others were dozing. We got down to our rock in an hour and a quarter, and found the lad not a little surprised at our absence, though he had by no means broken his heart over us. He said he had made a gigantic fire to light us down, and shouted with all his might; we neither saw one nor heard the other. I am told we looked a ghastly crew, and no wonder; it was our fourth night out.

We feasted at our cave, and performed some very necessary ablutions. The exceedingly neat and cleanly persons of the natives are infested by certain agile creatures whose rapidity of motion is only equalled by their numbers and voracity. It is positively dangerous to approach too near them, and one has to study the wind, so as to get on their weather side. In spite of all precautions, my unfortunate companion and myself were being rapidly devoured alive, and it was to save the remainder of our wretched carcases that we performed as above; not that we expected more than a temporary lull in our tortures. The interiors of the inns are like the exterior of the natives, swarming with this section of animated creation. It is said that once, when these tormentors were filled with a unanimous desire, an unsuspecting traveller was dragged bodily from his bed! This needs confirmation. One word more, and I have done with this vile subject. We returned from our ablutions, and found the Frenchmen engaged in conversation. 'Ah!' said a certain aged individual, 'as to fleas, I don't pretend to be different to any one else – *I have them.*' This will give the reader a notion of what he may expect in Dauphiné. I verily believe he spoke the truth.

We got down to La Ville in good time, and luxuriated there for several days; but at last it was necessary to part, and I walked southwards to the Viso, while Macdonald went to Briançon.

It will be seen that the ascent of Mont Pelvoux is of a rather monotonous character. From the point where we crossed the narrow glacier to the time we stepped on the plateau of snow, it was one long stretch of more than six hours' continuous climbing, without any break whatever. We came down very fast, and did not rest for a minute; and yet that piece took us four hours.

To those who ascend mountains for views I confidently recommend the Mont Pelvoux; a glance at the map will show that, with the single exception of the Viso, whose position is unrivalled, it is better situated than any other mountain of considerable height for viewing the whole chain of the Alps. Our view included the whole, and extended from the Graians to the Tyrol.

But there is, apart from this, a hearty satisfaction to be felt in making an ascent, which is payment enough in itself. 'What is the use of going up mountains?' is a question which is often put. To such I would say: go up a good-sized mountain, and you will know; and perchance it may be, that it will cause you, as it does me now, to look back with pleasure on the past, and forward with hope to the future.

✳︎ (From 'The Ascent of Mont Pelvoux' by Edward Whymper. *Peaks, Passes and Glaciers*, Second Series, Vol. II.)

A. C. Ramsay

2 ❋ Llyn Llydaw

Approaching Llyn Llydaw, the full grandeur of this wonderful valley
bursts on the beholder. A lake rather more than a mile in length and of a
green colour, like some of the lakes of Switzerland, runs obliquely across
the valley. Around it rise the cliffs of Lliwedd, Cribgoch, and Pen Wyddfa,
seamed with veins of white quartz, looking like streaks of snow on the tall
black rocks that circle the vast amphitheatre, the scarred sides and ragged
outlines of which, sharply defined against the sky, may well seem, till
attempted, hopelessly inaccessible to the unpractised climber. In every
season and phase of weather, there is a charm in this valley to the lover of
the mountains. In quiet sunshine, when the rocks, and perhaps a lazy
ferry-boat, are reflected in the still water; or while the wanderer scales the
crags amid the seething mists; or when the pitiless rain, or hail, or snow,
comes driving down the valley; but best of all, in a threatening evening,
when the gathered clouds, like the roof of a vast cavern, hang heavily from
side to side on the edges of hills; and a streak of light caught from the
setting sun, shows redly behind the dim peak of Snowdon, grimly reflected in the sombre waters of the lake.

The signs of glacier ice are so evident in Cwm Llydaw that it is needless
to describe all the details. At the outflow of the lake there are moraine-like
mounds, formed of earthy matter, stones, and angular and subangular
blocks, which even now partly dam up the lake, and when I first knew it,
raised it to a still higher level, ere the channel of the brook was sacrilegi-
ously deepened to lower the water, for the sake of saving a few pounds in
the construction of an ugly causeway. Close to the outflow, the once
beautiful little islets of rock, feathered with heath and grasses, are now
united to the mainland, and a broad ugly black rim round the lake marks
alike the extent of the drainage, and the barbarism of the perpetrators of
this unhappy outrage on the most beautiful scene in North Wales. Between the upper part of Cwm-dyli and the north end of Llyn Llydaw, above
the brook, there are magnificent *roches moutonnées*, once overflowed by
the glacier; their sides and summits, from 200 to 300 feet above the lake,
being still strewn with moraine débris and numerous *blocs perchés*,
scattered on the rocks. On the little peninsula below, the striae running

east-north-east show the direction of the flow of the glacier, which, un-
checked by the hill beyond, passed right over the rocky barrier. From
signs higher up the hill, I believe that at one period the ice must have been
here at least 500 feet thick, and I incline to think that it was even much
thicker. On the opposite side of the lake, the moraine heaps, of large
blocks, clay, and angular stones sometimes scratched, are remarkably
apparent; and in the great recess below the cliffs of Lliwedd, the rocks are
wonderfully rounded, and dotted with moraine matter and scattered blocks,
at least 500 feet above the level of the lake. In the curve of that recess there
are striations somewhat converging towards the bottom, in the manner
that might be expected to be produced by ice pressing both down the
greater slope, and outwards towards the mouth of the valley; and well
up, on the broken spur of rock that runs from Lliwedd towards the efflux
of the lake, the striae turn suddenly round more easterly, where once the
ice flowed high across the ridge and escaped down Cwm-dyli into Nant
Gwynant.

❄ (From 'The Old Glaciers of Switzerland and Wales' by A. C. Ramsay,
F.R.S., *Peaks, Passes and Glaciers*, I.)

Philip C. Gosset

3 ❊ The Death of Bennen

It has often occurred to me, when walking on hard snow in winter, that a
mountain ascent at that period of the year might be made with much less
difficulty and trouble than in summer. With this view I made several
excursions in winter, and came to the conclusion that the mean temperature at a certain elevation, up to 8,000 feet, is not so low as might be
expected. In some cases I believe it to be higher than in the plain of
Switzerland. The plain is covered with fog for weeks in winter. In the
morning the fog lies close to the earth, at noon it rises to the height of a
few hundred feet, and in the evening it comes down again. During three
weeks running, often longer, you cannot see the sun, and the ground is
frozen hard. Above the fog the sun is shining brightly on the mountain
peaks. It is therefore easy to understand that unless the fog is kept off by a
strong N.E. wind (which is generally not the case in winter at least), the
temperature of the upper regions is higher than that of the plain. As an
example tending to prove this assertion, I may mention that I have found
flowers blooming on arêtes on the Rothhorn and Niesen at the height of
7,000 feet, when there was not a flower in the plain of the Canton of
Berne (on December 31, 1861, and on February 4, 1860). Amongst these
flowers were the *Gentiana verna* and *Viola calcarata*.

My friend B. was familiar with mountains in winter; he had been up the
Æggischhorn and Riederhorn in December, 1863: easy as these points may
be to reach in summer, in winter, if the snow is not hard, the question is
very different. On February 28, 1864, we left Sion with Bennen to mount
the Haut-de-Cry. We started at 2.15 A.M. in a light carriage that brought us
to the village of Ardon, distant six miles. We there met three men that were
to accompany us as local guides or porters, Jean Joseph Nance, Frederic
Rebot, who acted as my personal guide, and Auguste Bevard. We at once
began to ascend on the right bank of the Lyzerne. The night was splendid,
the sky cloudless, and the moon shining so as to make walking easy
without the use of a lantern. For about half-an-hour we went up through
the vineyards by a rather steep path, and then entered the valley of the
Lyzerne, about 700 feet above the torrent. We here found a remarkably
good path, gradually rising and leaning towards the Col de Chéville.

Having followed this path for about three hours we struck off to the left, and began zigzagging up the mountain side through a pine forest. We had passed what may be called the snow-line in winter a little above 2,000 feet. We had not ascended for more than a quarter of an hour in this pine forest before the snow got very deep and very soft. We had to change leader every five or six minutes, and even thus our progress was remarkably slow. We saw clearly that, should the snow be as soft above the fir region we should have to give up the ascent. At 7 A.M. we reached a chalet, and stopped for about twenty minutes to rest and look at the sunrise on the Diablerets. On observing an aneroid, which we had brought with us, we found that we were at the height of about 7,000 feet: the temperature was − 1° C.

The Haut-de-Cry has four arêtes: the first running towards the W., the second S.E., the third E., and the fourth N.E. We were between the two last-named arêtes. Our plan was to go up between them to the foot of the peak, and mount it by the arête running N.E. As we had expected, the snow was in much better state when once we were above the woods. For some time we advanced pretty rapidly. The peak was glistening before us, and the idea of success put us in high spirits. Our good fortune did not last long; we soon came to snow frozen on the surface, and capable of bearing for a few steps and then giving way. But this was nothing compared to the trouble of pulling up through the pine wood, so instead of making us grumble it only excited our hilarity. Bennen was in a particularly good humour, and laughed loud at our combined efforts to get out of the holes we every now and then made in the snow. Judging from appearances, the snow-field over which we were walking covered a gradually-rising Alp. We made a second observation with our aneroid, and found, rather to our astonishment and dismay, that we had only risen 1,000 feet in the last three hours. It was 10 o'clock: we were at the height of about 8,000 feet; temperature = −1·5 C. During the last half-hour, we had found a little hard snow, so we had all hope of success. Thinking we might advance better on the arête, we took to it, and rose along it for some time. It soon became cut up by rocks, so we took to the snow again. It turned out to be here hard frozen, so that we reached the real foot of the peak without the slightest difficulty. It was decidedly steeper than I had expected it would be, judging from the valley of the Rhone. Bennen looked at it with decided pleasure; having completed his survey, he proposed to take the eastern arête, as in doing so we should gain at least two hours. Rebot had been over this last-named arête in summer, and was of Bennen's opinion. Two or three of the party did not like the idea much, so there was a discussion on the probable advantages and disadvantages of the N.E. and E. arêtes. We were losing time; so Bennen cut matters short by saying: *'Ich will der Erste über die arête!'* Thus saying, he made for the E. arête; it looked very narrow, and, what was worse, it was considerably cut up by high rocks, the intervals between the teeth of the arête being filled up with snow. To gain this arête, we had to go up a steep snow-field, about 800 feet high, as well as I remember. It was about 150 feet broad at the top, and 400 or 500 at the bottom. It was a sort of couloir on a large scale. During the ascent we sank about one foot deep at every step. Bennen did not seem to like the look of the snow very much. He asked the local guides whether avalanches ever came down this couloir, to which they answered that our position was perfectly safe. We had mounted on the northern side of the couloir, and having arrived at 150 feet from the top, we began crossing it on a horizontal curve, so as to gain the E. arête. The inflexion or dip of the couloir was slight, not above 25 feet, the inclination near 35°. We were walking in the following order: Bevard, Nance, Bennen, myself, B., and Rebot. Having crossed over about three-quarters of the breadth of the couloir, the two leading men suddenly sank considerably above their waists. Bennen tightened the rope. The snow was too deep to think of getting out of the hole they had made, so they advanced one or two steps, dividing the snow with their bodies. Bennen turned round and told us he was afraid of starting an avalanche; we asked whether it would not be better to return and cross the couloir higher up. To this the three Ardon men opposed themselves; they mistook the proposed precaution for fear, and the two leading men continued their work. After three or four steps gained in the aforesaid manner, the snow became hard again. Bennen had not moved – he was evidently undecided what he should do; as soon, however, as he saw hard snow again, he advanced and crossed parallel to, but above, the furrow the Ardon men had made. Strange to say the snow supported him. While he was passing I observed that the leader, Bevard, had ten or twelve feet of rope coiled round his shoulder. I of course at once told him to uncoil it and get on the arête, from which he was not more than fifteen feet distant. Bennen then told me to follow. I tried his steps, but sank up to my waist in the very first. So I went through the furrows, holding my elbows close to my body, so as not to touch the sides. This furrow was about twelve feet long, and as the snow was good on the other side, we had all come to the false conclusion that the snow was accidentally softer there than elsewhere. Bennen advanced; he had made but a few steps when we heard a deep, cutting sound. The snow-field split in two about fourteen or fifteen feet above us. The cleft was at first quite narrow, not more than an inch broad. An awful silence ensued; it lasted but a few seconds, and then it was broken by Bennen's voice, '*Wir sind alle verloren.*' ['We are all lost.'] His words were slow and solemn, and those who knew him felt what they really meant when spoken by such a man as Bennen. They were his last words. I drove my alpenstock into the snow, and brought the weight of my body to bear on it. I then waited. It was an awful moment of suspense. I turned my head towards Bennen to see whether he had done the same thing. To my astonishment I saw him turn round, face the valley, and stretch out both arms. The ground on which we stood began to move slowly, and I felt the utter uselessness of any alpenstock. I soon sank up to my shoulders and began descending backwards. From this moment I saw nothing of what had happened to the rest of the party. With a good deal of trouble I succeeded in turning round. The speed of the avalanche increased rapidly, and before long I was covered up with snow. I was suffocating when I suddenly came to the surface again. I was on a wave of the avalanche, and saw it before me as I was carried down. It was the most awful sight I ever saw. The head of the avalanche was already at the spot where we made our last halt. The head alone was preceded by a thick cloud of snow-dust; the rest of the avalanche was clear. Around me I heard the horrid hissing of the snow, and far before me the thundering of the foremost part of the avalanche. To prevent myself sinking again, I made use of my arms much in the same way as when swimming in a standing position. At last I noticed that I was moving slower; then I saw the pieces of snow in front of me stop at some yards' distance; then the snow straight before me stopped, and I heard on a large scale the same creaking sound that is produced when a heavy cart passes over frozen snow in the winter. I felt that I also had stopped, and instantly threw up both arms to protect my head in case I should again be covered up. I had stopped, but the snow behind me was still in motion; its pressure on my body was so strong, that I thought I should be crushed to death. This tremendous pressure lasted but a short time; I was covered up by snow coming from behind me. My first impulse was to try and uncover my head – but this I could not do, the avalanche had frozen by pressure the moment it stopped, and I was frozen in. Whilst trying vainly to move my arms, I suddenly became aware that the hands as far as the wrist had the faculty of motion. The conclusion was easy, they must be above the snow. I set to work as well as I could; it was time, for I could not have held out much longer. At last I saw a faint glimmer of light. The crust above my head was getting thinner, but I could not reach it any more with my hands; the idea struck me that I might pierce it with my breath. After several efforts I succeeded in doing so, and felt suddenly a rush of air towards my mouth, I saw the sky again through a little round hole. A dead silence reigned around me; I was so surprised to be still alive, and so persuaded at the first moment that none of my fellow-sufferers had survived, that I did not even think of shouting for them. I made vain efforts to extricate my arms, but found it impossible; the most I could do was to join the ends of my fingers, but they could not reach the snow any longer. After a few minutes I heard a man shouting; what a relief it was to know that I was not the sole survivor! to know that perhaps he was not frozen in and could come to my assistance! I answered; the voice approached, but seemed uncertain where to go, and yet it was now quite near. A sudden exclamation of surprise! Rebot had seen my hands. He cleared my head in an instant, and was about to try and cut me out completely, when I saw a foot above the snow, and so near to me that I could touch it with my arms, although they were not quite free yet. I at once tried to move the foot; it was my poor friend's. A pang of agony shot through me as I saw that the foot did not move. Poor B. had lost sensation and was perhaps already dead. Rebot did his best: after some time he wished me to help him, so he freed my arms a little more so that I could make use of them. I could do but little, for Rebot had torn the axe from my shoulder as soon as he had cleared my head (I generally carry an axe separate from my alpenstock – the blade tied to the belt, and the handle attached to the left shoulder). Before coming to me Rebot had helped Nance out of the snow; he was lying nearly horizontally, and was not much covered over. Nance found Bevard, who was upright in the snow, but covered up to the head. After about twenty minutes the two last-named guides came up. I was at length taken out; the snow had to be cut with the axe down to my feet before I could be pulled out. A few minutes after 1 o'clock P.M. we came to my poor friend's face ... I wished the body to be taken out completely, but nothing could induce the three guides to work any longer, from the moment they saw that it was too late to save him. I acknowledge that they were nearly as incapable of doing anything as I was. When I was taken out of the snow the cord had to be cut. We tried the end going towards Bennen, but could not move it; it went nearly straight down, and showed us that there was the grave of the bravest guide the Valais ever had, and ever will have. The cold had done its work on us; we could stand it no longer, and began the descent. We followed the frozen avalanche for about twenty-five minutes, that being the easiest way of progressing, and then took the track we had made in the morning; in five hours we reached Ardon.

❋ (From 'Narrative of the Fatal Accident on the Haut-de-Cry, Canton Valais' by Philip C. Gosset. Vol. I.)

4 ❄ *In the Cause of Science*

ELECTRICAL ADVENTURES. – On the 10th July, I visited the Col de la Jungfrau from the Æggischhorn, in company with my wife, and Messrs. John Sowerby and W. G. Adams of Marlborough College. We had with us as guides, J. M. Claret of Chamounix, and a young man from the hotel. The early morning was bright and gave promise of a fine day, but as we approached the col, clouds settled down upon it, and on reaching it we encountered so severe a storm of wind, snow, and hail, that we were unable to stay more than a few minutes. As we descended, the snow continued to fall so densely that we lost our way, and for some time we were wandering up towards the Lötsch-sattel. We had hardly discovered our mistake when a loud peal of thunder was heard, and shortly after I observed that a strange singing sound like that of a kettle was issuing from my alpenstock. We halted, and finding that all the axes and stocks emitted the same sound, stuck them into the snow. The guide from the hotel now pulled off his cap, shouting that his head burned, and his hair seemed to have a similar appearance to that which it would have presented had he been on an insulated stool under a powerful electrical machine. We all of us experienced the sensation of pricking or burning in some part of the body, more especially in the head and face, my hair also standing on end in an uncomfortable but very amusing manner. The snow gave out a hissing sound, as though a heavy shower of hail were falling; the veil in the wide-awake of one of the party stood upright in the air; and on waving our hands, the singing sound issued loudly from the fingers. Whenever a peal of thunder was heard the phenomenon ceased, to be resumed before its echoes had died away. At these times we felt shocks, more or less violent, in those portions of the body which were most affected. By one of these shocks my right arm was paralysed so completely that I could neither use nor raise it for several minutes, nor indeed until it had been severely rubbed by Claret, and I suffered much pain in it at the shoulder joint for some hours. At half-past twelve the clouds began to pass away, and the phenomenon finally ceased, having lasted twenty-five minutes. We saw no lightning, and were puzzled at the first as to whether we should be afraid or amused. The young guide was very much alarmed, but Claret, who has no kind of fear, and who had twice previously heard the singing (unaccompanied by the other symptoms), laughed so heartily at the whole affair that we kept up our spirits. No evil effects were felt afterwards, beyond the inconvenience arising from the burning of our faces, which, though there had been no sun, were almost of livid hue when we arrived at the Æggischhorn. Principal Forbes mentions his having heard the singing noise from his bâton whilst crossing the St. Théodule, and, as I have said, Claret had also heard it before; but, with these exceptions, I can hear of no one who has met with these curious and interesting phenomena. It has been suggested that our bodies became, as it were, Leyden jars for the time, and that the thunder peal discharged us. Neither travellers nor guides were sorry when they got their final discharge.   ROBT. SPENCE WATSON.

GREEN SHADOWS ON SNOW. – On the 16th of September, last year, I ascended the Gross Glockner in company with two friends. At 5.30 A.M. we were upon the long ridge which forms the snowshed of the Pasterze and Leiter glaciers. The morning, upon the mountains, was perfectly clear and cloudless, though the valleys were filled with mist. The sun had not yet shown himself above the mountain ramparts which bounded our view towards the east, but a gorgeous fringe of fiery orange light, which rested upon the whole length of the mountain range, heralded his rising. I had been looking at this magnificent effect of the sunrise, when, happening to turn, I was surprised to see that our shadows upon the white snow at our feet were of a pale, though decided, green colour. Wishing to make certain of the fact, I asked one of my friends to look at the shadows and tell me what colour they were; and he immediately answered that they were green. This colour they retained for about ten minutes, until the sun had shown himself above the eastern range of mountains.

E. THURSTAN HOLLAND.

PHOSPHORESCENT SNOW. – On the 11th September, 1862, in company with my friends Messrs. Martineau and Donaldson Hudson, I crossed the mountains between the Fusch Thal and Möll Thal, taking the ordinary route to Heiligen-blut. We left Fusch late in the afternoon, and before we reached the Raurisr Tauern night had overtaken us, and it became so dark that we had considerable difficulty in finding our way. After we had crossed the Tauern and commenced our descent towards Heiligen-blut, we came upon several large patches of recently fallen snow. By this time it must have been between eight and nine o'clock, but it was too dark for us to see our watches. As we were crossing one of the patches of snow, I observed that the snowy particles which fell from my shoes appeared like a number of bright phosphorescent sparks. When I first saw these snowy sparks, I was walking in front of the party, but in order to observe the phenomenon better I dropped behind, and Hudson took my place. As I followed him, I saw clearly that at almost every step the snowy particles which he lifted with his feet fell in a little luminous shower. Except that the sparks were of a pale phosphorescent yellow colour, the effect was much the same as that of the sparks seen at night when a horse strikes his shoe against a stone. At one time also, I fancied that a large mass of snow was slightly luminous, but I cannot be certain whether it was so in reality, or whether I was deceived by the whiteness of the snow having suddenly caught my eyes through the darkness.   E. THURSTAN HOLLAND.

✳ (From *Notes and Queries*, Vol. I.)

A STRANGE SIGHT ON SNOWDON. – Mr. Howard Barrett writes: 'It has recently been my good fortune to witness a phenomenon amongst the hills of North Wales sufficiently rare to deserve record and to interest mountaineers who are students of nature as well as climbers.

'On January 20 last my friend Dr. Ambrose Fleming and myself left the Pen-y-gwryd Inn (near the foot of Snowdon) to walk up the Glydr Vach. The rain was steadily descending as we set out, and everything fifty yards distant from the observer was hidden in a thick and impenetrable mist that was driving up from the westward before a strong wind. We reached the summit just at noon, and the sun, which for the last half-hour had been making unsuccessful efforts to pierce the thick veil of clouds and vapour, was just then on the point of succeeding. We of course clambered up the minute aiguille, or natural cairn of splintered rock, that forms the actual summit, and which was just large enough to accommodate us both, and then looked northward and down towards the deep valley in which lies Lake Idwal. But both lake and valley were at first wholly obscured by great volumes of thin cloud and scud driving before the wind. Then all at once the sun, behind us and at no great altitude, burst forth through the clouds with brilliant rays, and we saw, to our astonishment, a circular rainbow, beautiful and complete; and within this, framed as it were by the glowing spectrum, the shadows of ourselves and the upper part of the little peak on which we stood distinctly projected upon the mist. We waved our arms, and at once the shadowy arms wildly answered us. At one time the rainbow was reduplicated, the primary one being completely and concentrically surrounded by a secondary circle. The colours of the inner rainbow were very bright and in the order of the primary bow; the outer one was fainter. As the wind cleared the valley wholly of mist these appearances vanished, and in their stead, and occupying much the same positions in the field of vision, lay Llyn Idwal far beneath, with Llyn Ogwen and both the Carnedds in the remote distance. But again the scud drove up and filled the valley, and once more the iris-circled phantoms reappeared; and this alternate vanishing and reappearance continued for several minutes, until once more the sun was obscured by a mass of clouds.

'Owing to a certain degree of astigmatism in my eyes, to me the bow or bows looked rather ovoid than circular, but to my companion they appeared quite circular. An attempt made by Dr. Fleming, to whom the solution of optical problems comes naturally, to determine the angle subtended by the diameter of the primary bow, brought it out as probably not much above 20°. It would be interesting to learn if any other members of the Club have ever met with similar phenomena, for I imagine that, in the nature of things, it is given only to mountaineers, to those who ascend church steeples or topmasts of ships, or who go up into the air in balloons, to behold such things. I suppose we are most of us familiar with shadows upon cloud or mist – the spectre of the Brocken, for instance – but during eleven or twelve summers in the Alps I have never seen a circular rainbow.

'I have since become aware that in the "Philosophical Magazine" for January 1884 (p. 61) an interesting article by Professor Tyndall occurs, describing experiments made by him in the laboratory to produce circular rainbows by artificial light thrown upon artificial mist. His attention had been drawn to the subject by an observation made at the Bel Alp on one occasion, when his own shadow was projected at night time by a lamp behind him on to the mist, and was seen to be surrounded by a luminous but uncoloured circle.

'Since I wrote the above Professor Tyndall's interesting article on "Rainbows" has appeared in the February number of the "Nineteenth Century". From this I gather that the phenomenon I have recorded has been even more rarely observed, or certainly more rarely described, than I had supposed.

'The Professor has to go back as far as 1835, and as far afield as the Ghâts of the Deccan, to find a recorded instance of the coloured circular rainbow. In the "Philosophical Transactions" for that year Colonel Sykes gives a vivid description of a phenomenon identical with that observed by myself and Dr. Fleming. He was at the top of "a precipice from 2,000 to 3,000 ft. perpendicular," forming the N.W. scarp of the hill-foot of Hurreechundurghur. From here he observed a brilliant circular rainbow, throwing out a fainter secondary bow; and, to complete the resemblance of the two instances, "shadows in distinct outline of myself," he says, "my horse, and people appeared in the centre of the circle, as a picture, to which the bow formed a resplendent frame." Also in a recent issue of the "Proceedings of the Royal Geographical Society" Mr. E. Colborne Baber describes the position on a mountain of West China (11,000 ft. in height) whence the phenomenon is frequently observed, and where it is called by the natives the "Fo-Kuang", or "glory of Buddha". He himself was not lucky enough to see it, but he gives the account of Baptist missionaries who did, and were much impressed by the spectacle.

'Thus has the glory of Buddha been made manifest even among the gentle undulations of Wales.'

❈ (From *Alpine Notes*, Vol. XI.)

Edward Whymper

5 ❄ The Fatal Accident on the Matterhorn

'Sir, – After the direct appeals which I have received from the President of the Alpine Club and from yourself to write an account of the accident on the Matterhorn, I feel it is impossible to remain silent any longer, and I therefore forward to you for publication a plain statement of the accident itself, and of the events that preceded and followed it.

'On Wednesday morning, the 12th of July, Lord Francis Douglas and myself crossed the Col Théodule to seek guides at Zermatt. After quitting the snow on the northern side we rounded the foot of the glacier, crossed the Furgge Glacier, and left my tent, ropes, and other matters in the little chapel at the Lac Noir. We then descended to Zermatt, engaged Peter Taugwalder, and gave him permission to choose another guide. In the course of the evening the Rev. Charles Hudson came into our hotel with a friend, Mr. Hadow, and they, in answer to some inquiries, announced their intention of starting to attack the Matterhorn on the following morning. Lord Francis Douglas agreed with me it was undesirable that two independent parties should be on the mountain at the same time, with the same object. Mr. Hudson was therefore invited to join us, and he accepted our proposal. Before admitting Mr. Hadow I took the precaution to inquire what he had done in the Alps, and, as well as I remember, Mr. Hudson's reply was, "Mr. Hadow has done Mont Blanc in less time than most men." He then mentioned several other excursions that were unknown to me, and added, in answer to a further question, "I consider he is a sufficiently good man to go with us." This was an excellent certificate, given us as it was by a first-rate mountaineer, and Mr. Hadow was admitted without any further question. We then went into the matter of guides. Michel Croz was with Messrs. Hadow and Hudson, and the latter thought if Peter Taugwalder went as well that there would not be occasion for anyone else. The question was referred to the men themselves, and they made no objection.

'We left Zermatt at 5.35 on Thursday morning, taking the two young Taugwalders as porters, by the desire of their father. They carried provisions amply sufficient for the whole party for three days, in case the ascent should prove more difficult than we anticipated. No rope was taken from Zermatt, because there was already more than enough in the chapel at Lac Noir. It has been repeatedly asked, "Why was not the wire-rope taken which Mr. Hudson brought to Zermatt?" I do not know; it was not mentioned by Mr. Hudson, and at that time I had not even seen it. My rope alone was used during the expedition, and there was – first, about 200 ft. of Alpine Club rope; second, about 150 ft. of a kind I believe to be stronger than the first; third, more than 200 ft. of a lighter and weaker rope than the first, of a kind used by myself until the Club rope was produced.

'It was our intention on leaving Zermatt to attack the mountain seriously – not, as it has been frequently stated, to explore or examine it – and we were provided with everything that long experience has shown to be necessary for the most difficult mountains. On the first day, however, we did not intend to ascend to any great height, but to stop when we found a good position for placing the tent. We mounted accordingly very leisurely, left the Lac Noir at 8.20, and passed along the ridge connecting the Hörnli with the actual peak, at the foot of which we arrived at 11.20, having frequently halted on the way. We then quitted the ridge, went to the left, and ascended by the north-eastern face of the mountain. Before 12 o'clock we had found a good position for the tent, at a height of 11,000 ft.; but Croz and the elder of Taugwalder's sons went on to look what was above, in order to save time on the following morning. The remainder constructed the platform on which the tent was to be placed, and by the time this was finished the two men returned, reported joyfully that as far as they had gone they had seen nothing but that which was good, and asserted positively that had we gone on with them on that day we could have ascended the mountain, and have returned to the tent with facility. We passed the remaining hours of daylight – some basking in the sunshine, some sketching or collecting, and when the sun went down (giving, as it departed, a glorious promise for the morrow) we returned to the tent to arrange for the night. Hudson made tea, myself coffee, and we then retired each one to his blanket bag; the Taugwalders, Lord Francis Douglas, and myself occupying the tent, the others remaining, by preference, outside. But long after dusk the cliffs above echoed with our laughter and with the songs of the guides, for we were happy that night in camp, and did not dream of calamity.

'We were astir long before daybreak on the morning of the 14th, and started directly it was possible to move, leaving the youngest of Taugwalder's sons behind. At 6.20 we had attained a height of 12,800 ft., and halted for half an hour, then continued the ascent without a break until 9.55, when we stopped for fifty minutes, at a height probably of about 14,000 ft. Thus far we had ascended by the north-eastern face of the mountain, and had not met with a single difficulty. For the greater part of the way there was, indeed, no occasion for the rope; and sometimes Hudson led, sometimes myself. We had now arrived at the foot of that part which from Zermatt seems perpendicular or overhanging, and we could no longer continue on the same side. By common consent, therefore, we ascended for some distance by the arête – that is by the ridge descending towards Zermatt – and then turned over to the right, or to the north-western face. Before doing so we made a change in the order of ascent; Croz now went first, I followed, Hudson came third, Hadow and old Taugwalder were last. The change was made because the work became difficult for a time, and required caution. In some places there was but little to hold, and it was therefore desirable those should be in front who were least likely to slip. The general slope of the mountain at this part was less than forty degrees, and snow had consequently accumulated and filled up the irregularities of the rock face, leaving only occasional fragments projecting here and there. These were at times coated with a thin glaze of ice, from the snow above having melted and frozen again during the night. Still it was a place over which any fair mountaineer might pass in safety. We found, however, that Mr. Hadow was not accustomed to this kind of work, and required continual assistance; but no one suggested that he should stop, and he was taken to the top. It is only fair to say that the difficulty experienced by Mr. Hadow at this part arose, not from fatigue or lack of courage, but simply and entirely from want of experience. Mr. Hudson, who followed me, passed over this part, and, as far as I know, ascended the entire mountain without having the slightest assistance rendered to him on any occasion. Sometimes, after I had taken a hand from Croz or received a pull, I turned to give the same to Hudson; but he invariably declined, saying it was not necessary. This solitary difficult part was of no great extent, certainly not more than 300 ft. high, and after it was passed the angles became less and less as we approached the summit; at last the slope was so moderate that Croz and myself detached ourselves from the others and ran on to the top. We arrived at 1.40 P.M., the others about 10 min. after us.

 'I have been requested to describe particularly the state of the party on the summit. No one showed any signs of fatigue, neither did I hear anything to lead me to suppose that anyone was at all tired. I remember Croz laughing at me when I asked him the question. Indeed, less than ten hours had elapsed since our starting, and during that time we had halted for nearly two. The only remark which I heard suggestive of danger was made by Croz, but it was quite casual, and probably meant nothing. He said, after I had remarked that we had come up very slowly, "Yes; I would rather go down with you and another guide alone than with those who are going." As to ourselves, we were arranging what we should do that night on our return to Zermatt.

'We remained on the summit for one hour, and during the time Hudson and I consulted, as we had done all the day, as to the best and safest arrangement of the party. We agreed that it would be best for Croz to go first, as he was the most powerful, and Hadow second; Hudson, who was equal to a guide in sureness of foot, wished to be third; Lord F. Douglas was placed next, and old Taugwalder, the strongest of the remainder, behind him. I suggested to Hudson that we should attach a rope to the rocks on our arrival at the difficult bit, and hold it as we descended, as an additional protection. He approved the idea, but it was not definitely settled that it should be done. The party was being arranged in the above order while I was making a sketch of the summit, and they were waiting for me to be tied in my place, when some one remembered that we had not left our names in a bottle; they requested me to write them, and moved off while it was being done. A few minutes afterwards I tied myself to young Taugwalder and followed, catching them just as they were commencing the descent of the difficult part described above. The greatest care was being taken. Only one man was moving at a time; when he was firmly planted the next advanced, and so on. The average distance between each was probably 20 ft. They had not, however, attached the additional rope to rocks, and nothing was said about it. The suggestion was made entirely on account of Mr. Hadow, and I am not sure it even occurred to me again.

'I was, as I have explained, detached from the others, and following them; but after about a quarter of an hour Lord F. Douglas asked me to tie on to old Taugwalder, as he feared, he said, that if there was a slip Taugwalder would not be able to hold him. This was done hardly ten minutes before the accident, and undoubtedly saved Taugwalder's life.

'As far as I know, at the moment of the accident no one was actually moving. I cannot speak with certainty, neither can the Taugwalders, because the two leading men were partially hidden from our sight by an intervening mass of rock. Poor Croz had laid aside his axe, and in order to give Mr. Hadow greater security was absolutely taking hold of his legs and putting his feet, one by one, into their proper positions. From the movements of their shoulders it is my belief that Croz, having done as I have said, was in the act of turning round to go down a step or two himself; at this moment Mr. Hadow slipped, fell on him, and knocked him over. I heard one startled exclamation from Croz, then saw him and Mr. Hadow flying downwards; in another moment Hudson was dragged from his steps, and Lord F. Douglas immediately after him. All this was the work of a moment; but immediately we heard Croz's exclamation Taugwalder and myself planted ourselves as firmly as the rocks would permit; *the rope was tight between us, and the shock came on us both as on one man.* We held; but the rope broke midway between Taugwalder and Lord F. Douglas. For two or three seconds we saw our unfortunate companions sliding downwards on their backs, and spreading out their hands endeavouring to save themselves; they then disappeared one by one, and fell from precipice to precipice on to the Matterhorn Glacier below, a distance of nearly 4,000 feet in height. From the moment the rope broke it was impossible to help them.

'For the space of half an hour we remained on the spot without moving a single step. The two men, paralysed by terror, cried like infants, and trembled in such a manner as to threaten us with the fate of the others. Immediately we had descended to a safe place I asked for the rope that had broken, and to my surprise – indeed, to my horror – found that it was the weakest of the three ropes. As the first five men had been tied while I was sketching, I had not noticed the rope they employed, and now I could only conclude that they had seen fit to use this in preference to the others. It has been stated that the rope broke in consequence of its fraying over a rock: this is not the case; it broke in mid-air, and the end does not show any trace of previous injury.

'For more than two hours afterwards I thought every moment that the next would be my last; for the Taugwalders, utterly unnerved, were not only incapable of giving assistance, but were in such a state that a slip might have been expected from one or the other at any moment. I do the younger man, moreover, no injustice when I say that immediately we got to the easy part of the descent he was able to laugh, smoke, and eat as if nothing had happened. There is no occasion to say more of the descent. I looked frequently, but in vain, for traces of my unfortunate companions, and we were in consequence surprised by the night when still at a height of about 13,000 feet. We arrived at Zermatt at 10.30 on Saturday morning.

'Immediately on my arrival I sent to the President of the Commune, and requested him to send as many men as possible to ascend heights whence the spot could be commanded where I knew the four must have fallen. A number went and returned after six hours, reporting they had seen them, but that they could not reach them that day. They proposed starting on Sunday evening, so as to reach the bodies at daybreak on Monday; but, unwilling to lose the slightest chance, the Rev. J. M'Cormick and myself resolved to start on Sunday morning. The guides of Zermatt, being threatened with excommunication if they did not attend the early mass, were unable to accompany us. To several, at least, I am sure this was a severe trial; for they assured me with tears that nothing but that which I have stated would have prevented them from going. The Rev. J. Robertson and Mr. J. Philpotts, of Rugby, however, not only lent us their guide, Franz Andermatten, but also accompanied us themselves. Mr. Puller lent us the brothers Lochmatter: F. Payot and J. Tairraz, of Chamounix, also volunteered. We started with these at 2 A.M. on Sunday, and followed the route we had taken on Thursday morning until we had passed the Hörnli, when we went down to the right of the ridge and mounted through the séracs of the Matterhorn Glacier. By 8.30 we had got on to the plateau at the top, and within sight of the corner in which we knew my companions must be. As we saw one weather-beaten man after another raise the telescope, turn deadly pale, and pass it on without a word to the next, we knew that all hope was gone. We approached; they had fallen below as they had fallen above – Croz a little in advance, Hadow near him, and Hudson some distance behind; but of Lord F. Douglas we could see nothing. To my astonishment, I saw that all of the three had been tied with the Club, or with the second and equally strong, rope, and consequently there was only one link – that between Taugwalder and Lord F. Douglas – in which the weaker rope had been used.

'The letters of the Rev. J. M'Cormick have already informed you respecting the subsequent proceedings. The orders from the Government of the Valais to bring the bodies down were so positive that four days after the events I have just related twenty-one guides accomplished that sad task. The thanks of all Englishmen are due to these brave men, for it was a work of no little difficulty and of great danger. Of the body of Lord F. Douglas they, too, saw nothing: it is probably arrested in the rocks above. No one can mourn his loss more deeply or more sincerely than myself. Although young, he was a most accomplished mountaineer, hardly ever required the slightest assistance, and did not make a single slip throughout the day. He had only a few days before we met made the ascent of the Gabelhorn – a summit considerably more difficult, I believe, to reach than the Matterhorn itself.

'I was detained in Zermatt until the 22nd of July, to await the inquiry instituted by the Government. I was examined first, and at the close I handed in to the Court a number of questions which I desired should be put to the elder Taugwalder; doing so because that which I had found out respecting the ropes was by no means satisfactory to me. The questions, I was told, were put and answered before I left Zermatt; but I was not allowed to be present at the inquiry, and the answers, although promised, have not yet reached me.

'This, Sir, is the end of this sad story. A single slip, or a single false step, has been the sole cause of this frightful calamity, and has brought about misery never to be forgotten. I have only one observation to offer upon it. If the rope had not broken you would not have received this letter, for we could not possibly have held the four men, falling as they did, all at the same time, and with a severe jerk. But, at the same time, it is my belief no accident would have happened had the rope between those who fell been as tight, or nearly as tight, as it was between Taugwalder and myself. The rope, when used properly, is a great safeguard; but whether on rocks, or whether on snow or glacier, if two men approach each other so that the rope falls in a loop, the whole party is involved in danger, for should one slip or fall he may acquire, before he is stopped, a momentum that may drag down one man after another and bring destruction on all; but if the rope is tight this is all but impossible.

'I am, Sir, your obedient servant,

'Haslemere, Aug. 7.'   'EDWARD WHYMPER.'

❋ (From *Notes and Queries*, Vol II. The letter appeared first in *The Times* of 8 August 1865.)

Clinton Dent

6 ❄ The First Ascent of the Dru

In July last year, J. Oakley Maund and I arrived at Chamonix with one fixed determination. Either we would climb the Dru, or, at the worst, would, as far as in us lay, prove its inaccessibility. By my wish our first attempts were to be made by the old route leading towards the lower peak. And here let me state, lest I forget it, that the weather was on nearly all occasions of such a description that no parliamentary expressions can possibly do justice to it. Time after time we were baulked by snow, wind, or rain. Day after day we sat waiting in vain for the favourable moment, till hope deferred, and a long course of table d'hôte dinners, without exercise, combined to make the heart sick. A couple of fine days would occur, and a start be effected. Then came the rain again, and we had to return, soaked and despondent. What time we were not being rained upon on the Montanvert, we were steaming and drying over Couttet's kitchen fire. On hydropathic principles we found this state of the elements an excellent cure for the mountain fever. Enough! Let me record what we did achieve in the rare intervals of decent weather.

Our first attempt was made with Johann Jaun and Andreas Maurer as guides. A lank-visaged porter, somewhat weak in the joints, who must have echoed Hamlet's interrogation as to the necessity of bearing fardels, carried our tent up to the grass slopes by the Charpoua Glacier. Here are many and excellent camping places. Dried dwarf rhododendron bushes abound, and water is plentiful, especially on the Moine side of the slopes. Leaving the porter at 2 A.M. still in a prostrate condition, we wended our way up the glacier, which was in first-rate order. All were in high spirits at the prospect of, at least, a good climb. Not a bit of it. The rock face over which access to the lower peak is alone possible was covered with snow in the most treacherous condition imaginable. The guides most properly refused to go on, pointing out that to descend in the afternoon, with the snow soft and loosely bound to the rocks, would be unwarrantably dangerous. Back we went, therefore, and met the sniggers and sneers of the worthy Chamoniards with an imperturbability bred of long experience.

Twice again within the next fortnight we tried, with the same guides. Result the same, except that we didn't go so far and got more wet. The excellent Jaun now left us, and Alexander Burgener came on as chief guide. Following his advice, a complete change of tactics was adopted. We decided to abandon all idea of attacking the lower peak, and made up our minds to try the higher east summit by our old '74 route.

And now let me digress for a moment and give credit where credit is due. It is due to the Messrs. Pendlebury's guides, especially, I believe, to Peter Baumann, who, in 1873, on his first inspection, marked out the true line of ascent as far as it was visible. Again, and above all, the whole of our success is due to Burgener's sagacity and great guiding qualities. I knew that any guide was immeasurably superior to an amateur in the knack of finding the way. I was aware that in quickness on rocks the two could hardly be compared. But I had always thought that the amateur excelled in one great requisite – pluck. This record will, I hope, show that in one instance at least this was an error. But for Burgener's indomitable obstinate pluck we should never have climbed the Dru.

Leaving the Montanvert about 1 A.M. we reached the rocks below the col somewhat late, for our route up the glacier was bad. There was a great deal of reconnoitring, and a considerable amount of talking. However we had a good climb, and settled the best route up some part of the couloir leading to the ridge. There was still too much snow on the rocks. A fancied insufficiency of guiding power – a decidedly insufficient supply of rope – and a strong idea that a new route was not to be worked out at a first attempt – combined to drive us back to Chamonix the same evening.

Après cela le déluge – and for a long time all mountaineering was impossible. Desperate were our attempts to amuse ourselves. Lawn tennis, with parti-coloured balls and wooden bats, in front of Couttet's was the fashion for a while. Then we went a cray fishing, Maund driving us to Chatelard in Couttet's basket carriage, and chirrupping pleasantly to an ancient spotted grey steed. Then I chirrupped him back again – and next day the spotted grey was '*très malade*', and my right arm very stiff. Under Maund's able tuition, and following his experienced directions at the fishing ground, we caught nothing.

Then I fell a musing and studied human nature, and wondered at the various imperfections of development the muscle, known to anatomists as the gastrocnemius, could exhibit in the legs of our countrymen, and marvelled why they took such pains in their costume to display its usually unsymmetrical proportions; and wondered why Couttet's barometer kept on rising, and pondered over —. Suffice it that at last Maund, to my infinite regret, left, from motives of fraternal duty, coupled with the rooted conviction that the rain would probably go on till the winter snows came.

And so it came to pass that with J. W. Hartley, and Alexander Burgener, and Andreas Maurer, as guides, I found myself one August day at a new and improved camping place, a good deal higher than our old bivouac. We left it at 3.45 A.M. and got early on to the rocks. A tremendous day we had. Bit by bit the best routes were worked out. Snow still lay thick everywhere. The rocks themselves were fearfully cold, and glazed with th in layers of slippery ice. It was a day of exploration. First the guides climbed to the col. Then Burgener and I climbed ropeless to the same spot. To those in search of excitement I recommend above everything these rocks when glazed. But for a growing conviction that the upper crags were not so bad as they looked, we should never have persevered that day. We reached at last a great knob of rock close to the col, and for a time Burgener and I sat alone, silently staring at the precipices of the upper peak. This was the turning-point of our year's climbing. Up to that moment I had only felt doubts as to the inaccessibility of the mountain. Now a certain feeling of confident elation began to creep over me. The aspect of a mountain varies marvellously according to the beholder's frame of mind. These same crags had been, at one time or another, deliberately pronounced impossible by each of us severally. Good judges had ridiculed the idea of getting up them. Yet, somehow, they looked different that day. Here and there we fancied we could trace short bits of practicable rock. Gradually, uniting and communicating passages developed themselves. At last we turned and looked at each other; the same train of ideas had been independently coursing through our minds. Burgener's face flushed, and we rose almost together, exclaiming *'Es muss möglich sein.'* The rest of the day was devoted to bringing down our ladder from the col to a point much lower and nearer the main peak. Then followed one of the nastiest descents I ever experienced. We had made our way over the great snow patches, for the stones fell too freely in the couloir to render that safe. At one time we had 150 feet of rope paid out between one position of comparative security and the one next below it. One step, and the snow would crunch up healthily and give good hold. The next, and the leg plunged in as far as it could reach. Yet another, and a layer of snow, a foot deep, would slide hissing off, and expose bare black ice beneath, or treacherous loose stones. Not till 9 P.M. did we reach Chamonix. But I had seen all I wanted, and now I would have staked my best hat on the possibility of climbing the mountain. The usual atrocious weather which kept us back after this attempt was in consequence doubly vexatious.

Perhaps the monotonous reptition of failures on our peak influences my recollection of what took place subsequently. Perhaps – as I sometimes think, even now – an intense desire to accomplish our ambition, ripened into a realization of actual occurrences, which really were only efforts of imagination. Anyhow when, on September 7, we once more sat before the camp fire, I could hardly persuade myself that so much had taken place since the attempt last mentioned. It seemed but a dream, whose reality could be disproved by an effort, that we had gone to Zermatt in a storm and hurried back again in a drizzle; that we had left Chamonix and tried the peak again in a tempest; that I had returned to England utterly dispirited and downcast; that I had posted back after forty-eight hours' sojourn in my native hand, on receiving by telegraph the welcome intimation that the weather at last looked promising. A confused jumble and whirl of thoughts crowded the brain. I heard the parting farewell from our pleasant party as the diligence lumbered away from Chamonix; this was chased away by the slow heavy clank of the railway carriages entering the station. I rubbed my eyes and looked up. Was that the Dru clear and bright above? The outline seemed strangely familiar. Surely that was Hartley there, occupied in the congenial employment of greasing his face with the contents of a little squeeze-bottle – and there was Burgener. But what was this shapeless sleeping mass? Gradually it dawned on me that I was but inverting a psychological process and trying to make a dream out of a reality. Hartley was there; Burgener was there; and the uncomely bundle was the outward form of the most incompetent guide in the Alps Not till after did we learn that our friend had previously distinguished himself with Maund on the north face of the Breithorn. Not till the next day did we fully realize how bad a guide might be. We kicked him and he awoke. Then he made the one true remark I heard him utter. He said he had been drunk the day before. Then he relapsed; and during the remainder of the time he was with us enunciated nothing but falsehoods.

From four in the morning the next day till seven in the evening when we reached our bivouac again, we worked incessantly. Not so the Driveller – for so we christened our new guide appropriately. Hartley dragged him up the glacier. Twice we pointed out to him half-hidden crevasses, and twice he acknowledged our courtesy by disappearing into them. Finally on the rocks we unroped and let him be. For seven hours he crouched under a little rock, not daring to move up or down, or even to take his knapsack off his back.

For the first time on this occasion we climbed above the col and bore off to the left on to the real rock peak. At first it was easy, but progress was distressingly slow, with only one guide and a short rope, for the Driveller far below had most of that commodity encircling his person. Hartley must have enjoyed his day. Unfortunately for him he was by far the lightest member of the party. Accordingly, we argued, he was less likely to break the rickety old ladder than we were. He was the lightest, so he was most conveniently lowered over nasty places when they occurred.

In the good old times if you wanted your chimneys swept you summoned a master sweep. This worthy would come attended by a satellite, in the shape of a boy. The boy was of such size and shape that he fitted tolerably tightly into your chimney. He then clambered up and did the work, while the master sweep remained below to encourage, preside over, and subsequently to profit by his apprentice's exertions. On much the same principle did we climb this part of the mountain. Hartley was the boy, while Burgener and I, however unworthily, enacted the role of the master sweep. Gallantly did our friend fulfil his duties. Whether climbing up a ladder slightly out of the perpendicular, leaning against nothing, and with overhanging places above; whether let down by a rope tied round his waist so that he dangled like the sign of the Golden Fleece outside a haberdasher's shop; or hauled up before he was ready, with his raiment in an untidy mass round his neck; in each and all of these exercises he was equally at home; and would be let down or would come up, smiling. Over one place, where Burgener and I exerted ourselves to the utmost to hold the ladder against a slightly overhanging rock-face, with an ugly-looking bunch of great icicles above, we must have spent an hour. On a later occasion by a deviation of about fifteen or twenty feet we climbed to the same spot in a few minutes with perfect safety, without using any ladder.

Once more, on September 11, and for the last time, we sat on the rocks just above the camping place. Never had we been so confident of success. Instructions had been given to our friends below to look out for our appearance on the summit between 12 and 2 P.M., the next day. Hartley had brought a weakly little stick which, it was arranged, was to crown our labours, and decorate the summit, on the morrow. But the old source of disquietude harassed us. Our eyes turned anxiously to the west. There, a single huge belt of cloud hung heavily right across the sky – livid in colour above, but tinged a crimson red below. Hartly was despondent at the prospect it suggested. But perhaps its very watery look hinted to my mind that it might be a Band of Hope. From below the smell of savoury soup was wafted gently up, 'stealing and giving odour'. We took courage, then descended and took sustenance.

At 4 A.M. on September 12 we left. Kaspar Maurer, younger brother of Andreas before mentioned, now accompanied us, for our old enemy the Driveller had been sent away with a flea in his ear – an almost unnecessary adjunct, as anyone who had slept in the same tent with him could testify. Notwithstanding that Maurer was ill, we mounted rapidly, for the way was tolerably familiar, and we all meant business. Our position now was this. By our exploration of September 8 we knew that from the col it was possible to ascend to a considerable height on the main mass. Again, from telescopic observations and the slope of the rocks we were certain that the final arête was easy. Immediately above the col the only choice was to cross over rather on to the south-east face while ascending. A projecting buttress of rock, some two or three hundred feet in height, cuts off the view on to the face from the col. We hoped by turning straight up behind this to hit off the arête just above the point where it merges into the precipitous N.E. wall. The rocks behind this buttress are visible only from near the head of the Charpoua Glacier, but we had never properly examined them.

We followed the couloir running up from the head of the glacier, keeping well to the left to a little below the col. At this point it became necessary to cross the couloir, and for that purpose we employed the long ladder, which we had placed in position the day before. Right glad were we to see the rickety old structure, albeit it creaked and groaned dismally under our weight, and ran its splinters into our persons at all points of contact. Yet there was a certain companionship about this same weather-beaten ladder, and I felt as if it was almost a hardship that it could not share more in our promising success. Next we fastened a double rope, about 20 ft. in length, and swung ourselves down a rough cleft as if we were barrels of split peas going into a ship's hold. Up again, and the excitement waxed stronger as we neared the doubtful part. Then Alexander lay flat on his stomach, and wriggled round a projecting rock, disappearing suddenly from view. We followed, progressing like the skates down the panes of glass in an aquarium tank, and found ourselves huddled together on a little ledge. An overhanging rock above compelled us to assume the anomalous attitudes enforced on the occupant of a little-ease dungeon. What next? An eager look up, and part of the doubt was solved. There was a way – but such a way. A narrow flat couloir, its angle plastered with ice from top to bottom, invited, or forbade, further progress. Above, a pendulous mass of great icicles, black and long like a bunch of elephants' trunks, crowned the gully. We tucked ourselves away on one side, and the guides performed the best feat of rock climbing I can imagine possible. Unroped they worked up, hacking out the ice, their backs and elbows against one sloping wall and their feet against the other. The masses of ice dashing down, harder and harder as they ascended, showed how they were working. Suddenly a slip above – a shout – a crash of falling ice. Then a brief pause, broken after a few minutes by a triumphant yell from above, and the end of a rope dangled down close to us. Using this latter aid considerably, we mounted and found the top of the couloir blocked up by a great overhanging boulder, dripping still where the icicles had just been broken off. 'Come on,' said voices from above. 'Up you go,' said a voice from below. I leaned as far back as I could, and felt for a hand-hold. There was none. Then right, then left – still none. So I smiled feebly, and said, 'Wait a minute.' Thereupon, of course, they pulled with a will, and struggling and kicking like a spider irritated with tobacco smoke, I topped the rock gracefully. How the first man did it, is, and always will be, a mystery to me. Then we learned that a great mass of ice had broken away under Maurer's feet while in the couloir, and that he must have fallen had not Alexander pinned him to the rock with one hand. From the number of times that this escape was described to me during the next day or two I am inclined to think it was a near thing. 'The worst is over,' said Alexander. I was glad to hear it, but, looking upwards, had my doubts. The higher we went the bigger the rocks seemed to be. Still there was a way, and it was not so unlike what I had often pictured.

Another tough scramble, and we stood on a comparatively extensive ledge. Already we had climbed more than half of the only part of the mountain as to the nature of which we were uncertain. A few steps on, and Burgener grasped me suddenly by the arm. 'Do you see the great red rock up yonder?' he whispered, hoarse with excitement; 'in ten minutes we shall be there, and on the arête – and then –' I felt that nothing could stop us now; but a feverish anxiety to see what was beyond, to look on to the last slope, which we knew must be easy, impelled us on, and we worked harder than ever to overcome the last few obstacles. The ten minutes expanded into something like thirty before we really reached the rock. Of a sudden the mountain seemed to change its form. For hours we had been climbing the hard dry rocks. Now these appeared to vanish, and – blessed sight – snow lay thick, half hiding, half revealing the last slope of the arête. A glance showed that we had not misjudged. Even the cautious Maurer admitted that as far as we could see all was well; but he added, 'Up above there, possibly –' And now, with the prize almost within our grasp, a strange desire to halt and hang back came on. Alexander tapped the rock with his axe, and let out his pent-up excitement in a comprehensive anathema of Chamonix guides. Already we could anticipate the half-sad feeling with which we should touch the top itself. The feeling soon gave way. 'Forwards,' we cried, and the axe crashed through the layers of snow into hard blue ice beneath. A dozen steps, and then a bit of rock scrambling; then more steps along the south side of the ridge – some more rock, and we topped the first eminence. Better and better it looked as we went on. 'See there!' cried Alexander, suddenly; 'the actual top.' There was no mistaking the two huge stones we had so often looked at from below. A few feet below them, and on our left, was one of those strange arches formed by a great transverse boulder, and through the hole we saw blue sky. Nothing could lie beyond, and, still better, nothing could be above. On again, while I could hardly stand still in the great steps the leader hacked out. A short troublesome bit of snow-work followed, where the heaped-up cornice had fallen back from the final rock. Then Hartley courteously allowed me to unrope and pass him, and in a second I clutched at the last broken rocks, and hauled myself up on to the flat sloping summit. There for a moment I stood alone, gazing down on Chamonix. The dream of five years was accomplished. The Dru was climbed.

Our first care was to level the telescope in the direction of Couttet's hotel. There was not much excitement there, but in front of the Imperial we were pleased to think we saw somebody gazing in our direction.

Accordingly with much pomp and ceremony the stick (which I may here state was borrowed without leave) was fixed up. Then to my horror Alexander produced from a concealed pocket a piece of scarlet flannel, like unto a baby's undergarment, and tied it on. I protested in vain. In a moment the objectionable rag was floating proudly in the breeze. Determined that our ascent should not be questioned by any subsequent visitors, we left the following articles: one half-pint bottle containing our names, preserved by a paper stopper from the inclemency of the weather; two wooden wedges (use unknown), two ends of string, three burnt fusees, divers chips, one stone-man, the tenpenny staff and the infant's petticoat.

Of the view I can say but little. I remember that Chamonix looked very nice from this distance. I remember that the Aiguille Verte seemed much less above us, and the lower peak much more below us (at least 80 ft.), than we had expected. Anyhow, I know that the comparative meagreness of the panorama did not affect our spirits, nor detract from the completeness of the expedition. The Dru is essentially a mountain to be climbed for its own sake. After three-quarters of an hour, i.e., at 1.15 P.M., we turned to descend, and very difficult the descent proved. In three places we fixed ropes to assist. Two of these still hang on the rocks, are securely fastened, are new club ropes, and will be found very serviceable in indicating the right route. We followed precisely the same line of rocks as in the morning, and noticed few, if any, places where this route was capable of improvement or even alteration. Not till nearly five o'clock did we reach our abandoned store of provisions, and very short work we made of them. Since ten in the morning we had partaken of nothing but one crushed sandwich. Ignoring the probability of being benighted on the rocks we caroused merrily on tinned meat and seltzer water. The sun was sinking low behind the Brevent range, and the rocks were all darkened in the grey shadows ere we packed up and resumed our journey. Very little time was lost in descending. But before we had reached the breakfast place at 7 P.M. darkness had overtaken us. When within a few feet of the glacier the mist, which had been long threatening, swept up from below and cut off all view. The crevasses just by the top of the glacier were so complicated, and the snow bridges so fragile, that we decided not to go on. So we sat down under an overhanging rock, and made believe that we enjoyed the fun. Hartley somewhat transparently imitated the action of a man going to sleep. The guides, as was their wont when inactive, wrangled over the dimensions of the different chamois they had shot, each of course outvying the other. Meanwhile I considered what I would have for breakfast next day, and finally stirred up Hartley. For two hours or so we discussed with some warmth the relative merits of kidneys and 'ferras' as articles of diet. Meanwhile the temperature sank, and slowly and gradually we became exceedingly chilly and uncomfortable. The end came sooner than we expected. By the time that Alexander had, in imagination, shot a chamois about the size of an elephant, and I had nearly carried my point about the kidneys, and was passing on to the subject of fried eggs, the mist lifted and disclosed the glacier feebly lit up by the rising moon. Instantly we sprang to our feet, and fondly imagined that an hour or so would see us back at the camp. Not so, however. The snow was all hard frozen, and in the dim light it was found necessary to cut steps nearly the whole way down the glacier. From 9 P.M. till 2.30 A.M. on the morning of the 13th, were we thus occupied. Charmingly comfortable was the tent that night. From the circumstance that the invariable struggle for the best pillow was unusually brief, and that Hartley did not dispute my final proposition that kidneys, if not cooked *à la brochette*, were to all intents and purposes wasted, I am inclined to think that we were not long in dropping off to sleep. By nine o'clock, however, we were at the Montanvert, where my old friend the landlord received us with more than his usual affability. Champagne was produced, for our success had already been reported, and notwithstanding that the summit is invisible from the inn, mine host was pleased to give us credit for telling the truth. Not so, however, the other Chamonix guides, many of whom maintained that we had merely reached a point on the south-east face of the lower peak. In spite of, or perhaps in consequence of, these early libations, we skipped down with more than our wonted nimbleness, and by 10 o'clock we were at Chamonix. There, I am pleased to record, the first man to congratulate us was M. Loppé, without whose kindly sympathy and constant encouragement I doubt if we should have ever persevered to our successful end.

Those who follow us, and I think there will be many, will perhaps be glad of a few hints about this peak. Taken altogether, it affords the most continuously interesting rock climb with which I am acquainted. There is no wearisome tramp over moraine, no great extent of snow fields to traverse. Sleeping out where we did, it would be possible to ascend and return to Chamonix in about 16 to 18 hrs. But the mountain is never safe when much snow lies on the rocks, and at such times stones fall freely down the couloir leading up from the head of the glacier. The best time for the expedition would be, in ordinary seasons, in the month of August. The rocks are sound, and are peculiarly unlike those on other mountains. From the moment the glacier is left, hard climbing begins, and the hands as well as the feet are constantly employed. The difficulties are therefore enormously increased if the rocks be glazed or cold, and in bad weather I should think the crags of the Dru would be as pretty a place for an accident as can well be imagined.

The lower peak I am certain can be climbed, but not by the tempting couloir which runs up between the two points. This may be followed for some distance, but then it will, I believe, be found best to bear off to the left. I know this way has been repeatedly tried, but then so had our line of ascent. Every bit of the mountain must be explored before any final conclusion as to its inaccessibility from this side is come to. It would be feasible to lower oneself down by a long rope from the higher on to the lower peak, and very probably the way down from this latter might prove easier than the way up. Let anyone in search of excitement insure his life and try. I am not sure that I should care to do so. If there be much snow on these lower rocks, as there was during the greater part of this last season, their ascent will be unjustifiably dangerous.

One remark in a former paper on this mountain should be here corrected. There, I stated (and it was my belief till last year) that we, in our second attempt, were very near the summit of the lower peak. I must plead guilty to an egregious mistake. We were probably not very much above the level of the col.

Ideas as to what is fair in mountain climbing are somewhat peculiar. I have been asked repeatedly whether we used 'artificial aid' in the Dru. Now by artificial aid seems to be meant driving in pegs into rocks where there is no hand or foot hold. Such a proceeding is considered highly improper. To cut a step in ice is right, but to do anything of the sort on rock is in the highest degree immoral. Again, a ladder to bridge a crevasse may be used without animadversion, but its employment over a rock cleft is tabooed. In fact, anything but hobnails, rope, axes, and a ladder for a bergschrund is 'artificial aid'. Rockets and target practice in general at rock peaks is usually only mentioned to be condemned, while grapnels, chains, and crampons are the inventions of the fiend. Why this should be so is hard to see. Perhaps we must not consider too curiously. For my own part if it could be proved that by no possible means could a given bad passage be traversed without some such aid, nor turned by another route, I should not hesitate to adopt one of these expedients. At the same time I believe that no such place exists. Emphatically I say that this is the case on the Aiguille du Dru. We used our ladders repeatedly and frequently, but only to shorten our way up, while exploring the mountain. When we actually climbed it we used one ladder in one place, and this particular place could have easily been turned by descending some little way and remounting by another route. We saved perhaps an hour by the use of the ladder; an hour late in the season is invaluable. Those who follow will find for themselves the truth of what I state; and if they can climb the peak without 'artificial aid', they will at least give us the credit for being able to do likewise. We have only shown one way up. There may be a dozen others, though I doubt it. In descending we noticed only a few places where the route would be easier. Still in a first ascent late in the season there is little time for deliberation. Promptness is essential, and the line chosen has often to be followed when the climbers are conscious that it is far from the easiest.

My task is nearly done. Space, and consideration for my readers, alike forbid any account of the festivities that took place at Couttet's in the evening. I believe there were fireworks; I rather think some cannon were let off. I am under the impression that a good many bottles were uncorked. Perhaps this last may be connected with a hazy recollection of all that actually took place. Yet visions as of dancing forms in the salon rise up, with the villagers and guides crowding at the windows to witness the graceful exercise of valsing in thick boots; and there, in the midst of the throng, I seem to see Maurer, resplendent in a shirt the front of which was like unto a petrified bath towel, a coat many sizes too large, his face beaming with smiles, and shining from the effects of drinks offered hospitably on all sides; close by, Alexander, displaying similar physiognomical phenomena, his natural free movements hampered by the excessive tightness of some garments with which an admirer of smaller girth had presented him, yet withal exceedingly well pleased with himself. Let us leave them there. They did their work well, and may be pardoned for a little swagger.

The days grow shorter apace; the sun has barely time to make the icefields glisten ere the cold shadows creep over again. Snow lies thick on ledge and cranny, and only the steepest mountain faces show dark through the powdery veil. Bleak night winds whistle around the crags, and whirl and chevy the wreathing snow-clouds, making weird music in these desolate fastnesses. The clear satiating air, the delicate purity of the Alpine tints, have given way to fog, mist, slush, and smoke-laden atmosphere. Would you recall these mountain pictures? Draw close the curtains, stir the coals into an indignant crackling blaze, and fashion in the rising smoke the mountain vista. How these scenes crowd back into the mind, with a revivability proportionate to the impression originally made! What keener charm than to pass in review the memories of these simple, wholesome pleasures; to see again, as clear as in the reality, every ledge, every hand and foot hold; to feel the fingers tingle and the muscles instinctively contract at the recollection of some tough scramble on rock or glacier?

I have endeavoured to give the impressions made by our expedition. I only wish that anyone could derive a hundredth part of the pleasure in reading that I have had in writing them.

❊ (From 'The History of an Ascent of the Aiguille du Dru' by C. T. Dent. Vol. IX.)

W. Penhall

7 ❅ The Matterhorn from the Zmutt Glacier

It was on reading, some three years ago, Mr. Whymper's account of the Matterhorn in 'Scrambles in the Alps', that I first conceived the idea of finding a new way up the mountain. I was surprised to learn that, notwithstanding their repeated failure on the Breil ridge, neither Mr. Whymper nor Professor Tyndall had ever attempted the north-western face; all he says is, 'The ghastly precipices which face the Zmutt Glacier forbade any attempt in that direction.'

Then I ascertained that in the first ascent from Breil the Italian guides actually got on to the upper part of this Zmutt face, though Mr. Grove gives a very unfavourable account of their route. Still his opinion was based on an inspection of the slope from above, and everybody knows what inaccurate impressions are got under such circumstances.

The fact remained that no one had given the Zmutt face or ridge a single trial. At that time, however, I had never been even to the Stockje, and my plans were of the vaguest possible kind. Moreover, when at Zermatt, later in the year, none of the guides I spoke to seemed to jump, as I had expected, at my 'happy thought', and I contented myself with going up by the ordinary route. Later, however, when descending from the Dent Blanche, I carefully examined the north-western rocks of the Matterhorn, and the impression I got was that a way might be found. I consequently decided to make an attempt the following year.

In the winter I found Mr. Conway was bent on the same expedition, and we accordingly engaged Ferdinand Imseng for the month of August, 1878. Our programme was a most ambitious one, including, besides the Matterhorn, new routes for the Weisshorn, Rothhorn, and Dom.

Before trying the first of these we considered four or five days of uninterrupted fine weather indispensable, and as they never came we left Zermatt, having again only looked at the Matterhorn. I was delighted, however, to find that Imseng was really very anxious to see what could be done, though he would not venture an opinion as to the probable result.

Last year I was unable to get away so soon as I should have liked, and I anxiously read the letters I had from Imseng about once a week during the summer, each telling me in wonderful German that the Matterhorn had not been done, though he generally hinted someone was on the point of starting, and that I had better be quick. At last he wrote to say he had been up the Weisshorn, from Zinal, and that the gentleman he accompanied in that expedition was about to turn his attention to the Stockje.

I hurried at once to Zermatt, where I arrived on Friday, August 29, when I found Imseng was assisting at a festive entertainment under the Riffelhorn. I saw him in the evening, and he was in most exuberant spirits, the cause of which was soon explained, he had just concluded a most enjoyable day by winning thirty francs at a sort of bottle-breaking pool, which formed the closing feature of the banquet.

Then we discussed our plans, and decided that if the weather kept fine we would make an early start the following Monday morning so as to give time for examining the face, and then sleeping out as high as possible we would try and reach the summit on the Tuesday.

Louis Zurbrücken, of Macugnaga, with whom Imseng has done a good deal of chamois hunting, was engaged as second guide. The next day I went for a training walk up Castor, with Zurbrücken, and from what I could make out of his guiding qualities, I felt very glad I had secured him.

On Monday, September 1, we got up at 2.30 to find the valley full of clouds, but not wishing to throw away the slightest chance, we set off half an hour later with a porter carrying blankets, and walked somewhat despondently up through the pine forests, looking in vain for a single star to encourage us. Presently Imseng reminded me that the evening before I had said there was no need to tell the other guides where we were going, as our first attempt was so likely to come to nothing. 'Well,' he said, 'we did as you told us, but unfortunately we did not all say the same.' Then I found they had construed what I said into directions to deceive, so one had given out we were going to Zinal, another that the Dent d'Hérens was our destination, while the porter had still further drawn on his imagination and explained quite proudly that he had mentioned to several of his friends that we were going chamois hunting, but where he did not know exactly. He seemed to think his fabrication very ingenious because it happened to be the 1st of September, and the absence of rifles or any offensive weapons a perfectly unimportant detail.

We agreed that after all this preamble something must be done, and we pushed on; but when we came to the highest châlets the weather looked so very unpromising that we devoutly wished ourselves back in bed, and we all crawled into a hay barn and went to sleep. On looking out at 7.30 I found the Matterhorn was nearly free from clouds, though all the other mountains were still covered; we thought the wind had changed a little, and we started once more. Hitherto we had formed no plan as to our exact route, and when we got nearly opposite the Stockje we waited and consulted. I wanted to go much further up the glacier and try the middle of the face. Imseng's only objection to this was that if we went that way probably we should find no suitable place to pass the night, while on the arête we should.

This seemed reasonable, so I gave in, and we turned up a rather steep slope of hard snow on our left; after three-quarters of an hour we reached some rocks which brought us to the arête, about 1,500 feet above the glacier. The rocks of the arête were climbed without difficulty, and above them after half an hour of snow we came to hard ice, up which we had to cut steps for 2 hrs., until in fact we reached the first of the rocky teeth visible from Zermatt.

Here we left our knapsacks and the porter, and passed the first and second teeth without difficulty, the third was more troublesome, and then we saw we should have to leave the arête and go to the left or Zermatt side, over a very objectionable looking slope of loose rocks, with some ice and snow at intervals. It was a place of no extraordinary difficulty, but as the slightest slip would probably have landed the whole party somewhere in the neighbourhood of the Matterhorn Glacier, we thought it unwise to attempt to pass it so late in the day, when the sun had been on it for several hours. We decided, therefore, to go no further that day, and turned our attention to the rest of the route. So far as we could see it would be necessary to leave the arête again, higher up, and then go to the right of it, and one thing we did not like was that a great many stones fell from that region, and then swept down a curious curved gully into the great couloir which descends from below the teeth where we were standing, obliquely across the face to the head of the Tiefenmatten Glacier. The central part of the face seemed freer from falling stones.

However we reasoned that by keeping as far as possible on the arête we should not long be exposed to falling stones, especially as we should be up there in the early morning. We could find no slab of rock large enough for us all to sit down upon, so we had reluctantly to retrace our steps down the ice slope to a patch of rocks where we could pass the night, and we calculated that having good steps ready made we should be able to reach the teeth again in little more than half an hour.

The sunset was one of the most perfect I have ever seen in the Alps, not a single cloud was visible, not a breath of wind stirring.

The panorama round the great glacier below us was magnificent, but all our attention was centred on one object in it, and straining my eyes at the gaunt slopes above, I fancied, as the light failed, I could make out not one, but half-a-dozen possible routes. The guides were most confident, saying that, with such weather, it must succeed. So after an excellent repast we spread out the blankets and tried to compose ourselves for the night.

The place was only prospectively a suitable one, the rock was far from flat, and after the sun had set we found half an hour's rest quite as much as we could endure at a time, so we got up and tramped backwards and forwards over a very limited exercise ground, and then lay down to shiver again.

About 10 P.M. we felt distinctly there was a wind, and soon we agreed it was rather strong and more than rather cold. Imseng, always hopeful as to the weather, said the wind invariably rose about that time, and it would subside before sunrise. I had never before heard that such was the case, but the sky was so clear I hoped he might be right, still, how we should have got through that night I don't know but that we had a small spirit lamp on the Russian principle which would just boil a soldier's mess tin. Zurbrücken and the porter held a blanket to keep off the wind, and Imseng and I cooked. First we made chocolate till that was all gone, then we went in for mulled wine. The third brew of this exhausted the spirit, and being once more unoccupied our attention returned to the weather. The moon first surrounded itself with a broad bright band, and shortly disappeared, then the stars over the Tiefenmatten Joch were obscured, and though the hour of sunrise was approaching, the wind increased instead of abating. It seemed madness to think of going up, and stop still we could not.

When it was light a few flakes of snow fell, and, expecting a storm, we began the descent at once. We did not take the same route as in going up, but left the arête immediately, and traversed the rocks obliquely, so as to get a better view of the central part of the face. After we had examined it pretty carefully for about ten minutes a mist formed and concealed it entirely, so we continued the descent, and left the rocks at a point which appears almost immediately under the summit when viewed from the Stockje. We skirted under the rocks, and finally reached the Zmutt Glacier by the same snow slope up which we had gone the day before.

We glanced up from time to time only to see the upper part of the mountain entirely covered with watery clouds.

As we went down we met Mr. Mummery coming up with Alexander Burgener. We thought for a moment of going to the Stockje and waiting for a time in the hope we might be able to get up the next day. The weather had, however, so thoroughly disgusted us, that we went on. Mummery was wiser and waited. Leaving the guides on the highest grass slopes I ran down to Zermatt; soon after I got there I began to think I had the best of it, for a few drops of rain fell and the wind came in gusts, banging the shutters about and raising a cloud of dust. Yet the storm did not burst, but seemed to think better of it, and passed off. About 6 o'clock Imseng came up to me and said very seriously that Zurbrücken had just been to consult the priest, and the opinion of that worthy was that it would be fine the following day, and – would I like to start again after table-d'hôte? I confess I should hardly have proposed it myself, but as he suggested it I agreed, and after several delays, owing to the provisions, the guides' supper, &c., we found ourselves at 10 o'clock once more trudging up the too familiar path; we were all half asleep, and the events of the two previous days seemed like a dream. When we were above the pine forests some rhododendron bushes looked very inviting, and we called a halt for 10 min.; we lengthened it into 20, and then went on. After reaching the glacier we took exactly the same route as in descending the day before, and at 3.30 we were close to the place where we had to take to the rocks. Here we waited 1 hr., and had breakfast, the spirit lamp being again brought into requisition.

The first few steps after getting on to the rocks were difficult, and probably a better place might be found higher up; afterwards we climbed on cautiously, as at places the rocks were loose; we kept well to the right where, although steeper, they became firm, and in 1 hr. and 5 min. we were at the side of the couloir. We found the point where we came upon it unfavourable for crossing, and accordingly went up parallel to it for 20 min., to a place where it is very narrow, and then a dozen steps in the snow took us across in less than 5 min. The character of the rocks changed at once, they were no longer loose, but smooth and much steeper, at the same time offering enough small cracks to make climbing quite safe and agreeable. We kept in the middle of a wide ridge ending almost precipitously, and as we went on more care was necessary, owing to the increasing steepness. I had my axe attached round my wrist by a thick piece of cord, and had paid no attention to the fastening for some time, when suddenly it snapped, leaving the loop still on and in about six leaps the axe was in the couloir below. Though I regretted extremely the loss of an old friend closely connected with all my previous climbs, I believe I got on better without it. Thinking such would be the case, Imseng suggested I might carry a little more, and while we were making a fresh disposition of the knapsacks, we noticed Mummery on the arête just at the highest point we had reached two days before.

About 1¾ hrs. from the point where we crossed the couloir we found ourselves standing on a narrow ledge of rock just below a small precipice which there was no possibility of ascending. Although we were conscious that every minute was of the utmost value, we were here compelled to call a halt in order to decide upon the direction of our further advance.

This was the point we had observed carefully during our descent on the previous day. From the position we then occupied we were only able to command a view of the precipice itself, and of the rocks on its left; we had remarked the impossibility of ascending the former, and the latter had struck us as of an exceedingly forbidding nature, both on account of their seeming steepness and smoothness. We had determined that the best way would probably lie round the rocks on the right, which I have said we were unable to see. From the ledge where we now stood we were able to examine the latter with precision. The rocks were of a most unattractive nature. They combined in themselves all the qualities which are most hateful in rocks: they were very steep, they were very smooth, in texture they were hard, and they were of that dark colour which many of us associate with the most difficult bits of climbing we have come across. We could not see to what they led, or what would be the nature of the climbing above them. We felt that certainty of success here would not be assured, and turned to examine the alternative route.

Here we were met by long slopes of smooth rocks, rising one above another in apparently endless succession. Our choice then lay between this and the short piece of bad rock followed by – we knew not what.

We could not afford to hesitate for long, and we at once commenced to tackle the latter, led on by the delusive hope of finding an easier way when the corner was turned.

For the first few yards the difficulties we had to surmount were of no great moment, but every step we took was the parent of more abominable offspring; the ledges and cracks which alone gave a trifling foothold, became every moment fewer and smaller, and as a natural consequence our rate of advance, slow enough at first, became scarcely perceptible. After $\frac{3}{4}$ hr. of this kind of work we found ourselves a hundred feet from where we started, the precipice still unsurmounted, the patch of snow which we knew lay above it still far out of reach, and further progress absolutely impossible. We descended a few feet to a perilously small ledge, where we waited, conversing rather with blank looks than audible words.

Happily there was now no doubt as to what we had to do; the only course clearly was to descend once more to the foot of the precipice. It was easy enough to come to this decision, but to carry it into effect was a matter of no small difficulty.

Any attempt to describe the events of the hour which followed would be pure waste of time. Many of my readers must have been in similar positions, and their memories will assist them in picturing to themselves what language is unable to convey. By those who do not know what slopes of this kind are like, any endeavour to give an idea of our position would be at once dismissed as incredible.

For 1 hr. and 5 min. we were forced to descend with the utmost care, each being obliged to devote his whole attention to himself and give up all idea of assisting his companions.

At last we found ourselves once more on the ledge we had so unfortunately abandoned, with considerable increase of fatigue, considerable diminution of flesh at the ends of our fingers, and two hours of valuable time lost.

We again waited a few minutes before trying the way to the left. On starting again we got on better than we had anticipated for the first half-hour, when suddenly we came upon fresh and unexpected difficulty; the rocks were no longer wet, but covered with a thin coating of ice. They would not have been particularly easy under the best of circumstances, and with this additional complication they required the greatest caution. Fortunately this did not last long, and we were soon standing on a narrow strip of snow that we had not noticed before. The appearance of the upper part of the mountain changes constantly, and from this point we were amazed at the size of the crags above us on our left, and I am still puzzled as to why they form no feature of the distant view.

One thing made us quite happy: the rest of our way was clear, there was nothing to prevent us from getting to the part of the face at which we knew the Italians must have traversed it in their first ascent. So on we went over the same sort of smooth rocks, of which we had already had so much, then passing another patch of snow we bore to the left, and on nearing the broad couloir which separated us from the arête, again struck straight up the face.

Presently Imseng pointed out a good place for crossing the couloir, where some rocks in the middle, almost overhanging, would give us protection if stones should fall. As luck would have it, some did fall just as we reached the spot mentioned, and we escaped them entirely; but as we watched them down the couloir up which we knew the other party had come, but an hour before, the guides began to institute a comparison between their way and our own.

The fact was, the sun had just reached the rocks above. A few rapid steps took us to the arête, and 2 min. afterwards we saw a rope attached to the top of a steep gully in the couloir. We regarded it with great curiosity and interest, feeling sure it had been there for fifteen years, but the next day we learned that Mummery's party had been up a little higher, and then finding it impossible to get on to the arête, had attached the rope in descending to this place.

Our work was practically over, so we proclaimed a halt, but though not sorry to sit down, we were restless to get really to the top, particularly when a shout from the shoulder told us the other party were rapidly descending, so after a few minutes we scrambled on, and in little more than $\frac{1}{2}$ hr., we were at the southern end of the final ridge – time 3 P.M.

It was not unpleasantly cold, so having considerably lightened the knapsacks and wine tin, we enjoyed the view for a good half hour, and then moved on to the true summit, and prepared to descend. The top, though from all accounts it changes its appearance rapidly, looked just the same as it did in 1877, but soon after leaving it I noticed the mountain had made great progress in one respect: the number of ropes above the shoulder had been largely increased In one place there were three ropes and a rusty chain all together. Now I think one of the hardest things one tries to do on a mountain is to help oneself with a rope; of course anybody can come down like a sailor, but my experience is that if I take the rope in one hand and try at the same time to hold on to the rocks, at one moment the rope is slack and I get my fingers on to a small projection; the next it is made tight from below, my hand is wrenched from the rocks, and there is nothing for it but to leave go altogether, or else trust to it entirely; another objection is that the permanent rope gets mixed up with the rope with which the party is attached. Now though I should like to see all such artificial aids removed from every mountain in the Alps, I have only referred to this subject to make one protest. I heard before leaving Zermatt that negotiations had already been opened with the Swiss Alpine Club, with a view to building a hut on the Zmutt ridge. If this is done, ropes at the bad places are sure to follow, and the way will soon be marked out by the same scatter of broken glass and sardine boxes which at present disgraces the northern route.

Let us try and keep one side of the Matterhorn at any rate for those who really admire the most wonderful mountain in the Alps, and who like to climb it for its own sake, and then we can give up the other arêtes to be decorated, if necessary, with chains and ladders from top to bottom, and so formed into the cockneys' high road from Breil to Zermatt!

From the shoulder we went down at a good pace so as to reach the glacier before it got dark; this was just accomplished, and then having finished up everything we had in the way of food, to excuse ourselves for not going on at once, we said to one another we would wait till the moon rose, after that we stumbled on over the glacier and down the most abominable short cuts, finally reaching Zermatt at 9.45.

Refusing to answer any questions till the following morning we went off to bed, and I confess for my own part I could scarcely keep awake while I undressed. This was hardly to be wondered at. We had had two hours' sleep on Sunday night; none on the arête on Monday night; we had walked all Tuesday night, and Wednesday of itself would have been a tiring day even if one had started fresh.

What a night's rest in the Alps will do is wonderful, but I was disgusted when, on looking out at 9 next morning, I saw my guides sitting on the wall as if they had been up hours. I must now give them their due. Of Imseng it is almost superfluous to speak; he has been engaged in several of the most difficult expeditions that have been done of late years, and the only charge I have ever heard brought against him is that of rashness. Even this is, in my opinion, unfounded, for I know no guide who is quicker in detecting real danger when it exists, or in taking the best means to avoid it.

Zurbrücken is a younger man, and I had never before seen him on a hard mountain, but I am sure his activity, sureness of foot, and weight-carrying capabilities will soon give him an acknowledged position among the best guides of his district. If I might be allowed to read a moral from the expedition I have just tried to describe, I should say it goes to prove what has been pointed out before, that a rock face ought never to be condemned from mere inspection. Any competent mountaineer might, I believe, look at the Matterhorn from the Stockje and report the face perilously steep, and raked with falling stones; yet if he proceeded to climb it, he would find that up the middle of it there lies a way, quite as free from the danger of stones as many expeditions now frequently made.

The time we took will be very little guide to those who follow.

Let a good walker sleep at the Stockje and cross the glacier so as to be on the rocks soon after daybreak; in less than 5 hrs. he may reach the summit, and I feel confident he will look back to the climb as one of the most interesting in the Zermatt district.

Two routes having now been made up the Zmutt side, the question naturally arises which is the better? I will not attempt to answer this, but simply say, so far as my observation goes, Mr. Mummery's way is the longer, and though easier for the first 3 hrs., is exposed to greater danger from stones in the upper part; while the face affords more continuous difficulty and less real danger.

❄ (Vol. IX.)

W. W. Graham

8 ❄ The Dent du Géant

From the time I first saw the wonderful rock tower of the Dent du Géant, I had a secret wish to attempt the ascent, but the repeated failures of so many first-class climbers and the reputation of inaccessibility which it had thus gained, made me postpone the attack in favour of some more easily climbed peak. Then, too, the chaffing advice of more experienced mountaineers, 'Oh, if you've got a spare week, go and try the Géant,' was a damper to any slight sparks of enthusiasm left. However, when the news arrived at Zermatt that the much-tried peak had been done, I determined to make use of M. Sella's staircase, as it was somewhat unkindly termed, the report being that he had festooned the peak with rope, not to mention iron stanchions and other aids to climbing.

Accordingly, when next at Chamonix, I engaged Alphonse Payot and Auguste Cupelin, whom I found very keen on going, it being a new excursion for the Chamonix list, and on August 14 last we left the Montenvers early in the morning. Our start was delayed by a heavy shower, but we got off at last, and taking the left side of the séracs, which we found to be quite an hour shorter than the other route, easily reached the snow field at the foot of the peak. Then, however, it began to snow very hard, which put climbing out of the question, and a rush was accordingly made for the cabane in hopes of its clearing up before the next day.

I now found myself face to face with the problem how to kill time till tomorrow morning. Of course we might have returned, but by sleeping at the cabane we hoped to gain some hours the next day. Well, I carved my name on the walls, I ate as slowly and I fear as much as I could, I discussed exhaustively every possible subject with Payot and Cupelin, till they went to sleep – the average guide's command of sleep is very remarkable – I smoked innumerable pipes, and 'still I was not happy'.

It was only 4 o'clock, and the snow was falling in that slow heavy way in which only snow can fall when you want to do something and it doesn't intend that you shall; I could not sleep, and at last I was driven to study the visitors' book. Strange to say, I found a good deal of amusement in turning over its pages, the entries being quite a study of national character. English entries were almost always short and gruff, 'So and so,

Montenvers to Courmayeur (or *vice versa*), time —, guides —.' German and Italian notices are more florid and make more of the difficulties, and the enthusiasm culminates in the French accounts. One man describes his guides, two of the least capable men of Chamonix, as *'les plus braves gens du monde'*; another commends himself to *'le bon Dieu'* before daring the 'perilous' descent to Courmayeur, while a third entry, too long for repetition, is quite a gem in its way. A previous notice by his friend described the author as having *'reculé'*. 'True,' he says when succeeding on the third attempt, *'j'avais reculé, mais – pour mieux sauter'*; and proceeds to chant quite a Nunc Dimittis over the accomplishment of what he calls his 'long-cherished vow'. Almost the last entry in the book was signed by the Sella family, who stated, with some prefatory flourishes to the glory of Italy, that they had made the first ascent of the Dent du Géant, and hoisted thereon the Italian flag. As, however, I knew that they had not reached the highest pinnacle, and the accounts of later ascents made no mention of going farther, I concluded to my great relief that I still had first chance of finishing off the peak.

Sleep came at last, and next morning the weather was worse than ever; fully eighteen inches of snow had fallen, and we were obliged to return damp and disconsolate to the Montenvers.

For the next two or three days the weather was only suitable for small excursions, but Saturday proved fine, and in spite of the protest of the guides that there was too much snow, believing that 'the better the day the better the deed', I determined to start early next morning. We did not intend to be again half frozen, so carried quite a small stack of wood and engaged as porter a youth whose sole name, christian or sur, was Pierre.

We started before two on August 20, a pitch-dark moonless night, the natural result being that we lost the track on the Mer de Glace almost immediately; owing to this delay, and to our taking it very easy, it was eight o'clock before we reached the col. Here we intended to send Pierre to the cabane with our 'impedimenta', but he wished to join the ascent *'comme volontaire'*, so after breakfast and a rest we started at nine to attack the mountain. The snow was in beautiful order, so that we were able to kick steps up a steep couloir, and before eleven we had reached the summit of the rock arête, where it abuts against the peak itself. Here was a beautiful shelter from the wind, which was very cold, and we discussed the probable route. The peak is, roughly speaking, a triangular wedge, the three faces looking N.W., S.W., and S.E. approximately. The S.E. face is as nearly perpendicular as possible; in fact, overhangs in at least one place, and consequently may be speedily dismissed. The N.W. face is practicable for a considerable distance, but, looking down from above, is nearly perpendicular for the last 200 or 300 feet. Finally there remained the S.W. face. By this and by its left-hand edge the Italians had ascended, and we could see about 200 feet of rope very near the top, but no others. Here Pierre's courage evaporated, so leaving him with our axes and provisions, we climbed a great slab of rock and worked our way straight upwards, our course lying along the right edge of the S.W. face. About half the ascent was accomplished without stopping and in silence only broken by a pant as one by one we raised ourselves up what may be best likened to a great staircase with very high narrow stairs; and I must say that it was the hardest climbing, from a muscular point of view, that I ever tried. Then, however, the character of the peak entirely changes. It becomes a surface almost as smooth as if it had been planed, whilst the rock, being a close quartz, offers no welcome cracks as hand or foot hold. This face has an inclination of 65° to 70° at least, and in most places more, and is only broken by two vertical clefts and a few very narrow ledges. We climbed three of these with the greatest difficulty, and reached the level of the rope we had seen, though we were still separated from it by the whole breadth of the face. We crossed very gingerly, the ledge being very narrow, and in most places there being absolutely no hand hold. Fortunately the face is not very wide, and we crossed in safety. Then we saw what we ought to have seen before, that the ropes stretched away below us for quite 300 feet, but, being laid in a cleft which was half full of frozen snow, they had been quite hidden. We now mounted merrily, the rope being a great assistance, and indeed in one place necessary, as there is a smooth slab quite fifteen feet high, and which could only be climbed by ladder or by nails driven in. The ascent of this cut our hands very badly, as the rope was a mass of ice. Then the way led round a large smooth slab on to the N.W. face; there the rope had become loosened at its upper end, and was hanging down useless. We hoisted Payot up and then he had to work along, hanging from the ledge by his hands till he reached the arête. We then passed him the rope and he fastened it more securely for the benefit of future climbers. We turned the corner, crept along a narrow ledge which overhung a magnificent precipice, and the difficulties were over. The rope was frozen to the rocks, but we were independent of it, as the slope decreased to about 40°, and we were able to go up, partly climbing, partly crawling. About 100 feet of this and we reached a rock step on which was cut the letter 'M', doubtless the point to which Maquignaz had ascended before bringing up M. Sella. With a jump we were up this and on the lower of the two little teeth on the summit ridge, the point which had been previously reached by the Italians, as was attested by a stone man and a tattered flag. Straight in front of us rose the other tooth, about twenty feet higher, but separated from us by an extremely awkward notch. The most obvious line of descent was blocked by a huge loose slab which vibrated, and we consequently had to let ourselves down a vertical drop of about fifteen to twenty feet, and then found ourselves on the little arête between the two teeth. This was of rock topped with ice and gradually narrowed from a foot to a few inches, with, on the right hand, an over-hanging precipice of quite 1,200 to 1,500 feet, on the other, a slope of 70° falling almost to the Mer de Glace. Boots had been previously removed, but we were compelled to bestride the arête, which was fortunately short. The other tooth rose perfectly smooth for about ten feet, after which it appeared fairly easy. I as the tallest and lightest mounted on Payot's shoulders, he being astride the ledge. Fortunately there was a small vertical crack by which to steady myself, but as I gently raised myself on Payot I felt very like a man about to undergo the 'long drop'. Then with a pull I was up, and with the aid of the rope raised Payot, and in a minute or two more we were on the top. We promptly set to work to raise a stone man, and in doing so found a splendid crystal, of which I took possession. We hoisted our flag, having borrowed a portion of the Italian flag-staff and utilizing my handkerchief. The view, though very fine, is limited on the Grandes Jorasses side, but the position, which resembled nothing so much as standing on the top of a huge pillar, was unique. On the east and south fell enormous cliffs, as I proved by lying down and dropping stones which fell without striking the face, while on the other two sides fell precipices which would have been called perpendicular anywhere else. In short, there was a far greater sense of isolation and out-of-the-worldness than I have ever felt on any of the loftier peaks. However, the wind was too cold for any stay, so after a dram and a yell, at 1.30 we started on the descent. This time we took care to follow the ropes, and the descent was quite easy in consequence. We soon reached the more broken rocks, where the ropes ceased, finding on one ledge quite a sackful of crystals, which, legend saith, were left by Alexander Burgener on his memorable attempt. We found another short rope behind a projecting rock, and creeping under this found ourselves once more at the spot where we had left our axes and Pierre. Time, 3 P.M. After a short halt we resumed the descent. The sun, however, had been hard at work, and our couloir was impracticable, every step starting an avalanche. We had to descend by the rock arête, which was very rotten, and covered with loose stones under the snow, which came down in showers at any false step. Pierre was very unsteady, nor was I much better, and we gave the guides plenty of trouble. 'Encore une chute de Pierre' (pierres), exclaimed Cupelin as Pierre slipped for about the twentieth time, a witticism which he repeated with a chuckle as often as occasion offered. At last we reached the foot of the rocks, and a grand glissade brought us once more down to the col. It was now 5.30, and though I wanted to go on, the guides said it would be dusk before we could clear the séracs, so we took up our quarters once more at the cabane. This time Morpheus was propitious, and I slept the sleep of the just. Next morning we reached the Montenvers without any other adventure than the fall of a snow bridge, which brought us all in a heap into a shallow crevasse. For the last mile or two I could see that Cupelin had something on his mind – a joke, I knew, and I waited patiently for its appearance. Just before entering the hotel, he pointed to the now distant Dent du Géant, and exclaimed with a perfect storm of chuckles, '*Nous aussi, nous avons reculé, mais – pour mieux sauter.*'

❋ (Vol. XI.)

A. F. Mummery

9 ❄ The Aiguilles des Charmoz and de Grépon

In a certain remote period, when a few unclimbed peaks were still to be found in the Alps, it was my good fortune to explore the various summits of the Charmoz, or rather of what used to be called the Charmoz, for the inventive genius of my successors has been so stimulated by the dearth of new routes that this peak has been hewn in twain, one half retaining the name of Charmoz, whilst the other and loftier has been dubbed the Grépon.

In company with Alexander Burgener and Benedikt Venetz, I made a very early start on July 15, 1880, and, being provided by M. Couttet with an admirable lantern (this expedition took place in the pre-folding-lantern age), we made very fair progress for the first half-hour. We then began to ascend something which Burgener averred was a path, but which insensible of, or possibly made bashful by, such gross flattery, hid itself coyly from view at every third step. After a long grind the grey light of morning began to overpower our lantern, so, finding a suitable stone, we carefully hid it and marked the spot with a sprig of pine. Sad to say, on our return, though we found many stones with many sprigs of pine on them, none had our lantern in the hole underneath, a circumstance much to be regretted, as from an item which subsequently appeared in my bill it seems to have been a lantern held in high esteem by Monsieur Couttet.

We soon got clear of the forest, and ultimately reaching a stream under the lateral moraine of the Nantillon Glacier, halted for breakfast. Here we discovered that three slices of meat, a tiny piece of cheese, ten inches of loaf, and a big bag of raisins were all the provisions the hotel porter had thought necessary. Luckily Burgener had been left in charge of the commissariat, and, as I prefer raisins on the side of a mountain to any other food, I was able to look on the porter's conduct with philosophy, a state of mind by no means shared by my companions.

We very injudiciously turned the lower ice fall by keeping to the right and ascending a couloir between the cliffs of the Blaitière and the precipitous rocks over which the glacier falls. The couloir proved very easy, but a rock buttress on our left being still easier we took to it and rattled to the top at a great pace. Immediately over our heads towered an endless succession of séracs, huge sky-cleaving monsters, that seemed almost in the act of falling. The spot was not a desirable one for a halt, so we turned to the left to see how we were to get on to the glacier. At one point, and one only, was it possible to do so. A sérac lurching over the cliff, and apparently much inclined to add to the pile of broken ice-blocks some hundreds of feet below, was the only available bridge. We scrambled along it, crossed a crevasse on avalanche débris, and dashed up a short ice slope to the open glacier. Ten minutes sufficed to take us into comparative safety, and we traversed to the island of rock, by which the ice fall is usually turned.

Here we made a halt and proceeded to search the knapsack for possibly hidden stores of food. Whilst Venetz and I were engaged in this duty, Burgener screwed himself and his telescope into a variety of extraordinary attitudes, and at length succeeded in making a satisfactory examination of our peak. An hour later we started again and tramped up to the base of the long couloir which leads to the depression between the two summits of the mountain, or, in modern language, between the Grépon and the Charmoz.

We crossed the bergschrund at a quarter to nine, and at once turning to the left, out of the couloir, worked our way up some good rocks for three-quarters of an hour, only one or two slabs offering any sort of resistance to our progress. By this time we had reached the top of a secondary ridge, which here abuts against the final cliffs of the mountain. We sat down on an ice-coated rock and producing our limited supplies of food, once more solemnly reviled the Chamonix porter. We then deposited the wine tin in a safe corner, and unanimously discarded coats and boots, which with two out of three hats and the same proportion of ice-axes, were packed away in a secure cleft. The baggage, consisting of a spare rope, two wooden wedges, the food, a bottle of Bouvier, a tin of cognac, and an ice-axe, was made over to me.

The two men began to worm their way up the cliff, Venetz usually being shoved up by Burgener and then helping the latter with the rope. Progress, however, was painfully slow, and when at last good standing ground was reached, the rope declined to come anywhere near me. Ultimately I had to make a difficult traverse to fetch it, as it was quite impossible to carry the ice-axe and knapsack without its aid. This sort of work continued for three-quarters of an hour, and then a longer delay suggested that there was something seriously wrong. An eager query brought back the reply that the next bit was quite impracticable, but, added Burgener, '*Es muss* gehen.' Anxious to see the obstacle which, though impracticable, was yet to be ascended, I swarmed up the edge of a great slab to a narrow ledge, then, working round an awkward corner, I entered a dark cold gully.

A mighty block, some forty feet high, had parted from the main mass of the mountain, leaving a rounded perpendicular couloir, which was now everywhere veneered with ice. A tiny stream trickled down the back of the gully, and about mid-height had frozen on to the rocks, forming a thick column of ice flanked on either hand by a fantastic fretwork of the same material. A green bulge of ice, about fifteen feet above, prevented our seeing the back of the gully beyond that point. Nothing could appear more hopeless, there was not even decent foothold where we stood, everywhere the black glazing of ice filled up and masked the irregularities of the rock below.

Some ten minutes later both men appeared to my inexperienced eye in extremely critical positions. Venetz, almost without hold of any sort, was gradually nearing the afore-mentioned green bulge; an axe, skilfully applied by Burgener to that portion of the guide costume most usually decorated by patches of brilliant and varied hue, supplying the motive power, whilst Burgener himself was cleverly poised on invisible notches cut in the thin ice which glazed the rock. Before, however, Venetz could surmount the green bulge, it became necessary to shift the axe to his feet, and for a moment he was left clinging like a cat to the slippery wrinkles of the large icicle. How he succeeded in maintaining his position is a mystery known only to himself, and the law of gravity. With the axe beneath his feet, he once more moved upwards, and with a desperate effort raised his head and shoulders above the bulge. *'Wie geht's?'* yelled Burgener. *'Weder vorwärts noch zurück,'* gasped Venetz, and to a further query whether he could help Burgener up, came the reply, *'Gewiss nicht.'* However, so soon as he had recovered his wind he renewed his efforts. Little by little his legs, working in spasmodic jerks, disappeared from sight, and at last a burst of patois, a hauling in of the rope, and Burgener advanced and disappeared. The whizz of icicles and other small fragments, and the hard breathing of the men showed they were advancing. Then Burgener shouted to me to squeeze well under cover for fear of stones, but as the crack to which I was holding only sufficed to shelter my nose, fingers, and one foot, I thought it wise to work back out of the gully on to the warm rocks, being, moreover, much persuaded to this line of conduct by my toes, which, un-protected by boots and with stockings long since cut to ribbons, were by no means unwilling to exchange frozen rock and ice for warmth and sun-shine.

Presently a startled shout and a great stone leapt into space, followed by a hoarse yodel to announce the conquest of the gully. As I scrambled back the rope came down with a swish, and I tied up as well as I could with one hand, while the other hung on to an ice-glazed corner. Having accomplished this important operation I began the ascent. Everything went well for the first few feet, then the hold seemed to get insufficient, and a desperate effort to remedy this ended in my swinging free, unable to attach myself to either rock or ice. A bearded face, with a broad grin, looks over the top of the gully, and cheerily asks, 'Why don't you come on?'

Then a few vigorous hauls, and I am above the green bulge, and enter a narrow cleft. Its smooth and precipitous walls were everywhere glazed with ice, and their parallel surfaces offered no grip or hold of any sort. It was just possible to jam one's back against one wall and one's knees against the other, but progress under these conditions was not to be thought of. After a few minutes had been allowed to convince a possibly sceptical Herr that the knapsack and the ice-axe were not the only impedimenta in the party, the persuasive influence of the rope brought me to more broken ground, and a scramble landed me in the sunshine.

The men were ruefully gazing at their torn and bleeding elbows, for it appears they had only succeeded in attaching themselves to the gully by clasping their hands in front of them, and then drawing them in towards their chests, thus wedging their elbows against the opposing walls. They were both very thoroughly 'blown', so we halted and circulated a certain flask. Then I lay down on the warm rocks and wondered how long my internal organs would take to get back into those more normal positions from which the pressure of the rope had dislodged them.

A quarter of an hour later we were once more *en route*. Above, a long series of broken cliffs, seamed by a fairly continuous line of vertical cracks, assured our progress as far as the ridge. How I crawled up great slabs hanging on to impossible corners – how at critical moments the knapsack hooked on to sharp splinters of rock, or the ice-axe jammed into cracks, whilst the holes in my toes got deeper and bigger, and the groove round my waist more closely approximated to the modern ideal of female beauty – is fixed indelibly on my mind; but I will limit myself to saying that on some rocks, in due accordance with the latest mountaineering fashion, I expostulated with Burgener on the absurdity of using a rope, at the same time taking very good care to see that the knot was equal to all emergencies. On other rocks I just managed to ascend by adopting new and original attitudes, which, despite certain adverse criticisms, I still believe would have won renown for any artist who could have seized their grace and elegance, and would, moreover, have afforded a very distinct departure from all conventional models. On yet other rocks a method of progress was adopted which has since, I regret to say, given rise to fierce disputes between the amateur and professional members of the party; it being alleged on the one hand that there is no difficulty in ascending such rocks if the climber be not hampered by a knapsack and ice-axe; and on the other, that a waist measurement of eighteen inches ought, for some mysterious reason, to be taken into account, and detracts from the climbing merit of its possessor. Without, however, entering into controversial matter of so painful a character, I may briefly say that at a quarter-past eleven we scrambled on to the ridge and feasted our eyes with a near view of the summit.

The more sanguine members of the party at once concluded that a projection on the left, of easy access, was the highest point; but certain gloomy dissentients averred that an ugly tooth on the right, of a most uncompromising character, was the true peak. Laughter was the portion of these unbelievers, and the easy crag was scaled amid a wild burst of enthusiasm, only, however, to find that here, as elsewhere, the broad and easy path is not for the faithful.

Returning to the gap where we had attained the ridge, we made our way to the foot of the real summit. Venetz was promptly lifted up to Burgener's shoulders and propelled onwards by the axe; but the first attack failed, and he recoiled swiftly on to Burgener. The despised Herr was then used to extend the ladder, and by this means Venetz was able to reach indifferent hold, and ultimately to gain the summit. At 11.45 A.M. we all crowded on to the top, the men rejoicing greatly at the reckless waste of gunpowder with which Monsieur Couttet welcomed our arrival. Burgener, as a fitting recognition of this attention, planted our one ice-axe on the highest point, whilst the rank and file of the expedition diligently sought stones wherewith to build it into an upright and secure position. To this a handkerchief of brilliant pattern and inferior repair, the product into which the Zermatt wash had resolved two of more ordinary dimensions and colour, was securely lashed.

Whilst these details were being satisfactorily completed, the heavy luggage of the party was quietly sunning himself in a comfortable nook, and absorbing that mixture of sunlight, atmosphere, glittering lake, and jagged ridge, which make up a summit view. Long hours of exertion urged to the utmost limit of the muscles, and the wild excitement of half-won but yet doubtful victory, are changed in an instant to a feeling of ease and security, so perfect that only the climber who has stretched himself in some sun-warmed, wind-sheltered nook, can realize the utter oblivion which lulls every suspicion of pain or care, and he learns that, however happiness may shun pursuit, it may, nevertheless, be sometimes surprised basking on the weird granite crags. To puzzle one's brains at such moments by seeking to recognize distant peaks, or to correct one's topographical knowledge, or by scientific pursuits of any sort, appears to be sacrilege of the most vicious sort. To me it seems the truer worship to stretch with half-shut eyes in the sun, and let the scenery

Like some sweet beguiling melody,
So sweet we know not we are listening to it

wrap us in soft delight, till with lotus-eaters we had almost cried —

Let us swear an oath . . .
. . . to live and lie reclined
On the hills like gods together, careless of mankind.

But Burgener did not altogether share this view, and at 12.30 P.M., he insisted on our sliding down a doubled rope on to the ridge below the summit. All went merrily till we reached the ice couloir. Here Burgener tried to fix one of our wooden wedges; but do what he would, it persisted in evading its duties, wobbling first to one side and then to another, so that the rope slipped over the top. We all had a try, driving it into cracks that struck our fancy, and even endeavouring to prop it up with ingenious arrangements of small stones. Someone then mooted the point whether wedges were not a sort of bending the knee to Baal, and might not be the first step on those paths of ruin where the art of mountaineering becomes lost in that of the steeplejack. Whereupon we unanimously declared that the Charmoz should be desecrated by no fixed wedges, and finding an insecure knob of rock we doubled our rope round it, and Venetz slid down. I followed, and to prevent as far as possible the chance of the rope slipping off the knob, we twisted it round and round, and held the ends fast as Burgener descended.

By 2.20 we rejoined our boots, and ideas of table d'hôte began to replace those of a more poetic type. We rattled down the rocks, and raced across the glacier in a way that we subsequently learnt created much astonishment in the minds of sundry friends at the opposite end of M. Couttet's telescope. The further we got the faster we went, for the séracs that looked unpleasant in the morning now lurched over our heads in a way that made Burgener's *'schnell, nur schnell,'* almost lift one off one's feet. After the usual habit of séracs they lurched and staggered, but did not fall, and we got down to the lower glacier much out of breath, but otherwise uninjured. Reaching the neighbourhood of our lantern we sought diligently but found it not, so we made for a châlet Burgener knew of.

We found the fair proprietress feeding pigs. She brought us milk, and though of unexceptionable quality the more fastidious members of the party would have liked it better had not some of the numerous denizens of her abode and person previously sought euthanasia in the flowing bowl.

Happily the zigzags did not take long to unwind, and at 5.30 P.M. we were warmly welcomed by Monsieur and Madame Couttet and much excellent champagne.

Whilst on the summit of the Charmoz, I had been struck by the two sharp and towering pinnacles of the Grépon, and made various inward vows to scale them. I was, however, due in England before time could be found for their ascent, and the attack had to be postponed till 1881.

On August 3 of that year I was remorselessly ejected from my bed at 1.30 A.M., and informed that there was not a cloud or even a rag of mist for laziness and a love of slumber to modestly shelter beneath, so reviling guides, mountains, and early starts, I got into my clothes and came down to the chill and comfortless salon. I then found that neither hot tea for the Monsieur nor breakfast for the guides was forthcoming. Doubtless the just retribution awarded by Providence (or M. Couttet) to those who bring Swiss guides to Chamonix.

We got on very slowly at first, our progress being much hindered by a bottle lantern. Happily, before the loss of time became really serious, Venetz took advantage of a smooth rock and some interlaced brambles, and went head-over-heels, no one exactly knew where, though, from some remarks he let fall, I gathered that it was one of the least desirable quarters of Hades. When he reappeared the lantern was no more, and we were able to make better progress, till, after a weary grind, we reached the Nantillon Glacier.

At the foot of the couloir leading to the col between the Charmoz and the Grépon we halted for breakfast. This couloir, though not absolutely free from falling stones, is fairly easy, and it was not till about 70 feet below the col, when we had traversed to the right and assaulted a great slab, that we met with our first serious difficulty, and found it necessary to put on the rope. Both Venetz and I made sundry attempts, but, so soon as we got beyond the sure and certain support of Burgener's axe, progress upwards became impossible, and though we reached points within a few feet of broken and fairly easy rock, we were forced on each attempt to return. Whilst still doubtful whether a yet more determined attack might not conquer our enemy, Venetz wisely climbed back into the couloir and up to the col to see if any more convenient line could be discovered. He soon called on us to follow, and, leaving Burgener to pick up the rope and knapsack, I scrambled round and found Venetz perched some 10 feet up a huge slab. This slab rests like a buttress against the great square rock, which shuts in the col on the Grépon side with a perpendicular wall. Its foot, accessible by a broad and convenient ledge, is about 20 feet below the col, whilst its top coincides with a curious hole in the ridge above and to the right of the col. From this, once attained, we believed the summit was accessible.

So soon as Burgener had brought round the rope and knapsack, Venetz tied up and set to work. At one or two places progress was very difficult, the crack being in part too wide to afford any hold, and forcing the climber on to the face of the slab. I subsequently found that at the worst point my longer reach enabled me to get a slight hold of a small protuberance with one finger, but how Venetz, whose reach is certainly a foot less than mine, managed to get up has never been satisfactorily explained. At the next stage the crack narrows, and a stone has conveniently jammed itself exactly where it is wanted; beyond, the right-hand side of the crack gets broken, and it is a matter of comparative ease to pull oneself on to the top. This top then forms a narrow, but perfectly easy and level, path to the hole in the ridge. We found this hole or doorway guarded by a great splinter of rock, so loose that an unwary touch would probably be resented with remorseless severity, and the impertinent traveller hurled on to the Nantillon Glacier. Squeezing through, we stepped on to a little plateau covered with the débris of frost-riven rock.

Burgener then proposed, amid the reverent and appreciative silence of the company, that libations should be duly poured from a bottle of Bouvier. This religious ceremony having been fittingly observed (the Western form, I take it, of the prayers offered by a pious Buddhist on reaching the crest of some Tibetan pass), we proceeded to attack a little cleft overhanging the Mer de Glace, and cleverly protected at the top by a projecting rock. Above this we found ourselves in a sort of granite crevasse, and as this, as far as we could discover, had no bottom, we had no bottom, we had to hotch ourselves along with our knees against one side, and our backs against the other. Burgener at this point exhibited most painful anxiety, and his *'Herr Gott! geben Sie Acht'* had the very ring of tears in its earnest entreaty. On my emergence into daylight his anxiety was explained. Was not the knapsack on my shoulders, and were not sundry half-bottles of Bouvier in the knapsack?

We now boldly struck out on to the Nantillon face, where a huge slice of rock had been rent some 16 inches from the mass of the mountain, leaving a sharp, knife-like edge, destructive of fingers, trousers, and epidermis, but affording a safe and certain grip. This led us on to a spacious platform, whence a scramble of some 20 feet brought us to the sharply-pointed northern summit. Burgener self-denyingly volunteered to go down and send me up a stone wherewith to knock off the extreme point of the mountain, but the pleasing delusion that I was to occupy the convenient seat thus afforded was quickly dispelled. Stones were hauled up by Venetz in considerable quantities, and the construction of a stone man – or, having regard to its age and size, I ought, perhaps, to say a stone baby – was undertaken. A large red handkerchief was then produced, and the baby was decorously draped in this becoming and festive attire. These duties finished, we partly scrambled and partly slid back on to the big platform, and proceeded to enjoy ourselves, feeling that our work was over, our summit won, and that we might revel in the warm sunshine and glorious view.

That night my dreams were troubled by visions of a great square tower –

the great square tower that at the other end of the summit ridge had thrust its shoulders above the snows of the Col du Géant, and though the men had stoutly maintained that our peak was highest, I felt that the delights of an untroubled mind must be for ever abandoned if up that tower I did not go. After breakfast, I sought for Burgener, but I found that he was invisible, an essential portion of his clothing being so terribly damaged that the protracted exertions of the local tailor were requisite to his public appearance. However, in response to my urgent entreaties, Venetz retired to bed, and Burgener emerged resplendent in the latter's garments.

It turned out that Burgener had to be in Martigny the next morning but one, so, to give him time on our return from the Grépon to drive over the Tête Noire, we resolved to go up to Blaitière-dessous that evening and make an early start. The tailor duly accomplished his labours and released Venetz, and about four o'clock, with the addition of a porter we strolled up to the châlet.

We got under way at two o'clock the next morning, and, following the route just described, reached the base of the first summit. Passing to the right of this we dropped down a fifteen-feet step and crawled up a smooth rock to the edge of the great cleft which divides the summit ridge into two equal sections. After a careful examination, as there did not appear any other method of descent, we fixed our spare rope, having first tied two or three knots at suitable intervals. Venetz went down first, and after he had made a short inspection he called on us to follow. Burgener descended next, and I brought up the rear in company with the knapsack and an ice-axe. I found the first twenty feet very easy, then I began to think that the Alpine Club rope is too thin for this sort of work, and I noted a curious and inexplicable increase in my weight. To add to these various troubles the axe, which was held by a loop round my arm, caught in a crack and snapped the string. Luckily, by a convulsive jerk, I just managed to catch it in my left hand. This performance, however, greatly excited Burgener, who, unable to see what had happened, thought his Herr and not merely the ice-axe was contemplating a rapid descent on to the Mer de Glace. Having restored our spirits by a quiet consideration of the contents of a certain flask, we set off in pursuit of Venetz, who had carried away our only remaining rope. A convenient flake had split from the mountain on the Nantillon side and offered a fairly easy zigzag path to the top of the tower, which shuts in the great cleft on this side.

We here found one of the many excellences of the Grépon peculiarly well developed. On the Mer de Glace face, from ten to twenty feet below the ridge, a broad road suitable for carriages, bicycles, or other similar conveyances, led us straight along to the last gap, thus obviating the necessity of following the ridge and climbing up and down its various irregularities. It is true that this desirable promenade was only to be reached by rounding a somewhat awkward corner, which my companion professed to think difficult, and its continuity was interrupted at another point by a projecting shoulder, which pushed one's centre of gravity further over the Mer de Glace than was wholly pleasant; but, the passage of these minor obstacles excepted, we were able to walk arm in arm along a part of the mountain which we had expected to find as formidable as anything we had encountered. Reaching the last gap we rejoined Venetz and proceeded to examine the final tower.

It was certainly one of the most forbidding rocks I have ever set eyes on. Unlike the rest of the peak, it was smooth to the touch, and its square-cut edges offered no hold or grip of any sort. True, the block was fractured from top to bottom, but the crack, four or five inches wide, had edges as smooth and true as a mason could have hewn them, and had not one of those irregular and convenient backs not infrequently possessed by such clefts. Even the dangerous help of a semi-loose stone, wedged with doubtful security between the opposing walls, was lacking. Added to all this a great rock overhung the top and would obviously require a powerful effort just when the climber was most exhausted.

Under these circumstances, Burgener and I set to work to throw a rope over the top, whilst Venetz reposed in a graceful attitude rejoicing in a quiet pipe. After many efforts, in the course of which both Burgener and I nearly succeeded in throwing ourselves over on to the Mer de Glace, but dismally failed in landing the rope, we became virtuous, and decided that the rock must be climbed by the fair methods of honourable war. To this end we poked up Venetz with the ice-axe (he was enjoying a peaceful nap), and we then generally pulled ourselves together and made ready for the crucial struggle.

Our rope-throwing operations had been carried on from the top of a sort of narrow wall, about two feet wide, and perhaps six feet above the gap. Burgener, posted on this wall, stood ready to help Venetz with the ice-axe so soon as he should get within his reach, whilst my unworthy self, planted in the gap, was able to assist him in the first part of his journey. So soon as Venetz got beyond my reach, Burgener leant across the gap, and, jamming the point of the axe against the face of the rock, made a series of footholds of doubtful security whereon Venetz could rest and gain strength for each successive effort. At length he got above all these adventitious aids and had to depend exclusively on his splendid skill. Inch by inch he forced his way, gasping for breath, and his hand wandering over the smooth rock in those vague searches for non-existent hold which it is positively painful to witness. Burgener and I watched him with intense anxiety, and it was with no slight feeling of relief that we saw the fingers of one hand reach the firm hold offered by the square-cut top. A few moments' rest, and he made his way over the projecting rock, whilst Burgener and I yelled ourselves hoarse.* When the rope came down for me, I made a brilliant attempt to ascend unaided. Success attended my first efforts, then came a moment of metaphorical response, promptly followed by the real thing; and, kicking like a spider, I was hauled on to the top, where I listened with unruffled composure to sundry sarcastic remarks concerning those who put their trust in tennis shoes and scorn the sweet persuasion of the rope.

The summit is of palatial dimensions and is provided with three stone chairs. The loftiest of these was at once appropriated by Burgener for the ice-axe, and the inferior members of the party were bidden to bring stones to build it securely in position. This solemn rite being duly performed, we stretched ourselves at full length and mocked M. Couttet's popgun at Chamonix with a pop of far more exhilarating sort.

The aged narrative from which I have been reading ends abruptly at this point. Before, however, quitting the summit of one of the steepest rocks in the Alps I may, perhaps, be permitted to ask whether the love of rock-climbing is so heinous and debasing a sin that its votaries are no longer worthy to be ranked as mountaineers, but are to be relegated to a despised and special class of 'mere gymnasts'.

It would appear at the outset wholly illogical to deny the term 'mountaineer' to any man who is skilled in the art of making his way with facility in mountain countries. To say that a man who climbs because he is fond of mountaineering work is not a mountaineer, whilst a man who climbs because it is essential to some scientific pursuit in which he is interested, is a mountaineer, is contrary to the first principles of a logical definition, and I trust this club will not commit itself to so absurd a blunder. It may be freely admitted that science has a higher social value than sport, but that does not alter the fact that mountaineering is a sport, and by no possible method can be converted into geology, or botany, or topography. That the technique of our sport has made rapid progress is alleged against us as a sort of crime, but I venture to say, in reality, it is a matter, not for regret, but for congratulation. To emulate the skill of their guides was the ideal of the early climbers, and I trust it will still be the ideal that we set before ourselves. A terminology which suggests that as a man approaches this goal, as he increases in mountaineering skill, he ceases to be a mountaineer, stands self-condemned, and must be remorselessly eliminated from our literature.

* M. Dunod heard at Chamonix that I took three ladders of 10 feet each on this ascent ('*Annuaire Club Alpin Français*', 1886, page 99); it is needless to say that this is a Chamonix myth. It, however, led him to encumber himself with three ladders of 12 feet each. His ascent and all subsequent ascents have been made by the southern ridge of the Grépon; the ridge from the point described, page 168, to the real summit has not since been traversed.

But underlying all this sort of criticism would appear to be a recrudescence of Mr. Ruskin's original charge, that we treat the mountains as greased poles. This I venture, on behalf of rock-climbers generally, to most emphatically deny. Pleasure in the exertion of acquired skill is perfectly consistent with a keen appreciation of natural beauty, and this appreciation forms a chief part of the attraction which the more difficult ascents exert. It is true that few of us analyse with any care the complex web of motives which determines our choice of ascents, but, so far at all events as my experience extends, it justifies the belief that those best skilled in the mountain craft appreciate most keenly the glorious scenes amongst which we wander.

Mr. Leslie Stephen has pointed out, and probably most would agree, that the charm of mountain scenery is to be found in every step taken in the upper world. The strange interfolding of the snows, the gaunt, weird crags of the ridges, the vast blue icicle-fringed crevasse, or the great smooth slabs sloping downwards through apparently bottomless space, are each and all no less lovely than the boundless horizon of the summit view. The self-dubbed mountaineers, however, fail to grasp this essential fact. To them the right way up a peak is the easiest way, and all other ways are wrong ways. Thus, they would say, to take an instance from a well-known peak, if a man goes up the Matterhorn to enjoy the scenery, he will go by the Hörnli route; if he goes by the Zmutt ridge, it is, they allege, the difficulties and 'greasy poliness' of the climb that attract him. Now, this reasoning would appear to be wholly fallacious. Among the visions of mountain loveliness that rise before my mind none are fairer than the stupendous cliffs and fantastic crags of the Zmutt ridge. To say that this route with its continuously glorious scenery is, from an aesthetic point of view, the wrong way, while the Hörnli route which, despite the noble distant prospect, is marred by the meanness of its screes and its paper-besprinkled slopes, is the right, involves a total insensibility to the true mountain feeling.

The suspicion, indeed, sometimes crosses my mind that the so-called mountaineer confounds the pleasure he derives from photography or from geological or other research, with the purely aesthetic enjoyment of noble scenery. Doubtless, the summit of a peak is peculiarly well adapted to these semi-scientific pursuits, and if the summit is the only thing desired, the easiest way up is obviously the right way; but from a purely aesthetic standpoint, the Col du Lion, the teeth of the Zmutt ridge, or Carrel's Corridor, whilst affording as exquisite a distant prospect, combine with it the dramatic force of a splendid foreground of jagged ridge, appalling precipice, and towering mist-veiled height.

The importance of foreground cannot, I think, be over-rated, and it is obvious that the more difficult an ascent the bolder and more significant will usually be the immediate surroundings of the traveller. In other words, the artistic value of an ascent generally varies with its difficulty. This, necessarily, leads us to the conclusion that the most difficult way up the most difficult peaks is, from an artistic point of view, always the right thing to attempt, whilst the easy slopes of ugly screes may with propriety be left to the scientists, with M. Janssen at their head. To those who, like myself, take a non-utilitarian view of the mountains, the great ridge of the Grépon may be safely recommended, for nowhere can the climber find bolder towers, wilder clefts, or more terrific precipices; nowhere, a fairer vision of lake and mountain, mist-filled valleys, and riven ice.*

* The impression which the two ascents made on me, and which is more or less faithfully represented in my paper, was that the Charmoz was the harder climb of the two. Those, however, who have since explored the peaks tell me that the Charmoz is, relatively to the Grépon, quite easy. Continuous and violent snow-storms (from July 8 to 12, 1880) had glazed some of the rocks, and filled the deeper cracks with ice; this, added to the fact that we somewhat foolishly discarded our boots, doubtless accounts for the excessive difficulty we experienced, and also for the fact that my successors have found the distance from the top of the ice-gully to the ridge merely a pleasant scramble of a quarter of an hour. It also appears open to question whether the point I ascended is quite the highest; it seemed so to us, but we were very possibly mistaken.

❄ (Vol. XVI.)

C. E. Mathews

10 ❄ The Alpine Obituary

Some time since, when I had the pleasure of addressing my colleagues of
the Alpine Club on the growth of mountaineering, I ventured to remind
them that our obituary was a sad one, and that probably few of our
members 'had any idea of the number of lives lost in the Alps since
Edouard de la Grotte fell into a crevasse on the Findelen Glacier twenty-
five years ago'. I did not then enlarge upon the subject; it seemed to me
that to do so would serve no useful purpose. But the terrible accidents
which have recently occurred, and the facts that two of the victims of the
last season were members of our own Club, and that all of them were men
of ability and reputation, whom their friends or their country could ill
afford to lose, have convinced me that the time has come when the Alpine
death-roll should be looked fairly in the face.

It is lamentable that whenever a serious accident occurs in the Alps,
there is generally an outburst of ignorant and foolish criticism. The public
are warned against the folly of mountaineering; they are informed that we
wilfully run unnecessary risks; that we climb almost impossible peaks
from a pure spirit of bravado, from a desire to brag of our exploits, or from
some other motive of equal silliness and stupidity. Criticism is good for all
of us, but it is only really valuable in proportion to the knowledge of the
critic. There was a time when climbing was regarded by some people as a
proof of lunacy, but as the taste for mountaineering became more widely
spread and the climbers better known, the wiser critics have admitted that
we were men whose pursuit, whether dangerous or not, 'it would be
impertinent to treat otherwise than with serious and rational respect'.

Under these circumstances it is no longer necessary to justify the practice
of mountaineering. What does concern us is to inquire at what cost 'the
playground of Europe' has been added to the recognized amusements of
Englishmen; whether the game is worth the candle; above all, whether the
disasters which have chequered Alpine history are or are not attributable
to purely preventable causes.

It is not possible to contemplate with a light heart the grave list of
casualties which I now present in a tabulated form to the readers of the
Journal. In compiling it I have endeavoured to avoid all exaggeration; 'to

nothing extenuate nor set down aught in malice'. Many accidents have occurred in the Alps below the snow line, in sub-Alpine regions, on road, or lake, or river. With these I have nothing to do. Many a life has been lost in the attempt to investigate the structure of some particular rock, or to obtain possession of some coveted flower. Of these I take no count. The accidents to which I desire to call attention are those only which have happened to mountaineers at work, and which have proved fatal on the spot. Probably the list is not an exhaustive one, but ' 'tis enough; 'twill serve'.

In 1856, when mountaineering was in its infancy, a Russian gentleman, accompanied by two guides, was crossing the Findelen Glacier to Zermatt. He was duly roped; but the guides, ignorant of their work, held the two ends of the rope in their hands. The traveller fell into a concealed crevasse; the rope was at once jerked out of careless hands; and M. de la Grotte now lies in the old churchyard at Zermatt.

In 1860, two years after the Alpine Club had become a recognized institution, and when the means of avoiding a certain class of accidents should have been well-known, three English gentlemen were descending from the Col du Géant towards Courmayeur. It was late in the afternoon, and the snow was fresh and soft. The travellers were tied together, but the first and last guides held the ends of the rope in their hands. The leading guide, the well-known F. Tairraz, walked by the side of the party, taking hold of the rope from time to time. Everything being thus made ready for an accident, it immediately occurred. One of the travellers slipped; the first and last guides could, of course, render no assistance, and were only able to save themselves. All the travellers perished, and Tairraz declined to survive the disaster and perished with them.

There was then immunity from accidents for two years, but early in 1864, from ignorance of the state of winter snow, the gallant Bennen, whom some of the older members of the Club will so well remember, was lost with one of his Herrschaft in an avalanche on the Haut de Cry.

Then came the memorable accident on the first ascent of the Matterhorn, in 1865, when, owing to easily avoidable causes, four valuable lives were thrown away, and among them that of one of the ablest guides who ever wielded ice-axe in the Alps. Misfortunes came thickly in this eventful year, and before the season closed six more victims were added to the death roll.

The loss of Mr. Young on Mont Blanc in 1866 was perhaps the most inexplicable of recorded accidents, whilst that of Captain Arkwright and three of his guides on the Grand Plateau in the same year, was an exact repetition of the celebrated accident to Dr. Hamel's party more than sixty years ago.

Two lives were lost in 1868 two more in 1869, and in 1870 occurred that fearful disaster on Mont Blanc, when one Scotch and two American gentlemen, with eight guides, were either blown from the Calotte or perished miserably from cold and hunger. Another life was lost in 1871, two in 1872, two in 1873, two in 1874, two in 1875, and three in 1876.

In 1877 an accident occurred from an entirely new cause. Two members of the English Bar, accompanied by three well-known guides, attempted the Lyskamm from the Lysjoch. By this time contempt had followed familiarity. The leading guide led his party on to an overhanging cornice of snow, and every member of the expedition paid the penalty of the rashness of their leader.

Five lives were lost in 1878, five in 1879, four in 1880, five in 1881, and in spite of all experience, all knowledge, all warning, the season that has just closed has been as fruitful of disaster as any that has been recorded in our annals.

These are the facts, painful and inexorable. What lessons are to be drawn from them? If the pursuit of mountaineering – which does not add much to the book of human knowledge, but is admittedly followed for the health and pleasure of its votaries – if this sport, noble as it undoubtedly is, can only be obtained at such great sacrifices; if it is *necessary* that eighty-seven lives should be thrown away in a mere handful of years, in order that some hundred men should enjoy an annual holiday after this particular pattern, then the game is emphatically not worth the candle, and mountaineering should be discountenanced by all those who profess to regulate their lives on the principles of prudence and good sense.

But is it so? Is mountaineering really a pursuit containing so many elements of danger that a man of reasonable prudence ought to forgo it? or does the danger really result from the careless or wilful neglect of those precautions which observation and experience have proved to be necessary? Let this question be tested by reference to the death roll.

I suppose that it is an obvious truism that no sane man should undertake an expedition, even of the third or fourth order, unaccompanied by friend or guide; and yet on reference to our obituary it will be seen that eight of the fatal accidents there recorded have happened to gentlemen climbing alone. Is it reasonable or fair that our pursuit should be discouraged in consequence of accidents such as these?

Again, if there is any precaution better understood than another, and in respect of which the law has been laid down by competent authority with wearisome iteration, that precaution consists in the proper use of the rope. To cross a glacier unroped is to court danger, nor would any guide now consent for a moment to hold the end of a rope in his hand. If the strain came upon him, his hands would be useless. But, if the rope is fixed round his waist, he has both hands free, and by the proper use of the ice-axe he can arrest a slip under any ordinary circumstances. There is no accident on record – with one single exception – that has occurred on a glacier, by a fall into a crevasse, to a party properly roped together. I feel almost humiliated to have to enforce so elementary a mountaineering proposition. It is the first lesson the novice has to learn. Of course, a man may cross a glacier unroped without falling into a crevasse, just as a man may cross a rifle range while practice is going on, without being shot, but the difference between crossing a glacier with or without a rope is the difference between perfect safety and inexcusable rashness. The use of the rope is equally necessary on rocks. If the rocks are not very difficult, the slip of one member of a party can be easily arrested. If they are, in places of exceptional difficulty only one person should move at a time. Will it be believed that eighteen of the deaths here recorded are attributable to the neglect of this obvious and simple precaution? It was culpable negligence, and that only, which cost the lives of Elliott and of Moseley. Only one verdict could be given by an honest jury on deaths like these – 'Suicide, whilst in a state of sound mind.'

There is some difference of opinion as to the numbers of which a climbing party should be composed. But whatever number is right, two is unquestionably wrong. A sudden illness or a slight accident to one of the party, and the other is of little use. Imagine, for instance, a man who has sprained his ankle seven or eight hours from home. To leave the sufferer for many hours is very painful; to remain with him is practically useless. A party on any mountain of the first or second order should never be less than three. The typical party for comfort and safety consists of two travellers and two guides. With one traveller and one guide the latter is overweighted in more senses than one; with two guides the labour is equally divided. On reference to our obituary it will be seen that nine deaths have occurred in cases where the party has consisted of two persons only. In other words, the smaller the party the greater the risk of disaster.

During the past season the snow has been exceptionally bad. The attack on a new peak like the Aiguille Blanche de Peuteret, an obelisk of rock on the south side of Mont Blanc, demanded a strong party and favourable conditions of weather and of snow, but every precaution was disregarded. The state of Professor Balfour's health before he left England was such that some of his friends urgently pressed him not to climb. He took one guide only with him, and he made the expedition contrary to the express advice of Emile Rey, of Courmayeur, no mean authority, who not only declined to accompany him, but warned him of the state of the snow, and earnestly dissuaded him from the enterprise. The snow on the Wetterhorn was known to be in bad order when Mr. Penhall attempted it, also with one guide only, in August last. The expedition should not have been made.

Although we must ever mourn for the brave men who have rendered good service to the Club, and whose loss makes a gap that will not be easily filled, it is none the less our duty to see that the responsibility is put upon the right shoulders, and that our pursuit should not be held up to unmerited obloquy because some sanguine men persist in neglecting the ordinary safeguards which alone make that pursuit justifiable.

There is another cardinal mistake which is still too often made, which has resulted in many accidents, and if persisted in may result in many more. I mean climbing in bad weather. I fear that there are few members of the Club who can honestly plead not guilty to this charge. It is true that if a man has set his heart upon a particular peak, and he gets within an hour or two of the top of it before bad weather comes on, it is very hard to turn back. The average Englishman does not like to be beaten. But after all, is it not the truest courage to run away? Every climber knows the enormous difference between mountaineering in sunshine and in storm. The risks on what is ordinarily an easy mountain become tremendous in bad weather, and the climber is in the worst physical and mental condition for grappling with them. The worst accident we have to record, that on Mont Blanc in 1870, when eleven lives were lost, would have been avoided if the party had retreated before the storm began. I cannot help thinking that it is rather obstinacy than true courage which induces a man to persist in an enterprise when wind and weather are against him. The real bravery is to accept defeat. Under such circumstances, he who climbs and runs away, may live to climb another day. Every prudent man will, therefore, set his face against such a flagrant breach of the unwritten laws of climbing morality. And every prudent guide if asked to proceed under such circumstances will answer as Melchior Anderegg once did to a climber in my hearing – '*Es geht, Melchior!*' said my friend, when we came to an impracticable spot. '*Ja!*' replied Melchior, '*es geht, aber* ich *gehe nicht.*' ['It goes, Melchior!' 'Yes! It goes, but *I'm* not going!']

Many of the accidents in our obituary have resulted from avalanches. I know that some persons are of opinion that accidents from this cause are among those which are most difficult to avoid. I do not share in this view. Avalanches are of two kinds: those which result from the falling of fresh snow down a more or less steeply inclined plane, and those which result from the fall of ice from an overhanging glacier. In my judgement, no party should ever run the slightest risk of an accident from either. All of us know the 'Ancien Passage'. In settled weather, when the snow is old and in good order, no accident is possible at this spot, but after fresh snow, it is the playground of avalanches, as Captain Arkwright and his three guides found to their cost fourteen years ago. The risk is always great in working under an overhanging glacier. I remember, in the year 1870, ascending the Pizzo Bianco to inspect the east side of Monte Rosa. Mr. Morshead and myself had set our hearts on making the first passage over the Höchste Spitze, from Macugnaga, to the Riffel. We were advised by eminent guides.

After a long examination we were forced to admit that we could not get up without crossing the tracks of ice avalanches, and thereby incurring a serious risk, which, in our judgement, was not justifiable. As a matter of fact, some avalanches fell whilst our inspection was being made. I know that Dr. Taylor and the Messrs. Pendlebury made this excursion in 1872, after Ulrich and Christian Lauener and the veteran Almer had declined to have anything to do with it. Now if Dr. Taylor's party could have satisfied themselves that by a very early start they could get above the avalanche-tracks before the sun had power to loosen the overhanging ice, the ascent might have been less open to hostile criticism. But Dr. Taylor himself informed us that at 2 A.M. 'a deep roll from the Zumstein announced that the avalanches were waking early'. The excursion has been more than once repeated. Last year, however, the inevitable result occurred. Signor Marinelli and his two guides were in a dangerous position *late in the afternoon*. They fell in with the ice avalanches which Dr. Taylor had avoided, and were killed on the spot. In other words, the culpable neglect of ordinary precautions had its natural consequences.

I have already referred to the 'cornice accident' of 1877. This was clearly the result of bad guiding. Even good guides sometimes fail to take sufficient precautions. One would have thought that an accident so striking and so melancholy would have been warning enough for all time, and yet within the last three or four years two parties have been nearly sacrificed from precisely the same cause, on the Piz Palu and the Gabelhorn, and in each case were only saved by the skill and dexterity of the rear guide.

There can be no doubt that in these days men climb Alps who are not fitted for it, and who would be much better at home. They are not only often out of training, but altogether ignorant of the very alphabet of their art. Conceive a man who knows about enough of cricket to play in a match at a country school, thinking himself worthy to play at Lord's against Australian bowling; and yet men, whose pedestrian feats have not amounted to more than Skiddaw or the Glyddrs, sometimes rush out to the Alps and expect to be conducted safely to the top of the Weisshorn or the Matterhorn.

Accidents do not happen to men who understand their business, and do not neglect reasonable precautions. The pioneers of the Alpine Club learned their work slowly. They laboured in new fields and at great disadvantages. They had the dread of the unknown before them as well as its charm. Perhaps they were over-cautious, but they had their reward. Peak after peak fell before them; col after col was crossed. New expeditions were made season after season, often under circumstances of unusual difficulty; but there is not a blot upon their mountaineering escutcheon, there is not a single accident to record. This fact is worth earnest consideration. But, as Mr. Stephen has told us – and mountaineers never had a more prudent or more sagacious adviser – 'The modern race of mankind is in a too great hurry. It refuses to serve an apprenticeship to anything. It believes that by a little happy audacity and the expenditure of enough money it can leap over all preparatory stages. Mountaineering, like so many other things, has become a fashion with many who don't really care about it; and the mountains have taken a terrible revenge.'

What, then, are the conclusions to be drawn? Surely my readers will already have done so for themselves. Mountaineering is extremely dangerous in the case of incapable, of imprudent, of thoughtless men. But I venture to state that of all the accidents in our sad obituary, there is hardly one which need have happened; there is hardly one which could not have been easily prevented by proper caution and proper care. Men get careless and too confident. This does not matter or the other does not matter. The fact is, that everything matters; precautions should not only be ample but excessive.

> The little more and how much it is,
> And the little less and what worlds away.

Mountaineering is not dangerous, provided that the climber knows his business and takes the necessary precautions – all within his own control – to make danger impossible. The prudent climber will recollect what he owes to his family and to his friends. He will also recollect that he owes something to the Alps, and will scorn to bring them into disrepute. He will not go on a glacier without a rope. He will not climb alone, or with a single companion. He will treat a great mountain with the respect it deserves, and not try to rush a dangerous peak with inadequate guiding power. He will turn his back steadfastly upon mist and storm. He will not go where avalanches are in the habit of falling after fresh snow, or wander about beneath an overhanging glacier in the heat of a summer afternoon. Above all, if he loves the mountains for their own sake, for the lessons they can teach and the happiness they can bring, he will do nothing that can discredit his manly pursuit or bring down the ridicule of the undiscerning upon the noblest pastime in the world.

❄ (Vol. XI.)

Ellis Carr

11 ❄ Two Days on an Ice Slope

In venturing to write an account of our attempt on the Aiguille du Plan, I have felt myself somewhat handicapped by the necessity of describing a failure, and by the fear that, in the opinion of some, the fact that we did not reach the summit of our peak might deprive me of my chief if not sole justification for putting pen to paper.

In undertakings of all kinds it has been admitted that success often covers a multitude of sins in the methods adopted to attain it, while failure as often tends to emphasize those sins and bring them into relief; and it seems to me that mountaineering offers no exception to the rule, but, on the contrary, frequently affords striking examples of its application. Accepting, therefore, whatever risk there may be of the latter contingency in the present instance, I have endeavoured to record the details of an expedition which, though unsuccessful in the ordinary acceptation of the word, was, to myself at least, instructive, not only as a test of endurance, but as a lesson in that self-reliance on the mountains which can only come by experience.

Before leaving England Mr. Mummery and I discussed the possibility of making an ascent on the Aiguille du Plan from the Chamonix valley. The mountain excited our interest in the first place from its having received but little attention from climbers generally, and, secondly, from the fact that the summit had never been reached from the north-west side of that great ridge in the chain of Mont Blanc of which it forms a part, the side from which we proposed to approach it. Further, so far as we were aware, no one had ever attempted it since Mr. Baumann's defeat in August 1880. The description he gives in the *Alpine Journal* of his experience on the mountain, and its appearance when seen from a distance, led us to the conclusion that in no case could we expect to find the problem an easy one, nor lacking in interest and excitement (danger for its own sake we did not court), and this, added to the ever seductive charm of possibly making a new ascent, determined us to assign to the Aiguille du Plan a prominent place in our programme, when we met, as agreed, at the Montanvert in August.

A pleasant sojourn among the Graians with Messrs. Walker and Solly had occupied the latter part of July, and after waiting a day or two in vain for fine weather at Courmayeur, in the hope of traversing Mont Blanc, I accompanied them across the Col du Géant, arriving at the Montanvert on August 3.

With the exception of the rooms secured for us by the kind mediation of a friend at court, we found the hotel, I believe for the first time in its history, full to overflowing with English climbers and their families in residence, amongst whom were many personal friends, and it seemed as if the noble Alpine spirit (a judicious blend, by the way, of enthusiasm for the mountains and tender pity for the outsider), hunted out of its old haunts by the rush of trains, hotel omnibuses, and their teeming contents, had found, for a time at least, a congenial resting-place under the shadow of the Aiguilles, before being driven to take wing once more. That this will, sooner or later, be its fate is, alas! already but too apparent, as the daily storming of the hotel, in fine weather, by 200 to 300 birds of passage, of varied plumage (some of whom devour their meal with shouts prior to rejoining the ranks of the army crossing the glacier to the place from whence they came), already drives the poor roosters to take refuge with a luncheon bag on the mountain side, or, without any such visible means of support, to remote corners of the hotel, there to wait till the rush is over, and at least one of the salon windows can again be opened without incurring risk of personal violence.

Having determined to devote a day to a preliminary inspection of our mountain, we started from the hotel in company with Messrs. Slingsby and Solly at 6 A.M. on August 11. Our party followed the usual Charmoz route across the rocky spurs which descend from that mountain, and the weary valley of boulders beyond, as far as the right moraine of the Nantillons Glacier. Having traversed this glacier and a second smaller one lying at the base of the Aiguille de Blaitière, and after turning at its foot a rib of sharp rocks which forms its left bank, we found ourselves on the glacier immediately below the Aiguille du Plan, and for the first time in a position to obtian a full view of our mountain. Its appearance, from where we stood, was that of an enormous façade of most excessive and uncompromising steepness, crowned with towering pinnacles, and flanked on each side by projecting wings – on the left by the rocky wall of the Aiguille de Blaitière, and on the right by steep cliffs forming the base of a detached peak of the Plan itself. Access to the summit ridge was apparently completely cut off at both ends by these huge wings, really mountains in themselves; and as there were no subsidiary ridges or ribs of continuous rock to suggest a probable route, we were driven to the conclusion that only by the steep snow slopes on the face in front of us could the summit be reached from this side. Roughly speaking, it may be said that the upper face of the mountain is divided vertically into two parts, differing in their character, that next to the Aiguille de Blaitière consisting of smooth rocks interspersed with patches and streaks of snow, the other of a series of hanging glaciers and snow slopes running up to the highest peak, which, when seen from the N.W., stands somewhat behind the line of the summit ridge. The lower part of the face is unequally divided into two bays or cirques, the larger on the side next the Blaitière, by a huge rocky rib or buttress, which, rising from the glacier, cuts the face at right angles, terminating abruptly at the foot of the ice cliffs of the first hanging glacier of the series before referred to. Though, when seen from below, these ice cliffs appeared to be more or less broken, there were no dangerous-looking séracs, and at one point where there was a gap, we thought it might be possible to force a passage to the snow slopes above, could we once succeed in reaching the ice by way of the rock buttress. As there appeared to be no more promising alternative, and the rock buttress would most likely in any case command a comprehensive and near view of the face, we decided to make our reconnaissance in this direction.

On our way up to the glacier we deviated sufficiently to the right to obtain a glimpse into the bay or great couloir on the far side of the buttress, but at once rejected it, as it was completely blocked by a hanging glacier at the top, and would be swept throughout its entire length by any séracs which might fall.

On approaching the rocks at the foot of the buttress we found them exceedingly steep, and judged them, if not absolutely unclimbable, much too expensive in time so early in the day; so, turning a crevasse or two, we skirted them on the left for some distance, making our way up the glacier and keeping a look-out for a promising point of attack.

There did not appear to be much choice, the lower part of the rocks being smooth and offering an almost continuous and unbroken wall. We therefore continued our course up the glacier, before long reaching a point from which a better view could be obtained of the lower portion of the face opposite to us, and saw that it consisted for the most part of apparently inaccessible precipices, surmounted at their northern end by a hanging glacier, doubtless the same to which Mr. Baumann gained access by scaling the rocks of the Aiguille de Blaitière still further to the left.

Only on the right of this section of the face – i.e. on the side adjoining the great rock buttress – was a break in the line of cliffs, formed by a most formidable-looking ice couloir, up to the bergschrund at the base of which the glacier slope whereon we stood rapidly narrowed and steepened. Some distance above the bergschrund a rib of steep rocks divided the couloir into two parts. Above the point where this rib somewhat abruptly terminated, the inclination of the couloir, steep throughout, became more severe, and continued to increase, culminating at a point some 800 or 900 ft. above the bergschrund in an apparently perpendicular ice wall.

Of the two divisions of the couloir that on the left alone showed no traces of falling stones or ice, being somewhat removed from the direct line of fire from the glaciers above, while its neighbour on the right was less favourably situated, being in admirable position to receive most liberal contributions.

The awful steepness and great length of the couloir confirmed our decision to try first the rock buttress, though, should that fail, we felt that here would be our best alternative, as, supposing it possible by any means to surmount the ice wall, the snow slopes above seemed to offer a direct and comparatively easy and unbroken way to the summit.

Mr. Baumann's route by the rocks of the Blaitière we had rejected as too dangerous, for not only did the state of the ice cliffs put all idea of scaling them out of the question, but in the only gully by which the Blaitière rocks, traversed by him, could be reached, a large mass of snow, over which we should perforce have to pass, hung suspended and obviously on the point of falling bodily. In fact, later on we saw that it had done so. This route was also objectionable from the fact that it led to a portion of the face hopelessly remote from the summit, while Mr. Baumann's description of the rock-climbing above suggested anything but rapid progress in that direction. We therefore resumed our search for a breach in the outworks of the rock buttress on our right, determined to attain on this as high a point as time would allow. The only place we could discover which appeared at all promising was situated at the upper edge of a steep snow slope which ran some distance up the side of the buttress, and at whose base we were now standing. Here the rival claims of two small chimneys divided our attention, till on nearer approach we chose the one more to the left, as being of the two somewhat easier and leading to a better line of route above.

It took more time than we anticipated to reach the rocks, as the snow slope, after we had passed a bergschrund not far from its base, turned to hard ice, and, on coming to close quarters with our chimney we found careful climbing and consequent slow progress compulsory. The rocks above the chimney, though easier, were still much too difficult for speed, and at the rate the hours were slipping by we began to realize that unless matters improved, and that pretty soon, we should never reach the séracs before dark. Our efforts had hitherto been directed towards a gap on the ridge on the left of a rocky tower, which, if not turned, threatened to bar all further progress, and, in fact, on a nearer approach, we could see no alternative landing-place. Instead of becoming easier, the steepness and difficulty of the climb now rapidly increased, and we consequently decided to abandon all idea of reaching the séracs. In the hope, however, of obtaining a view of the point where the rock buttress joined the mountain, Mummery and I, divesting ourselves of our rucksacks, made our way up the rocks, crossing some steep smooth slabs, partially covered with snow, till we stood almost close to the base of the rocky tower. On our left was a steep gully, running up to the gap on the sky-line we had been aiming for, with smooth sides enclosing a sharp angle in which was some ice. An upright crack, on its opposite side, seemed to offer means of access to the desired gap could we once manage to get into the gully. It was possible to traverse towards it for some 15 to 20 ft., there being, so far, good hand- and foot-hold in the face of the rock. Beyond, however, the foot-hold entirely ceased, and the hand-hold was reduced to one oblique crack, from $\frac{1}{2}$ in. to $\frac{3}{4}$ in. wide, on the right of a steep slab. After inspecting this in turn, with the rope held hitched round an ice-axe placed in a crevice, we thought that by hardening our hearts, and with the stimulus of assured success beyond, the slab itself might 'go'. As this stimulus, however, was conspicuous by its absence, and the hand-holds of the rest of the traverse were even more sketchy, we turned back to the base of the tower and scrambled up to the ridge on its lower side. From the notch in which we found ourselves the tower was quite unclimbable, and a steep chimney which descended below us on the far side offered no prospect of turning it there. It was conclusive; so with the consciousness of having done our best for the buttress route, though it failed to appreciate our efforts, we returned to our companions, having kept them patiently awaiting us for more than an hour. The afternoon was well advanced, and we hurried down to traverse the valley of boulders under the Charmoz before dark, and to seek the assistance of mine host of the Montanvert in satisfying the vacuum which we, like nature, were beginning to abhor.

The rocks having failed us, vision of the ice couloir, which had haunted me more or less during the day, now took definite form, and as we descended the glacier I could not help glancing back from time to time at the sheeted spectre, with its sweeping shroud of ice, much as a schoolboy might look for some signs of relenting in the cold, stern face of the master whose frown he meant nevertheless to brave. I looked in vain. Far from appearing easier, the couloir in the evening light seemed steeper than ever, and though I consoled myself by reflecting on the frequently deceptive appearance of slopes viewed in full front, I felt that *there* would be the tug of war, if not the unconditional surrender.

Apart from this obstacle the ascent of the couloir to the foot of the snow slopes resolved itself into the task of cutting steps up some 1,000 feet of ice or névé at an angle increasing from about 30° to 50°, and we hoped, by making an early start from a *gîte* situated as near as possible to our work, we might gain the snow slopes in time to complete the ascent.

To neglect no detail which might contribute to success, the morning of the next day, August 12, was partially occupied in sharpening the dulled points of our axes, an operation we found both difficult and tedious on the intoxicated and deformed instrument known as the hotel grind-stone, one end of whose axle, scorning restraint, described complicated curves in the air on its own account, but expeditiously and, in the opinion of the operators at least, splendidly performed by means of an old file borrowed from the 'boots'. Our own axes finished, it was curious to note how many others required attention, and we might have continued filing and panting for the remainder of the afternoon but for our appointment with the ice couloir.

Solly having to prepare for his return to England, Mummery, Slingsby, and I started at 4 P.M., with a porter carrying the material for our camp. This comprised a silk tent of Mummery's pattern, only weighing 1½ to 2 lb.; three eider-down sleeping-bags, 9 lb.; cooking apparatus of thin tin, 1½ lb.; or, with ropes, rucksacks, and sundries, about 25 lb., in addition to the weight of the provisions. Though not unduly burdened the porter found the valley of boulders exceedingly troublesome, and in spite of three distinct varieties of advice as to the easiest route across them, made such miserably slow progress, often totally disappearing amongst the rocks like a water-logged ship in a trough of the sea, that we were forced to pitch our tent on the right moraine of the Nantillons Glacier instead of near the base of our peak, as intended. The *gîte*, built up with stones on the slope of the moraine, with earth raked into the interstices, was sufficiently comfortable to afford Mummery and myself some sleep. A stone, however, far sur-passing the traditional *gîte* lump in aggressive activity seemed, most undeservedly, to have singled out Slingsby as its innocent victim, and judging by the convulsions of his sleeping-bag, and the sighs and thumps which were in full swing every time I woke up, it must have kept him pretty busy all night dodging its attacks from side to side. His account of his sufferings next morning, when Mummery and I were admittedly awake, fully confirmed and explained these phenomena; but on going for the enemy by daylight he had the satisfaction of finding that he had suffered quite needlessly, the stone being loose and easily removed. We used Mummery's silk tent for the first time, and found that it afforded ample room for three men to lie at full length without crowding. The night, however, was too fine and still to test the weather-resisting power of the material, and as this was thin enough to admit sufficient moonlight to illuminate the interior of the tent, and make candle or lamp superfluous, we inferred that it might possibly prove to be equally accommodating in the case of rain or wind. It was necessary, moreover, on entering or leaving the tent, to adopt that form of locomotion to which the serpent was condemned to avoid the risk of unconsciously carrying away the whole structure on one's back. We started next morning about three o'clock, leaving the camp kit ready packed for the porter whom we had instructed to fetch it during the day, and pushed on to the glacier at the foot of our mountain at a steady pace, maintained in my case with much greater ease than would have otherwise been possible by virtue of some long single-pointed screw spikes inserted over night in my boot soles; and I may here venture to remark that a few of these spikes, screwed into the boots before starting on an expedition where much ice work is expected, appear to offer a welcome compromise between ponderous crampons and ordinary nails. They do not, I think, if not too numerous, interfere with rock-climbing, and can be repeatedly renewed when worn down. A slight modification in the shape would further facilitate their being screwed in with a box key made to fit.

Leaving the rock buttress, the scene of our reconnaissance on the 11th, on the right, we struck straight up the glacier basin between it and the Aiguille de Blaitière, which glacier appeared to me to be largely composed of broken fragments of ice mixed with avalanche snow from the hanging glaciers and slopes above. Keeping somewhat to the left, we reached the bergschrund, which proved to be of considerable size, extending along the whole base of the couloir, and crossed it at a point immediately adjoining the rocks on the left. The axe at once came into requisition, and we cut steadily in hard ice up and across the couloir towards the small rib or island of rock before mentioned as dividing it higher up into two portions. The rocks at the base of this rib, though steep, gritty, and loose, offered more rapid going than the ice, and we climbed them to a gap on the ridge above, commanding a near view of the perpendicular country in front of us. Far above us, and immediately over the top of the right-hand section of the couloir, towered the ice cliffs of the hanging glacier we had tried to reach on the 11th, and beyond these again, in the grey morning light, we caught the glimpse of a second and even a third rank of séracs in lofty vista higher up the mountain. As before observed, this section of the couloir seemed admirably placed for receiving icefalls, and we now saw that it formed part of the natural channel for snow and débris from each and all of these glaciers. We therefore directed our attention to our friend on the left, and after a halt for breakfast traversed the still remaining portion of the dividing ridge, turning a small rock pinnacle on its right, and recommenced cutting steps in the hard ice which faced us. As has been before remarked, it is difficult to avoid over-estimating the steepness of ice slopes, but, allowing for any tendency towards exaggeration, I do not think I am wrong in fixing the angle of the couloir from this point as not less than 50°. We kept the axe steadily going, and with an occasional change of leader, after some hours' unceasing work, found ourselves approaching the base of the upper portion of the couloir, which from below had appeared perpendicular. We paused to consider the situation. For at least 80 to 100 feet the ice rose at an angle of 60° to 70°, cutting off all view of the face above, with no flanking wall of rock on the right, but bounded on the left by an overhanging cliff, which dripped slightly with water from melting snow above. The morning was well advanced, and we kept a sharp look-out aloft for any stray stones which might fancy a descent in our direction. None came, and we felt gratified at this confirmation of our judgement as to the safety of this part of the couloir. However, the time for chuckling had not yet come. As I stated, we had halted to inspect the problem before us. Look as we might we could discover no possibility of turning the ice wall either to the right or left, and though, as we fondly believed and hoped, it formed the only barrier to easier going above, the terrible straightness and narrowness of the way was sufficient to make the very boldest pause to consider the strength of his resources.

How long *I* should have paused before beating a retreat, if asked to lead the way up such a place, I will not stop to enquire, but I clearly remember that my efforts to form some estimate of the probable demand on my powers such a feat would involve were cut short by Mummery's quiet announcement that he was ready to make the attempt. Let me here state that amongst Mummery's other mountaineering qualifications not the least remarkable is his power of inspiring confidence in those who are climbing with him, and that both Slingsby and I experienced this is proved by the fact that we at once proceeded, without misgiving or hesitation, to follow his lead. We had hitherto used an 80-ft. rope, but now, by attaching a spare 100-ft. length of thin rope, used double, we afforded the leader an additional 50 ft. Mummery commenced cutting, and we soon approached the lower portion of the actual ice wall, where the angle of the slope cannot have been less than 60°.

I am not aware that any authority has fixed the exact degree of steepness at which it becomes impossible to use the ice-axe with both hands, but, whatever portion of a right angle the limit may be, Mummery very soon reached it, and commenced excavating with his right hand caves in the ice, each with an internal lateral recess by which to support his weight with his left. Slingsby and I, meanwhile possessing our souls in patience, stood in our respective steps, as on a ladder, and watched his steady progress with admiration, so far as permitted us by the falling ice dislodged by the axe.

Above our heads the top of the wall was crowned by a single projecting stone, towards which the leader cut, and which, when reached, just afforded sufficient standing-room for both feet. The ice immediately below this stone, for a height of 12 or 14 ft., was practically perpendicular, and Slingsby's definition of it as a 'frozen waterfall' is the most appropriate I can find. Here and there Mummery found it necessary to cut through its entire thickness, exposing the face of the rock behind.

On reaching the projecting stone the leader was again able to use the axe with both hands, and slowly disappeared from view; thus completing, without pause or hitch of any kind, the most extraordinary feat of mountaineering skill and nerve it has ever been my privilege to witness.

The top of the wall surmounted, Slingsby and I expected every moment to hear the welcome summons to follow to easier realms above. None came. Time passed, the only sounds besides the occasional drop of water from the rocks on our left, or the growl of a distant avalanche, being that of the axe and the falling chips of ice, as they whizzed by or struck our heads or arms with increasing force. The sound of the axe strokes gradually became inaudible, but the shower continued to pound us without mercy for more than an hour of inaction, perhaps more trying to the nerves, in such a position, than the task of leading. The monotony was to some extent varied by efforts to ward off from our heads the blows of the falling ice, and by the excitement, at intervals, of seeing the slack rope hauled up a foot or so at a time. It had almost become taut, and we were preparing to follow, when a shout from above, which sounded, from where we stood, muffled and far away, for more rope kept us in our places. It was all very well to demand more rope, but not so easy to comply. The only possible way to give extra length was to employ the 100 ft. of thin rope single, instead of doubled, at which we hesitated at first, but, as Mummery shouted that it was absolutely necessary, we managed to make the change, though it involved Slingsby's getting out of the rope entirely during the operation. To anyone who has not tried it I should hardly venture to recommend, as an enjoyable diversion, the process, which must necessarily occupy both hands, of removing and re-adjusting 180 ft. of rope on an ice slope exceeding 60° at the top of a steep couloir some 1,000 ft. high. The task accomplished, we had not much longer to wait before the shout to come on announced the termination of our martyrdom. We went on, but, on passing in turn the projecting stone, and catching sight of the slope above, we saw at a glance that our hopes of easy going must for the present be postponed. Mummery, who had halted at the full extent of his tether of about 120 ft. of rope, was standing in his steps on an ice slope quite as steep as that below the foot of the wall we had just surmounted. He had been cutting without intermission for two hours, and suggested a change. Being last on the rope, I therefore went ahead, cutting steps to pass, and took up the work with the axe. The ice here was occasionally in double layer, the outer one some 3 to 4 ins. in thickness, which, when cut through, revealed a space of about equal depth behind, an arrangement at times very convenient, as affording good hand-holds without extra labour. I went on for some time cutting pigeon holes on the right side of the couloir, and, at the risk of being unorthodox, I would venture to point out what appear to me the advantages of this kind of step on very steep ice. Cut in two perpendicular rows, alternately for each foot, the time lost in zigzags is saved, and no turning steps are necessary; they do not require the ice to be cut away so much for the leg as in the case of lateral steps, and are therefore less easily filled up by falling chips and snow. Being, on account of their shape, more protected from the sun's heat, they are less liable to be spoiled by melting, and have the further advantage of keeping the members of the party in the same perpendicular line, and consequently in a safer position. They also may serve as hand-holds. To cut such steps satisfactorily it is necessary that the axe be provided with a point long enough to penetrate to the full depth required for the accommodation of the foot up to the instep, without risk of injury to the shaft by repeated contact with the ice.

As we had now been going for several hours without food, and since leaving the rock rib, where we had breakfasted, had come across no ledge or irregularity of any kind affording a resting-place, it was with no little satisfaction that I descried, on the opposite side of the couloir, at a spot about 30 or 40 feet above, where the cliff on our left somewhat receded, several broken fragments of rock cropping out of the ice, of size and shape to provide seats for the whole party. We cut up and across to them, and sat down, or rather hooked ourselves on, for a second breakfast. We were here approximately on a level with the summit of our rock buttress of the 11th, and saw that it was only connected with the mountain by a broken and dangerous-looking ridge of ice and névé running up to an ice slope at the foot of the glacier cliffs. The gap in the latter was not visible from our position. The tower we had tried to turn appeared far below, and the intervening rocks of the buttress, though not jagged, were steep and smooth like a roof. The first gleams of sunshine now arrived to cheer us, and getting under way once more, we pushed on hopefully, as the couloir was rapidly widening and the face of the mountain almost in full view. We had also surmounted the rock wall which had so long shut out the prospect on our left, and it was at this point that, happening to glance across the slabs, we caught sight of a large flat rock rapidly descending. It did not bound nor roll, but slid quietly down with a kind of stealthy haste, as if it thought, though rather late, it might still catch us, and was anxious not to alarm us prematurely. It fell harmlessly into the couloir, striking the ice near the rock rib within a few feet of our tracks, and we saw no other falling stones while we were on the mountain.

Leaving the welcome resting-place, Mummery again took the lead, and cut up and across the couloir, now becoming less steep, to a rib or patch of rocks higher up on the right, which we climbed to its upper extremity, a distance of some 70 or 80 feet.

Here, taking to the ice once more, we soon approached the foot of the first great snow slope on the face, and rejoiced in the near prospect of easier going. At the top of this slope, several hundred feet straight before us, was a low cliff or band of rocks, for which we decided to aim, there being throughout the entire length of the intervening slope no suspicious grey patches to indicate ice. The angle was, moreover, much less severe, and it being once more my turn to lead, I went at it with the zealous intention of making up time. My ardour was, however, considerably checked at finding, when but a short distance up the slope, that the coating of névé was so exceedingly thin as to be insufficient for good footing without cutting through the hard ice below. Instead, therefore, of continuing in a straight line for the rocks, we took an oblique course to the right, towards one of the hanging glaciers before referred to, and crossing a longitudinal crevasse, climbed without much difficulty up its sloping bank of névé. Hurrah! here was a good snow at last, only requiring at most a couple of slashes with the adze end of the axe for each step. If this continued we had a comparatively easy task before us, as the rocks above, though smooth and steep, were broken up here and there by bands and streaks of snow. Taking full advantage of this our first opportunity for making speed, we cut as fast as possible and made height rapidly. We still aimed to strike the band of rocks before described, though at a point much more to the right, and nearer to where its extremity was bounded by the ice cliffs of another hanging glacier; but, alas! as we approached nearer and nearer to the base of the cliffs, looming apparently higher and higher over our heads, the favouring névé, over which we had been making such rapid progress, again began to fail, and before we could reach the top of the once more steepening slope the necessity of again resorting to the pick end of the axe brought home the unwelcome conviction that our temporary respite had come to an end, and that, instead of snow above, and apart from what help the smooth rocks might afford, nothing was to be expected but hard, unmitigated ice.

We immediately felt that, as it was already past noon, the establishment of this fact would put a totally different complexion on our prospects of success, and, instead of reaching the summit, we might have to content ourselves with merely crossing the ridge. We continued cutting, however, and reached the rocks, the last part of the slope having once more become exceedingly steep. To turn the cliff, here unclimbable, we first spent over half an hour in prospecting to the right, where a steep ice gully appeared between the rocks and the hanging glacier; but, abandoning this, we struck off to the left, cutting a long traverse, during which we were able to hitch the rope to rocks cropping out through the ice. The traverse landed us in a kind of gully, where, taking to the rocks whenever practicable, though climbing chiefly by the ice, we reached a broken stony ledge, large and flat enough to serve as a luncheon place, the only spot we had come across since leaving the rock rib, where it was possible really to rest sitting. Luncheon over, we proceeded as before, choosing the rocks as far as possible by way of change, though continually obliged to take to the ice streaks by which they were everywhere intersected. This went on all the rest of the afternoon, till, when daylight began to wane, we had attained an elevation considerably above the gap between our mountain and the Aiguille de Blaitière, or more than 10,900 ft. above the sea.

The persistent steepness and difficulty of the mountain had already put our reaching the ridge before dark entirely out of the question, though we decided to keep going as long as daylight lasted, so as to leave as little work as possible for the morrow.

The day had been gloriously fine, practically cloudless throughout, and I shall never forget the weird look of the ice slopes beneath, turning yellow in the evening light, and plunging down and disappearing far below in the mists which were gathering at the base of the mountain; also, far, far away, we caught a glimpse of the Lake of Geneva, somewhere near Lausanne. I had turned away from the retrospect, when an exclamation from Slingsby called me to look once more. A gap had appeared in the mists, and there, some 2,700 ft. below us, as it were on an inferior stage of the world, we caught a glimpse of the snowfield at the very foot of the mountain, dusky yellow in the last rays of the sun. Mummery was in the meantime continuing the everlasting chopping, in the intervals of crawling up disobliging slabs of rock, till twilight began to deepen into darkness, and we had to look about for a perch on which to roost for the night. The only spot we could find, sufficiently large for all three of us to sit, was a small patch or lump of rocks, more or less loose, some 20 or 30 ft. below where we stood, and we succeeded, just as the light failed, or about 8.30 P.M., and after some engineering, in seating ourselves side by side upon it. Our boots were wet through by long standing in ice steps, and we took them off and wrung the water out of our stockings. The others put theirs on again; but, as a precaution against frost-bite, having pocketed my stockings, I put my feet, wrapped in a woollen cap, inside the rucksack, with the result that they remained warm through the night. The half-hour which it took me next morning to pull on the frozen boots proved, however, an adequate price for the privilege of having warm feet. As a precaution against falling off our shelf we hitched the rope over a rock above and passed it round us, and to make sure of not losing my boots (awful thought!) I tied them to it by the laces.

After dinner we settled down to spend the evening. The weather fortunately remained perfect, and the moon had risen, though hidden from us by our mountain. Immediately below lay Chamonix, like a cheap illumination, gradually growing more patchy as the night advanced and the candles went out one by one, while above the stars looked down as if silently wondering why in the world we were sitting there. The first two hours were passed without very much discomfort, but having left behind our extra wraps to save weight, as time wore on the cold began to make itself felt, and though fortunately never severe enough to be dangerous, made us sufficiently miserable. Packed as we were, we were unable to indulge in those exercises generally adopted to induce warmth, and we shivered so vigorously at intervals that, when all vibrating in unison, we wondered how it might affect the stability of our perch. Sudden cramp in a leg, too, could only be relieved by concerted action, it being necessary for the whole party to rise solemnly together like a bench of judges, while the limb was stretched out over the valley of Chamonix till the pain abated and it could be folded up and packed away once more. We sang songs, told anecdotes, and watched the ghostly effect of the moonlight on a subsidiary pinnacle of the mountain, the illuminated point of which, in reality but a short distance away, looked like a phantom Matterhorn seen afar off over an inky black arête formed by the shadow thrown across its base by the adjoining ridge. We had all solemnly vowed not to drop asleep, and for me this was essential, as my centre of gravity was only just within the base of support; but while endeavouring to give effect to another chorus, in spite of the very troublesome vibrato before referred to, I was grieved and startled at the sudden superfluous interpolation of two sustained melancholy bass notes, each in a different key and ominously suggestive of snoring. The pensive attitude of my companions' heads being in keeping with their song, in accordance with a previous understanding, I imparted to Mummery, who sat next to me, a judicious shock, but, as in the case of a row of billiard balls in contact, the effect was most noticeable at the far end, and *Slingsby* awoke, heartily agreeing with me how weak it was of Mummery to give way thus. The frequent necessity for repeating this operation, with strengthening variations as the effects wore off, soon stopped the chorus which, like Sullivan's 'Lost Chord', trembled away into silence.

The lights of Chamonix had by this time shrunk to a mere moth-eaten skeleton of their earlier glory, and I became weakly conscious of a sort of resentment at the callous selfishness of those who could thus sneak into their undeserved beds, without a thought of the three devoted explorers gazing down at them from their eyrie on the icy rocks.

From 2 to 4 o'clock the cold became more intense, aggravated by a slight 'breeze of morning', and while waiting for dawn we noticed that it was light enough to see.

Daylight, however, did not help Mummery to find his hat, and we concluded it had retired into the bergschrund under cover of darkness.

We helped each other into a standing position and decided to start for the next patch of rocks above, from there to determine what chance of success there might be in making a dash for the summit, or, failing this, of simply crossing the ridge and descending to the Col du Géant. There was very little food left, and, as we had brought no wine, breakfast was reduced to a slight sketch, executed with little taste and in a few very dry touches.

Owing to the time required to disentangle virulently kinked and frozen ropes, &c., the sun was well above the horizon when we once more started upwards, though unfortunately just at this time, when his life-giving rays would have been most acceptable, they were entirely intercepted by the ridge of the Blaitière. We started on the line of steps cut the night before, but soon after Mummery had recommenced cutting the cold, or rather the impossibility, owing to the enforced inaction, to get warm, produced such an overpowering feeling of drowsiness that Slingsby and I, at Mummery's suggestion, returned to the perch, and jamming ourselves into the space which had before accommodated our six legs, endeavoured to have it out in forty winks. Mummery meanwhile continued step-cutting, and at the end of about half an hour, during which Slingsby and I were somewhat restored by a fitful doze, returned, and we tied on again for another attempt.

Surmounting the patches of rock immediately above our dormitory, we arrived at the foot of another slope of terribly steep, hard ice some 200 ft. in height. At the top of this again was a vertical crag 14 ft. or 15 ft. high, forming the outworks of the next superior band of rocks, which was interspersed with ice-streaks as before. A few feet from the base of this crag was a narrow ledge about 1 ft. in width, where we were able to sit after scraping it clear of snow. Slingsby gave Mummery a leg up round a very nasty corner, as he climbed to a point above the crag whence he was able to assist with the rope to a still higher and narrower ledge. Beyond was another steep slope of hard ice, topped by a belt of rocks as before.

Before reaching this point the cold had again begun to tell upon me, and I bitterly regretted the mistaken policy of leaving behind our extra wraps, especially as the coat I was wearing was not lined. As there was no probability of a change for the better in the nature of the going before the ridge was reached, I began to doubt the wisdom of proceeding, affected as I was, where a false step might send the whole party into the bergschrund 3,000 feet below; but it was very hard, with the summit in view and the most labourious part of the ascent already accomplished, to be the first to cry 'Hold!' I hesitated for some time before doing so, and the others meanwhile had proceeded up the slope. The rope was almost taut when I shouted to them the state of the case and called a council of war. They returned to me, and we discussed what was practically something of the nature of a dilemma. To go on at the same slow rate of progress and without the sun's warmth meant, on the one hand, the possible collapse of at least one of the party from cold, while, on the other hand, to turn back involved the descent of nearly 3,000 ft. of ice, and the passage, if we could not turn it, of the couloir and its ghastly ice wall. Partly, I think, to delay for a time the adoption of the latter formidable alternative, partly to set at rest any doubt which might still remain as to the nature of the going above, Mummery volunteered to ascend alone to the rocks at the summit of the ice slope, though the chance of their offering any improved conditions was generally felt to be a forlorn hope. He untied the rope, threw the end down to us, and retraced his steps up the slope, in due time reaching the rocks some 100 or 130 ft. above, but, after prospecting in more than one direction, returned to us with the report that they offered no improvement and that the intersecting streaks were nothing but hard ice. He, however, was prepared to continue the attempt if we felt equal to the task. If we could at that moment have commanded a cup of hot soup or tea, or the woollen jackets which in our confidence in being able to reach the ridge we had left behind, I am convinced I should have been quite able to proceed, and that the day and the mountain would have been ours; but in the absence of these reviving influences and that of the sun, I was conscious that in my own case, at any rate, it would be folly to persist, so gave my vote for descending. As the food was practically exhausted, the others agreed that it would be wiser to face the terrible ordeal which retracing our steps involved (we did not then know that it meant recutting them) rather than continue the ascent with weakened resources and without absolute certainty of the accessibility of the summit ridge.

As Slingsby on the previous day had insisted on being regarded merely as a passenger, and had therefore not shared in the step-cutting, it was now arranged that he should lead, while Mummery as a tower of strength brought up the rear. Though it was past 5 o'clock, and of course broad daylight, a bright star could be seen just over the ridge of our mountain not far from the summit – alas! the only one anywhere near it on that day. We started downwards at a steady pace, and soon were rejoicing in the returning warmth induced by the more continuous movement. Before we had gone far, however, we found that most of the steps were partially filled up with ice, water having flowed into them during the previous afternoon, and the work of trimming or practically recutting these was at times exceedingly trying, owing to their distance apart, and the consequent necessity of working in a stooping and cramped position.

But if the work was tough the worker fortunately was tougher still, and Mummery and I congratulated ourselves on being able to send such powerful reserves to the front.

The morning was well advanced before the sun surmounted the cold screen of the Blaitière, but having once got to work he certainly made up by intensity for his tardy appearance.

The provisions, with the exception of a scrap or two of cheese and a morsel of chocolate, being exhausted, and having, as before stated, nothing with us in the form of drink, nothing was to be gained by a halt, though, as we descended with as much speed as possible, we kept a sharp look-out for any signs of trickling water with which to quench the thirst which was becoming distressing.

Since finally deciding to return, we had cherished the hope that it might still be possible to turn the ice wall by way of the great rock buttress, and made up our minds at any rate to inspect it from above. With this in view, when the point was reached where we had on the previous day struck the flank of the hanging glacier, instead of continuing in the tracks which trended to the right across the long ice slope, we cut straight down by the side of the glacier to its foot, and over the slope below, in the direction of the séracs immediately crowning the summit of the buttress.

On nearer approach, however, it was manifest that even if by hours of step-cutting a passage from the ice to the rocky crest below could be successfully forced, descent by the latter was more than doubtful, while the consequences of failure were not to be thought of.

Driven, therefore, finally to descend by the couloir, we cut a horizontal traverse which brought us back into the old tracks, a short way above the point where the ice began to steepen for the final plunge, where we braced ourselves for the last and steepest 1,000 ft. of ice. Slingsby still led, and on arriving at the spot below our second breakfast place, where I had last cut pigeon holes, joyfully announced that one of them contained water. He left his drinking cup in an adjoining step for our use as we passed the spot in turn, and the fact that it was only visible when on a level with our faces may give some idea of the steepness of the descent. The delight of that drink was something to remember, though only obtainable in thimblefuls, and I continued dipping so long that Mummery became alarmed, being under the impression that the cup was filled each time.

Mummery had previously volunteered, in case we were driven to return by the couloir, to descend first, and recut the steps and hand-holds in the ice-wall, and as we approached the brink we looked about for some projecting stone or knob of rock which might serve as a hitch for the rope during the operation. The only available projection was a pointed stone of doubtful security, somewhat removed from the line of descent, standing out of the ice at the foot of a smooth vertical slab of rock on the left. Round this we hitched the rope, Slingsby untying to give the necessary length. With our feet firmly planted, each in its own ice step, we paid out the rope as Mummery descended and disappeared over the edge. It was an hour before he reappeared, and this period of enforced inaction was to me, and I think to Slingsby, the most trying of the whole expedition. The want of food was beginning to tell on our strength, the overpowering drowsiness returned, and though it was absolutely essential for the safety of the party to stand firmly in the ice steps, it required a strong effort to avoid dropping off to sleep in that position. We were fortunately able to steady ourselves by grasping the upper edge of the ice where it adjoined the rocky slab under which we stood. This weariness, however, must have been quite as much mental as physical from the long-continued monotony of the work, for when Mummery at last reappeared we felt perfectly equal to the task of descending. The rope was passed behind a boss of névé ingeniously worked by Mummery as a hitch to keep it perpendicular, and I descended first, but had no occasion to rely upon it for more than its moral support, as the steps and hand-holds had been so carefully cut. I climbed cautiously down the icy cataract till I reached a point where hand-holds were not essential to maintain the balance, and waited with my face almost against the ice till Slingsby joined me. Mummery soon followed, and rather than leave the spare rope behind detached it from the stone and descended without its aid, his nerve being to all appearance unimpaired by the fatigues he had gone through. I had before had evidence of his indifference while on the mountains to all forms of food or drink, with the single exception, by the way, of strawberry jam, on the production of which he generally capitulates.

Rejoicing at having successfully passed the steepest portion of the ice wall without the smallest hitch of the wrong sort, we steadily descended the face of the couloir.

Here and there, where a few of the steps had been hewn unusually far apart, I was fain to cut a notch or two for the fingers before lowering myself into the next one below. At last the rock rib was reached, and we indulged in a rest for the first time since turning to descend.

Time, however, was precious, and we were soon under way again, retracing our steps over the steep loose rocks at the base of the rib till forced again on to the ice.

Oh, that everlasting hard ice slope, so trustworthy yet so relentlessly exacting!

Before we could clear the rocks, and as if by way of hint that the mountain had had enough of us, and of me in particular (I could have assured it the feeling was mutual), a flick of the rope sent my hat and goggles flying down to keep company with Mummery's in the bergschrund, and a sharp rolling stone, which I foolishly extended my hand to check, gashed me so severely as to put climbing out of the question for more than a week. As small pieces of ice had been whizzing down for some time from above, though we saw no stones, it was satisfactory to find our steps across the lower part of the couloir in sufficiently good order to allow of our putting on a good pace, and we soon reached the sheltering rock on the opposite side and the slopes below the bergschrund wherein our hats, after losing their heads, had found a grave. The intense feeling of relief on regaining, at 5.55 P.M., safe and easy ground, where the lives of the party were not staked on every step, is difficult to describe, and was such as I had never before experienced. I think the others felt something like the same sensation. Fatigue, kept at bay so long as the stern necessity for caution lasted, seemed to come upon us with a rush, though tempered with the sense of freedom from care aforesaid, and I fancy our progress down the glacier snow was for a time rather staggery. Though tired, we were by no means exhausted, and after a short rest on a flat rock and a drink from a glacier runnel found ourselves sufficiently vigorous to make good use of the remaining daylight to cross the intervening glaciers, moraines and valley of boulders, before commencing to skirt the tedious and, in the dark, exasperating stony wastes of the Charmoz ridge. Sternly disregarding the allurements of numerous stonemen, which here seem to grow wild, to the confusion of those weak enough to trust them, we stumbled along amongst the stones to the brow of the hill overlooking the hotel, where shouts from friends greeted the appearance of our lantern, and, descending by the foot-path, we arrived among them at 10.30 P.M., more than fifty-four hours after our departure on the 12th.

Their kindly welcome I shall not easily forget, and I was sorry to find they had suffered considerable anxiety for our safety, for though aware of our intention, if possible, to cross the range into Italy, they had heard by wire of our non-arrival at Courmayeur, and were discussing the desirability of sending out a search party when our light appeared.

Our failure to reach the summit may, I think, be fairly ascribed to three causes, which on a future occasion might be avoided or allowed for – firstly, our under-estimate of the exceedingly icy condition of the upper part of the mountain, owing to the impossibility of examining it sufficiently closely from the rock buttress; secondly, the low temperature, due to the sheltered position of the face; and thirdly, the neglect to take sufficient food and extra wraps.

We went prepared for a tough piece of ice work in the couloir; and had carefully chosen settled weather for the attempt, but as the neglect of some apparently less important item of the arrangements has often proved the undoing of carefully laid plans, so our omitting to take extra wraps, added to our want of sufficient previous knowledge of the difficulties of the expedition, sufficed to complete our discomfiture, and forced us to return when the most laborious part of the ascent had been accomplished, and success seemed within our grasp. Better, however, the slip 'twixt cup and lip than of a shivering and half-frozen climber from his steps on a steep and lofty ice slope, and the consciousness of the wisdom of our decision to return remains, to some extent, as a set-off against the disappointment of failure.

As regards any future attempts on the mountain from this side, I believe the best, if not the only, line of route to the summit must lie over the upper snow slopes and snow-streaked rocks of the face adjoining the hanging glaciers, passing to the right of the square-topped central peak which crowns the ridge immediately above; but I am also convinced that to reach these slopes at all from below will ever be the chief difficulty. Leaving

Mr. Baumann's route out of the question as offering a point of attack too remote from the summit, though it might possibly, under favourable conditions, give access to the snow slopes, the alternative appears to lie between the couloir and the rock buttress. The former, if free from ice thick enough for step-cutting, as photographs prove is sometimes its condition for hundreds of feet, might prove to be absolutely impossible, as the rocks are exceedingly steep and smooth, while the passage of the latter, if practicable under any conditions, will always, I am certain, be extremely difficult, and frequently entirely barred by the ice cliffs of the hanging glacier which dominates it.

It would, therefore, appear that the presence of ice below in the couloir and its absence at the same time on the slopes above, are the most favourable conditions for an ascent, apart from possible risk from avalanches, though whether such will ever be found to co-exist only the future can show. It should be borne in mind that the expedition is one for which fine settled weather is absolutely essential, and one where the endurance of every member of a party may be put to a severe test. In spite, therefore, of the risk of prophesying, I venture to predict that some time will elapse before an easy route is discovered up the N.W. side of the Aiguille du Plan.

❋ (Vol. XV.)

12 ❄ *What the Climber Eats*

The provisions to be carried for a single day's climbing from a centre will naturally vary with the taste of the individual and the capacities of the locality. Bread, butter, cheese, jam (or honey), meat, sugar, lemons (or strong lemon essence, not essential oil); wine (or cold tea and the like), brandy, biscuits, chocolate, prunes, or perhaps acid drops, may be mentioned as a fairly typical list.

Butter is generally carried in a strong glass or horn tumbler, but Silver & Co. make a round vulcanite box with a screw lid, which is preferable. The other provisions are usually wrapped in paper (destined ultimately to be littered over the mountain), but it is best to do them up in small linen bags brought out from England for the purpose. Oiled-silk bags are also useful for biscuits and sugar. A small wooden box with a screw top will be found handy for carrying salt. Southwell & Co.'s jam, in 4-oz. tins, enough for one meal, can be purchased of R. Jackson & Co.

The fresh meat usually to be had in the Alps is not appetizing, and does not improve by being knocked about in a guide's sack. Chickens are perhaps the best and most palatable form of fresh meat, when obtainable properly fattened, as they generally can be in the great Swiss centres; potted meat is now very frequently preferred, and individual taste will naturally decide the form to be chosen. Irish stew, mulligatawny, and ox-tail soups, curries, and other preparations, put up in Silver's self-cooking tins, will be found excellent on the mountain side, where a hot meal is especially agreeable; one tin contains enough for the substantial part of a meal for three men. It may be well sometimes to carry beef-tea lozenges (Brand & Co.) when circumstances are likely to necessitate a prolonged interval between meals. The *rations condensées accélératrices* (*formule du Dr. Heckle*), made by Gaucher, costing 3 francs a box, and more commonly known as Kola biscuits, have been found to delay the approaches of exhaustion. Kola chocolate is also recommended. Both can be obtained from Silver & Co.

Most climbers prefer to drink red wine on the mountain side. A little sugar and lemon, and lemon essence, with a couple of glasses of suitable liqueur, may be carried without perceptible addition to the weight of the packs; and with these, in addition to the red wine, the ingenious mountaineer may prepare a 'cup' which will be found very palatable, especially when the hard work of the day has been accomplished. Some men prefer cold tea or other non-alcoholic drinks, which may be made and carried in a variety of ways, according to individual tastes or prejudices.

Cold tea is infinitely superior when made with cold water instead of hot; indeed it is difficult to credit how great the difference is. The relative quantities of tea and water are the same in either case, but in cold water it has to remain soaking for several hours. We have made careful experiments with Darjeeling tea both in hot and cold water, the latter being left to soak from one to six hours, using the same quantity of tea and water in each case. We find that from four to six hours give the best results. With other descriptions of tea the time might vary somewhat. One ounce of tea to three pints of water is about the right proportion. It is advisable to carry a small muslin bag (which should be well soaked in boiling water before being used) to strain the tea from the leaves.

Some kind of soup will probably form part of every supper at an Alpine hut, and, if Silver's self-cooking tins are considered too heavy, Lazenby's pea, bean, julienne, and gravy soups are all good – so is Edward's desiccated soup (F. King & Co.), but it is more bulky. The same qualification applies to Nelson's soups, but they are packed in small tin boxes, useful for many purposes. All these soups require to be soaked in cold water for about fifteen minutes before being thrown into boiling water. Pea flour, which can be bought in small tins (Symington's or Brand's), is a valuable ingredient in any plain soup, and so are the French desiccated vegetables, which can be bought everywhere. Bovril is useful for strengthening other condensed soups. Dr. Koch's meat peptone is more portable than bovril, and possesses certain valuable digestive properties, but it is not so palatable, and takes longer to dissolve. It may be bought in packets of 200 grammes (price 3*s*.), calculated to make ten litres of soup (Cie. Peptones de Viande du Dr. Koch). A pint of soup can be readily made in a light tin apparatus, sold by Hill & Son, for which spirit is necessary. Inglis's Metropolitan heating bottle, price 2*s*. 6*d*. (J. H. Pontifex), is very portable and light; it is similar to Hill's apparatus, but smaller. Should it be requisite to make soup only, then Silver's self-cooking tins are more handy, especially if only one or two meals are required.

. . . *and Wears*

Coat. – Norfolk jacket (some prefer it made without the pleats) with as many pockets as possible, all made of light strong cloth and to button up.

On the outside there may be the two usual breast pockets, two small ticket pockets, and four side pockets. The last six should have flaps, and be lined with mackintosh. On the inside have two breast pockets (one being wide and deep enough to carry a map) and a large game pocket going all round the skirt and fastened by several buttons. The inlet to this pocket should be high up in the coat, to avoid snow getting in when on a sitting glissade. The sleeves should have tabs for buttoning tight round the wrist, the tabs being on the upper part of the wrist, not on the under part. There should also be three buttons at the wrists, enabling the sleeve to be opened wide and turned back in hot weather. The collar should have the usual tab to button across the neck. The band should be let into the coat, and not be loose all the way round. About 3 inches loose on each side in front and working through the loops is ample, one side being furnished with two buttons, the other with two holes to allow of varying the tightness. The tab for hanging up the coat should be made of doeskin, stitched on linen; such a tab will not stretch when, in hot walks, the coat is carried slung over the shoulder on the axe; this is better than wearing the coat and carrying the waistcoat.

❄ (From the Report of the Special Committee on Equipment for Mountaineers, Vol. XVI.)

J. N. Collie

13 ❅ *Early Days in the Cuillins*

It was over thirty years ago that I first went to Sligachan, and I went for the fishing. It so happened that the weather was fine, which meant no water in the Sligachan River and no fishing. So I wandered up the glen to see that most marvellous of lochs, Loch Coruisk, and explored some of the great corries amongst the hills.

It was during one of these expeditions into Coire Bhasteir under Sgurr nan Gillean that I saw two mountaineers, A. H. Stocker and a friend, climbing on the rock face of one of the pinnacles. Hundreds of feet above me, on what appeared to me to be rocks as steep as the walls of a house, they moved slowly backwards and forwards, but always getting higher till they finally reached the summit. In those days I knew nothing about climbing, and it seemed to me perfectly marvellous that human beings should be able to do such things. That evening I got as much information as I could from them, and, having asked many questions about mountaineering, I telegraphed to Buckingham for an Alpine rope, for I was told that without it rock-climbing was dangerous. A few days later my brother and I started out with our new rope, also with the intention of climbing Sgurr nan Gillean. We went straight for our peak, up into the Bhasteir Coire and on to the ridge. We never got to the summit; the narrow ridge and the tooth of Sgurr nan Gillean proved too much for us, and after climbing for hours on the face we gave up the attempt. Next day we returned to the mountain, again spending many hours trying, first to surmount the pinnacles of Sgurr nan Gillean, and finally the peak itself, but we were unsuccessful, and the end of the story is, we had to inquire from John Mackenzie, one of the guides at Sligachan, how people usually ascended the mountain. Following his advice on our third attempt, we conquered the peak by the ordinary route. That was my introduction to mountaineering. The temptation was too great, and for the next twenty-five years, mountain-climbing became more important to me than fishing and more delightful than wandering on the shores of Cornwall and the west, where from secluded sandy bays one could spend whole days bathing in the great waves that forever roll in from the Atlantic Ocean. Those were the far-off days of long ago, when the ridge of the Coolin had been only partially traversed. The great rock faces were virgin ground, and the only Ordnance map was the most inaccurate of all British maps. Contour lines ran through ridges hundreds of feet high, and the highest peak in the whole of the Coolin was not even marked on the map. There was, however, a corrected version that had been published privately by C. Pilkington, who had visited these mountains in 1880 and made the first ascent of the Inaccessible Pinnacle.

The inaccuracies of the Ordnance map were undoubtedly due to the difficulties met with on the upper slopes of the mountains, for only seven peaks out of a total of nearly two dozen had been measured by the Survey; moreover, they gave no heights to any of the passes between the various peaks.

After 1886 for several summers I went back to Skye, and with John Mackenzie spent many a long day wandering over the ridges and climbing the peaks and the rock faces.

I am sure that many British climbers do not appreciate the position John Mackenzie holds in the climbing world. He is the only real British climbing guide that has ever existed. Neither the Lake District nor North Wales has produced one. For over forty years he has climbed amongst the Coolin. He is a first-rate and very safe rock climber. His knowledge of the district is unique. Moreover, if he had had experience of ice and snow as well he would be equal to a good Swiss guide. His great love of the mountains, his keen pleasure in all the beauties of the Coolin, never fails: whether it is a distant view of the mountains, or a sunset fading away behind the Outer Hebrides, or the great slabs of gabbro bending over into space, or a still pool of clear water reflecting the rowan bushes and the peaks beyond, or the autumn colours on the rolling moors backed by the hills and the sea, all these do not pass by him unnoticed; he understands not only the joy of a hard climb, but can also appreciate the marvels that a beautiful mountain land is perpetually offering to one.

Thirty years is a long time, yet John and I have climbed, fished, and wandered together over Skye during a good portion of most of those years. Still in many ways Skye will always be a land where we shall find new experiences. We shall see fresh views of mountains, moors, and lochs, wonderful new effects of colour, of light and shade, we shall find new climbs, and again lure the trout and the salmon from the lochs and rivers as we used to do in the days when we were both younger.

It was in 1888 that I first made my way along the whole ridge and climbed all the peaks in the Coolin. The first ascent of the Bhasteir tooth was made, and in 1889, with W. W. King, the first traverse of the Alasdair Dubh gap from the S. was accomplished. During these expeditions I had collected a series of measurements of the heights along the ridge of the Coolin that were published some years later in the *Journal of the Scottish Mountaineering Club*. I shall always remember my first acquaintance with the peaks to the W. of Sgurr a Mhadaidh. The weather had been bad for some time, but the day before I had to leave Skye it cleared, so John and I started from Sligachan very early in the morning. We went over into Coire na Creiche and up into the Tairneilear to the Bealach Glac Mhor, then over the four peaks of Sgurr a Mhadaidh and on over the knife-edge of Sgurr a Ghreadaidh, then over Sgurr na Banachdich and so to the top of Sgurr Dearg. We tried first one end and then the other of the Inaccessiebl Peak, but a strong wind was blowing, and we finally came back to the N. end. After many attempts, John refused to be beaten, however, and after having taken off his boots, he successfully surmounted the difficult piece of the climb. I came up on the rope. This, I believe, was the fourth ascent, only Pilkington, Stocker, and Hart having been up before us.

In those days the Inaccessible Peak was considered to be the highest point in the Coolin, but from it Sgurr Alasdair was obviously higher. My aim on that day was to get to the summit of Sgurr Alasdair, so climbing down along the ridge, we made our way to the summit of Sgurr Mhic Coinnich, only to be stopped by a precipice on its S. face. This cost us about two hours, trying first to get down directly to the dip below, and next trying to find a traverse across the W. face of the mountain. Finally we reached the dip, went on to Sgurr Thearlaich and the summit of Sgurr Alasdair, where I found by my barometer that it was about thirty feet higher than the Inaccessible Peak; it is really fifty-five feet higher.

By this time the sun was setting. We had two alternatives for a route home to Sligachan, either going down to Glen Brittle and back over the Maam, or down to Coruisk and Harta Coire and Glen Sligachan. We chose the latter. Following the ridge to the S., we came to a great gap, the Alasdair Dubh gap, by which we were again stopped, so we hurried back and made our way down into Ghrunnda Coire, then crossed over towards Coir'an Lochain, and keeping to the left we finally arrived at the Coruisk River just as the last light of the sunset was fading out of the sky behind the black and jagged ridge of the Coolin. Everything was wrapt in gloom, and only the sound of the streams could be heard faintly up at the head of the corrie. One seemed cut off entirely from the outer world, and the lonely grandeur of the place and the stillness of the night was a thing I have never forgotten. But there was a long and weary way in front of us before we should see the lights of the hotel at Sligachan. Fifteen hundred feet of climbing up the steepest of slopes and rocks had to be surmounted before we got to the top of Druim nan Ramh. By starlight we found our way down into Harta Coire, and after floundering along the interminable Sligachan glen we got home just before midnight. It was one of the hardest days I have ever had amongst the mountains. How many miles we went and how many feet we climbed it is impossible to say, for in many place we traversed backwards and forwards and up and down in our endeavours to overcome the difficulties that we met with on that extraordinary ridge of the Coolin.

It was not till 1896, however, that I started climbing the rock faces in earnest; up till then they were practically untouched. On these precipitous slopes every kind of rock climbing can be found. Gaunt gullies, huge rock slabs set at most awe-inspiring angles, great cracks and towers are met with in all directions. For instance, a climb of nearly 3,000 feet on bare rock can be found on the S. face of Sgurr a Ghreadaidh. The slabs of rock on the N.E. face of Sgurr Dubh a Coir'an Lochain are magnificent, and the N.W. ridge of Sgurr Alasdair is in places quite sensational. These are only a few out of the many face climbs in the Coolin.

But the expeditions in the Coolin were by no means finished, and in 1899 I made a discovery that promised more first-rate scrambling. Major Bruce, Harkabir Thapa, and I had been up Sgurr Alasdair and been kept later than wc intended by the rescuing of sheep that were crag-bound and starving on the rock ledges above the upper Coire Lagan. On getting down to the loch in the corrie, the sun was already low down, throwing heavy shadows across the face of the cliffs on the S. side of the lower corrie. The discovery was of a great shadow across the middle of the face of these cliffs that obviously was thrown by a huge tower of rock standing out from the cliff. Having photographed it, I made up my mind that at some future date I would not only investigate this tower, but also the splendid rock face on which it stood. But Coire Lagan is a long way off from Sligachan, and I never went back there again till 1906, when, with Colin Phillip, I went to the lodge at Glen Brittle.

It is curious that this magnificent face of precipices in the lower corrie never seems to have attracted the attention of climbers. For in 1906 it was entirely untouched, though since then dozens of climbs up and down and over it have been made and described in mountaineering journals.

This great wall of rock is almost two-thirds of a mile long and about 1,000 feet high. It is built on a very large scale. The great slabs of rock are less cracked and as a rule bigger than elsewhere in the Coolin. From a climbing point of view it is certainly the most remarkable and interesting rock face in the whole range. When one is on it in the mist one is strongly reminded of the Chamonix Aiguilles. The deeply cut gullies that run up into it are, as a rule, bare of vegetation, and the magnificent texture of the gabbro allows one to climb with safety in more precipitous places than on any other kind of rock. The day after I arrived at Glen Brittle in 1906 I started for Coire Lagan to find out what kind of rock it was that threw that great shadow across the cliff face. John had not come over from Sligachan, so I had to investigate it alone. I soon saw that the rock was a very real and interesting tower quite removed from the great rock face, standing out in the most imposing way over the corrie below. From the top of the precipice to the bottom is at least 1,000 feet, perpendicular in many places, and a narrow knife-edge of rock, about 100 feet long, runs out from it rather less than half-way down. On each side of the knife-edge are steep clean slabs of rock that at their base overhang the gullies below. At the end of this knife-edge is placed the tower that casts its shadow across the great slab. I do not know of any great mass of rock like it in Great Britain. It is not part of the rock face, but stands away from it, and its face has a sheer drop of about 500 feet into the corrie below.

It has been named the 'Chioch', and the rock face on which it is has been called 'Sron na Ciche'.

I climbed up to just beneath the Chioch, but did not try to climb it direct, being alone. I attempted to get up the great slab on to the knife-edge, but soon came down again. I traversed first with the gully on the E. and then round into the gully on the W. side, but could get up neither; but it looked promising if one could get into the gully on the E. side of the Chioch, above a huge jammed block and high enough up to traverse out of the gully again across the face of the precipice to where the knife-edge abutted on to the cliff. As John was coming that evening, I decided to wait, hoping with his help, and a rope, to conquer it on the morrow. As it turned out, it was a climb full of excitement, for one never knew what was round the next corner. We traversed slabs, we worked up cracks, and went right away from the Chioch into the gully on the E. side, losing sight of the Chioch altogether. Then we fortunately found a queer traverse unlike any traverse I have ever seen, that led out of the gully across the perpendicular face of the cliff, and back in the direction of the Chioch. But the Chioch itself we could not see, until having got round several corners, suddenly it came into view and we found ourselves on the end of the knife-edge. We sat down on that knife-edge, and slowly made our way to the great rock tower at its end, up this we climbed, and John and I were mightily pleased with our climb. After that everyone at Glen Brittle had to climb it and I believe that during that July and August John and I made the first ten ascents of the Chioch.

Since then many other ways have been discovered for getting to the top, but I still have a great liking for the original route, for there are so many surprises in it, and one has the opportunity of seeing the Chioch from so many points of view during the ascent. The most curious and sensational way down was worked out later. After getting back along the knife-edge the gully on the W. side is descended. Almost at once one comes to a long drop that has to be done on the rope. The slabs on this side of the Chioch are extremely fine and sometimes overhanging. From the bottom of the drop a traverse takes one out of the gully to the right, round underneath the Chioch. Here a slab slopes down steeply, ending apparently in space over the great precipice that rises from the corrie up to the top of the

Chioch. If, however, one climbs down this slab one can drop out of sight over the end into a notch running diagonally across the face of the preci- pice. This notch has been formed by a dyke of soft rock that has weathered out of the harder gabbro. Indeed the weathering has gone so deep that as one works along the notch towards the western gully it finally becomes a cave through which one can go, and it ultimately leads one down into the gully below. This gully can then be followed as it runs across and down- wards till the foot of the great precipice is reached.

During 1906 and the years that followed there were few parts of the W. Coolin that John and I did not wander over. On Sron na Ciche alone we found enough new climbing to last for a long time; also the faces of rock in all the other corries besides Coire Lagan had to be investigated.

Anyone who wishes to spend a long summer day scrambling about on splendid rock will not be disappointed with the Coolin; and the rock-work can be varied from easy to the most difficult. The Coolin however must be treated with respect; for should anyone be caught in the mist whilst on the main ridge of the Coolin, and not know about the corries below, the descent into the corrie is by no means easy, for although the first two or three hundred feet may be at a moderate angle, it soon gets steeper, finally becoming precipitous and quite impossible, and the climber will be sur- prised to find that he may have to spend perhaps a couple of hours in the mist trying to get down a few hundred feet of a mere British hill by the easiest route.

But on fine days one can take one's ease on the Coolin, and should one weary of rock-scrambling one can sit on some ledge perched high up above the lower world, surrounded by huge crags making foregrounds full of strength and beauty, and looking out over low-lying moors to the outer islands, that seem to belong to some mysterious land in the far-off west. Or one can wait till the last glories of the sunset have faded from the great precipices and the corries are all in gloom before one finally leaves them.

For colour, for fine mountain form, for grandeur, and for mystery the Coolin never disappoint one. During the long summer days the great expanses of white clouds will float in the clear air undefiled with the smoke of towns, or the mists will curl tenderly over the moorlands, or rush with wild haste through the great gaps in the ridges of the Coolin; or in the melancholy autumn time the moors, rioting in all the marvellously rich colours of decay, will serve as a splendid contrast to the dark purple of the corries, that seem as if they were hung with royal velvet. But it is impossible to describe the strength and the beauty of the colouring in the island of Skye; it can only be understood by seeing it.

❄ (From 'The Island of Skye' by J. N. Collie. Vol. XXXII.)

Geoffrey Winthrop Young

14 ❉ *Mountain Prophets*

Mountaineering was a discovery. There were men, of course, right back through history, who were attracted by individual hills, and went – or tried to go – up them. Just as there were men before Newton's day who watched apples falling, and ate them. But it was not until the early part of the last century that a particular group of men made the discovery that a particular kind of mountain, the Alps, held something in it or on it that could be turned to the use, the pleasure and the health of the body and the mind of man. It was a discovery that released a new force for good; and of what other modern discovery could this be said? Steam, electricity, have brought evil greater than their benefit: mountaineering alone has revealed a natural force only for good.

It was perhaps fortunate that the discovery was not made until Victorian days, and then by a number of the leaders of thought. By the authority of their writing and by their dignity of approach to the new activity they set a seal of distinction upon climbing; and this preserved it as a practice respectable if inexplicable during the decades of popular derision and criticism. They also established a notable tradition of the spirit in which mountains must be climbed; and this, in our country alone, and in this sport more than in all others, has served to protect its force for good from the progressively corrupting infections of competition and publicity-hunting.

Perhaps it should be called a revelation, rather than a discovery; for it was in the nature of an apocalypse, a vision suddenly apparent in the hills, of a new relationship between man and the forces expressed in mountain forms. In its development also, mountaineering has followed the course of other revelation. It has had its primitive chroniclers, its greater prophets, its lesser prophets, its rationalizing period and its romantic revival. It passed, even in my memory, through yet another stage familiar to creeds, in which ritual, repetition and what is now termed 'slickness' threatened to take the place of the earlier inner spirit. It is not inconsistent with such a history that many of us as we grow older turn more frequently to the original, objective stories of the first explorers – some of *Peaks, Passes and Glaciers*, early ascents of Mont Blanc, and their like. These first chroniclers knew no bias, and they had not yet learned to adjust their astonished reports to this or that school, of rock specialists or winter sporters or cartographers – all our later zealous subdivisions. They wrote only for those who, like themselves, had already discovered that they liked mountains. And between the simple lines of narrative we feel ourselves free to write in our own emotions as we remember to have felt them in the like places.

The chroniclers were followed by the prophets, major and minor, who gave the message to the world. With their formulation of climbing doctrine, the divisions inevitable between human mind and mind began to show themselves: the scientific bias as in Forbes, Tyndall or Bonney, the aesthetic as in John Ruskin, the literary and rationalized as in Leslie Stephen, the encyclopaedic as in John Ball or Tuckett, the humane and adventurous as in A. W. Moore. And from among the group of these major prophets, my own generation selected its favourites, each of us according to his own mental or temperamental bias. Those whom I am calling the minor prophets, if only for clearness, did not write until our generation was already active on hills. Theirs was a different order of prophecy, their messages were differentiated from each other not by temperament or mentality, but by the diverse types and regions of mountaineering they discovered and proclaimed.

Like many mountain initiates, I was an impassioned reader of any and all mountaineering books and records. On reaching comparative freedom in Cambridge, I tore through whole libraries and past centuries of literature, to find any chance reference to hills. This was before the days of mountain anthologies, and I compiled my own, of which *The Voice of the Mountains* afterwards availed itself. Any echo of my own feelings could bring a thrill that was exquisite, not without a faintly jealous under-pang that anyone else should have felt just this before me. I found indeed that echo all too seldom; and after the first stage of fascination with the prophetic books was past, I even began to miss something further. But what it was I did not then stop to examine, for out of the magic of romantic anticipation I had fallen into the very fever of active climbing, and book lore had come to matter much less. It was at a later stage that I became clearer as to the character of my own feeling, and that I began to look in books for the reflection of that entrancing awe, for the suggestion at least that in mountains man is matching himself with forces greater than his own, and experiencing emotion of the highest order. In Ruskin alone did I find the awe unqualified and courageously set out, in magnificent passages of prose. But Ruskin had restricted himself to the spectator's point of view, and condemned the climbing of hills. Wan and pale, I decided, is the lover who only praises from afar with eye and tongue, who renounces all active initiative in the relationship and 'dares not put it to the touch, to win or lose it all'. Of the other great prophets, I knew them to be men of varied ability, I could feel that they wrote under an inspiration like my own, and yet, the more I read them, the more I became sure that they were suppressing an aspect of their experiences essential to any complete picture of their mountaineering. If if were so, I could not entirely acquit them; since, as pioneers and prophets, they had a clean slate of public opinion upon which to write, with nothing to consider but themselves, the hills and the full truth of the happenings between them. Historians, however, were beginning then to teach me that, in order to understand a past generation, I must move myself back into the mind of the then man in the there street, and read his own thought through the medium of the outlook imposed by his generation. So I set myself to recover the Victorian angle or, as we might now say, 'slant' upon climbing, and detect, if might be, its blind point.

To the intellectual Victorian human life was in its heyday. All men were still perfectable, and all knowledge still knowable; reason existed to discipline emotion, and any as yet unharnessed forces, in a universe ordered by the intellect, must be at least capable of classification under one of the headings already determined by the educated mind. Among the long-lived sages of my father's generation and society, were a number of Alpine pioneers; and when I came into the mountain world they were royally kind to me: John Llewellyn Davies, James Bryce, Alfred Wills, H. Montague Butler, Kenelm Digby, Frederic Harrison, Frederick Pollock, Thomas Fowell Buxton, George Prothero. And yet others of the pioneers I came to know on my own account, Dr. Bonney, Dr. Hornby, Hereford George, Frederick Morshead, Horace Walker, James Eccles, Evan Mackenzie, Douglas Freshfield, A. J. Butler, J. W. Hartley, C. E. Mathews, Leslie Stephen, Edward Whymper. It was not difficult therefore to reconstruct a general picture of the great generation in its youth, at the time when it 'discovered' the Alps. Confident, vital and cultivated, many of them dictators of thought in their several spheres, they had walked out of their academic or legal groves and found themselves upon heights as unexplored as the poles and as rich with romance as Xanadu. With a stride they, the men of the study, had outdistanced generations of explorers and sportsmen, had opened up an untrodden realm which artists acclaimed as a new world of beauty, and had launched a novel activity for mankind. They could be justifiably proud of the figure which the church, the law, science and literature were cutting in the field of adventure. With a humorous gravity they set themselves to evolve a new technique, that of climbing, and while they learned to tread the dangerous circles of the new-found paradise with all Dante's agile intensity, they took the poet's and the patron's pleasure in investing the leadership of their chosen peasant guides with an aura of infallibility appropriate to few but a Beatrice. The robust

1. The Matterhorn, whose challenging shape has attracted mountaineers through the ages. The Hörnli ridge, which Whymper climbed, is facing the camera; the great North Face is on the right.

← 2. The Fall, *Gustave Doré's interpretation of the Matterhorn accident of 1865.*

↑ *3. The Aiguille du Géant.*
*A photograph by the Abraham brothers, who were the most successful
mountain photographers around the turn of the century.*

↑ 4. *The Zmutt Ridge of the Matterhorn forms the left-hand skyline and was the route taken by Mummery in his race with Penhall. Penhall's desperate route followed the prominent sloping snow gully, now called the Penhall Couloir.*

→ 5. *Norman Collie's most famous discovery was the unique Cioch, in the Cuillin hills of Skye, shown here in the classic Abraham picture.*

↑ *6a. The Chamonix Aiguilles.*
   The peak on the right is the Plan,
   with its long glacial North Face,
   scene of 'Two Days on an Ice Slope'.

← *6b. Mummery tackling the Mummery*
   Crack of the Grépon.

7a and b. *The two men who dominated*
Victorian climbing:
(top) Edward Whymper
and (bottom) A. F. Mummery.

8. 'Whatever number is right, two is wrong.'
Victorian climbers tackle a crevasse below the Requin in this Abraham picture.

and exalted playfulness of the new pursuit was particularly sympathetic to the strong spiritual movement of the Arnoldian evangelicals, then at its height, and I have not yet seen it explained how it came that the great broad church dignitaries, such as Llewellyn Davies, Hort and Lightfoot, found themselves so immediately at home in the Alps, whereas the muscular evangelicals, Charles Kingsley, my own godfather Tom Hughes, author of *Tom Brown*, or the Arnolds, vented their enthusiasm only upon our own insular heights. But, whatever might have been their preferences or their mental bias, of one thing it was plain to me that these pioneers in their youth must have been supremely confident, that they were masters of the situation intellectually, that there was nothing in this new region of pleasing colours and shapes, nothing in the new range of experiences, which could fall outside their established categories. When therefore they sat down to share their discovery with the world, by training and by conviction they could do no other than fit in under one or the other heading of the Victorian synopsis all their fresh won material. They could not but label it Practical Science, Nature Study or Physical Exercise, according to the author's scientific or humanistic bias. The heading usually preferred is suggested by the titles chosen for many of the prophetic books – *The Playground of Europe, Vacation Rambles, Hours of Exercise*, although this last hesitates between two. Even a great mountaineer, I came to see, might not be able to free himself from his contemporary convention, when it came to publication; and who of this formidable generation was to be the first to disturb the accepted holiday narrative or the creditable glacier controversy with a version of the emotions not authorized by the age, and that before the critical contemporary audience of climbing bishops, logicians and dons?

Not Tyndall certainly, intent upon building a foreground of scientific problem to dominate every Alpine story. How I used to try and peer into that tantalizing background, which he left uncoloured and unfilled-in lest it might disturb the balance of a scientific presentment. And yet, the first conqueror of Pic Tyndall on the Matterhorn, the first man to ascend the incomparable Weisshorn, who built the chalet above Belalp so as to be able to look for the rest of his life upon the mountain he considered the most beautiful, and who built the chalet at Hindhead as the first settler to profit by the contrast of that near wild scenery throughout the London working year – surely behind the professorial façade was hidden a romantic of the first order!

Wherever the personality betrayed itself in some such way, or whenever I recalled the warm and unstudied talk of the great prophets themselves, I noticed how far more near was their approach to my own feeling than in their written word. Their vision and mine of hills clicked suddenly into the same focus, like the two eyes of a glass, and I saw the men themselves differently. It reminded me of the feeling when my father, after the sixty-five years of silence about the Alps which followed his Mont Blanc accident and the death of his brother, one evening began to talk of his first tour, in the Dolomites, with Sir George Otto Trevelyan; and how, crossing a low pass, he had seen a white slope hanging far above in the gathering dusk, and had felt compelled to leave the others, and, racing the darkness, had reached it, and so stood upon his first perpetual snow. As his deep musical voice stressed the word 'compelled', I understood him suddenly as I never had before. A very able review of *Mountain Craft* underlined the discovered difference for me further. It commented on certain passages of mine – 'Wills, Whymper, Tyndall, Leslie Stephen . . . they would have jeered at a philosophical examination of the art of climbing rocks.' That was true, I felt, of their printed attitude; but – what of the men themselves? Wills wrote some of the first prophetic books of Alpine exploration with very judicial restraint. But Wills also built the Eagle's Nest from which to view Mont Blanc at all seasons, and made of the Alpine glory far more than a vacation refreshment for his family and circle. His youngest son, Con Wills – too soon to leave us – had been a friend and opponent of mine at school; we had played in the School Rugby and Hockey teams as colleagues, and led opposing House teams as good enemies. Tall, athletic, darkly aquiline and gentle, with his father's silvery intonation, he was the first boy to speak to me of mountains, after I had discovered my own passion for them, and with bated breath he showed me, almost involuntarily, how sacred to him was the inherited feeling for Alpine glaciers and the wonder of climbing. Later, Sir Alfred proposed me for the Alpine Club, in those days a ceremonial process, and one which moved me with the first sense of a great honour won. And I could recall, although it had meant little to me at the time, during the long talk which preceded his proposing me, the perfectly modulated sentence – 'And they (the Alps) may even profoundly influence your philosophy of life – when you are old enough to have one!'

Leslie Stephen – he would have jeered, except perhaps in print? When I was an undergraduate, Dr. Montague Butler, with his unparalleled courtesy to younger men, had sent for me to Trinity Lodge to entertain Leslie Stephen. The red flame still smouldered behind the grizzled beard and deafness of his impatient age. I plunged into talk of the past; and under the cold lava of visible boredom a volcano stirred, and jetted sparks of old rivalries and exultant or poignant moments upon Rothorn and Schreckhorn; and it was in a fashion that, even to my then uncritical mind, told of emotions very little indicated by the temperate felicity of his Alpine style. I may take him indeed as the most instructive example of my one-time 'discontent', for I believe we can trace the convention actually at work upon his writing. Stephen was pre-eminent among the prophets.

There is no writing that recreates for us more actually the poetry of the hills, and much of the truth of the sensations we receive among them' than his *Alps in Winter* and *Regrets of a Mountaineer*. His gifted personality and his wholehearted devotion to climbing 'placed' mountaineering once and for all in cultivated opinion. His style enshrined it, pellucid and convincing, blending tenderness with an irony that 'half-suspected animates the whole'. But if we once begin to read him, as I did, with a close and affectionate suspicion, we may soon become aware of the dexterous brain playing battledore and shuttlecock with emotions he had experienced – but not approved. He sports with them impishly, too honest with himself to let them fall to the ground. I could almost fancy him muttering, in those embarrassingly audible asides – 'Aesthetic impulse? – hum – that's for our dusty Ruskin-and-art shelf . . . Emotional reaction? – brr – what am I saying – the Rousseau-and-sentimentality drawer, of course – and there's impropriety even in its pink-wool lining! . . Unknown forces? – dear me, where's that dreary pigeonhole "aneroids-and-Professor-Tyndall?" . . . Self-discipline, challenge to manhood? – an easy one – under Sport, of course; or wait, get it under Walking, for I find myself the rhythm of legs over flat surfaces stimulates thinking, that is, rational thinking! . . Accord with Nature? awe? – what *are* we getting. to? – quick! – where's my former clerical wastepaper basket? . . And now – to clear our minds after that – let's have a joke about food, or temper or the Ten Commandments!' And clear the air Leslie Stephen does, with a lively wit and a literary tact which set all of us laughing again with relief. For really it was a near thing, on that page; his veracious memory had almost led us over the safe Victorian edge, in spite of himself. Indeed there are passages where the rescue, when it came, came just too late.

A. W. Moore was also among the greater prophets. Many, like myself in the past, would have been surprised to find him there, since his *Alps in 1864* was only read by the elect, and not delivered to the world until a generation later. It is the significance of this very suppression, which makes his book the strongest instance of the losing battle fought between our greater prophets and their period, upon which I am commenting. In charm of presentment Moore is only second to Stephen. In skill and daring as a climber he would seem to have been surpassed only by the Rev. Charles Hudson among his contemporaries, and as a mountaineer of intimate vision, if we judge by the books, he overtopped them all. In his stories, almost alone, do we feel that we are at grips with the men as they were, no less than with the climbing as it was. But these stories were issued 'for private circulation only'. In the preface Moore apologizes for having 'sacrificed elegance', and explains that, had he intended the book for publication, he would have 'rewritten the book on an entirely different principle'. In fact, he felt its detail and human reactions to be too intimate and revealing: the convention of the age would not tolerate their realism. Private friends could be trusted of course to understand, but the ear of the public must not be alarmed. Moore was an Irishman, and too sincere, in his adventurous aspect, to tone down or dry-docket his memories under the accepted headings. So it came that one of the most direct books of mountain revelation remained all but unread for another forty years.

I have left Whymper, who was my own first prophet, to the last in this group. I find him even now very difficult to discuss. The Whymper whose early life, as I now read it in the Diaries, and whose long post-Matterhorn life of self-exploitation can be assigned quite simply to a particular nine-teenth-century period and class and type, refuses to become identified with the heroic figure, whose *Scrambles amongst the Alps* suddenly blared like a destroying trumpet round my narrow school walls, scattering them to all the four corners of a blue firmament behind high icy peaks. How did a personality so seemingly limited succeed in capturing the imagination of so many hundreds of us, in succeeding generations, with his one book? Was there possibly something even in the nature of his limitations as a man, which, when he came to write, left his message free of the convention of the period, or even gave it an unconventional appeal? Whymper, as we re-read him, we see to have been inferior to most of his fellow prophets in sensibility, in imagination, and in culture. His love of giving information might be expected to be boring to youth, and the artistry of his book, for all his work upon it, is patchy. And yet there are very few works upon a single and out of the way theme which have continued to be read with such enduring zest. His secret, does it lie in his fidelity? in his power of visualizing himself and his surroundings in words of snapshot precision, so that we feel it is all just happening to ourselves? We take part, dramati-cally, in the conflict in progress, on our one hand the obstinacy of the man, on our other the reality of the forces against him. It is the same relationship with hills, at once sympathetic and antagonistic, which we all come to know as mountaineers; and it is kept vividly before us, the flashlight representation of a flinty mountain and of a steely Whymper in continuous concussion; all illuminated by the sparks of perilous incident they struck out of one another. Whymper is egocentric: he never sees himself de-tachedly or as anywhere but in the centre of a picture; he seems to feel little but surface emotion and no sentiment; he reveals himself as a man unresponsive in relationships, either human or with nature; he is bold, self-confident and calculating. His mind, that of a first-rate journalist rather ahead of his period, governed an unimaginative and not wholly amiable temperament. His reactions, therefore, when mountaineering, not improbably conformed more nearly to the ideal upheld by nineteenth-century middle-class convention than those of any other great contempo-rary prophet. His writing of them, for the same reason, suffered less from the suppressions which warped other prophets' messages. He could represent his true self in his book, as he acted and as he reacted, frankly and without any mental reservation, and for that, the more convincingly. If ever memory recalled an impression that did not fit into his considered frame, he could not, unlike the more subtle prophets, take refuge in a tranquillizing joke or reflection. Where, as Leslie Stephen himself said of him, 'other writers have tried to give a scientific, or a poetical, or a humorous turn to their narratives – Whymper bullocked stoutly into the confusion of thought he had evoked, and its extent is made plain to us, as we read, by the clatter of melodramatized and worst written passages falling about us'. Whymper in life, and Whymper as a writer, was an honest egoist; he wrote himself – 'the book is entirely personal, all ego!' But nowhere in mountain literature do we receive a like impression of the unendingness of the mountain quest, or of the significance of the individual in comparison with it. Leslie Stephen can give us a shock of unreality by scrambling, when hard pressed by some remembered sensation, into his 'Sports' compartment, and remarking – 'Still, it is strictly sport – as strictly as cricket, or rowing, or knurr and spell. The game is won when a mountain top is reached; it is lost when one is forced to retreat' – a definition, by the by, which he himself rejected just as often as suited his text. But Whymper hardly for a page lets us feel that getting to the top of a mountain is more than an incident in the great duel. Perhaps he will treat it as a two-line introduction to the description of a panorama, or he may only mention the ascent casually in a footnote. All the time he is shouting at us: 'These are the Mountains, and this is Me! and thus went the unending contest between us!' And while he declaims – and postures not a little – he succeeds in representing the mountains as so very big and the charm and challenge of the mountain climbing as so enduring, that we almost lose sight of himself in the course of his own domineering narrative. Only in the end to find that we have practically confused him with the Matterhorn; and that, whether we like him or no, his sincerity and forthrightness have earned him a high form of immortality by identifying him in our memories with the greatness of the mountains, and of the mountaineering, which he interpreted.

Happily, I have never been forced to reconcile my early hero-worship with the idea that the Whymper of the diaries and of the after life was the real Whymper, and that it was only a brilliant journalistic talent which enabled him to deceive me for my good with simulacra, where the reality was not. I believe that the Alps did for him during a few years what they have done for many another among us. They brought out in him, as fighting and seafaring also bring out in those who practise them, unsuspected qualities of heroism; they made him for his time among them a being greater than himself. And I believe that his retentive mind kept, and his skilled pen reproduced, a true memory of that inspired period, when he came to write the picture of himself and his climbs into his great book. His was a writer's craft, and he used every device of illustration and emphasis to make the memory live. We do not need to remind ourselves of another famous single-book record of adventure, T. E. Lawrence's *Seven Pillars*, to know that lavish elaboration and artifice can be used effectively, and justifiably, to recreate a genuine atmosphere, provided only that that atmosphere has first been genuinely felt. Behind the craftsman and publicist there had been in fact the young Whymper of the mountains, with whom the fastidious Moore climbed as a companion, and of whom Stephen wrote in memorable praise – 'He was clearly the most advanced, and would, but for one melancholy circumstance, have been the most triumphant of us all . . . (his) book contains the most genuine utterance of the spirit in which the victory has been won.'

But the inspiration did not survive the satisfaction of his conquistador instincts, in the ascent of the supreme Matterhorn, or the depressing accompaniments of its tragic sequel. I do not myself think that Whymper's combative mountaineering passion was of the kind that normally survives long. His geographical and scientific interests were already lifting to en-tangle his climbing feet when he wrote *Scrambles amongst the Alps*. After the accident, however, there was to be no escape, from his role as the premier mountaineer. The resounding tragedy, coming as the close of a type of novel adventure in itself alarming to the safe Victorian age, gave him an international fame and platform. Its sombre halo never again for-sook him. As a journalist, an illustrator, and ambitious, it was inevitable that he should follow where fate pointed so obvious a way. There was something also in his rugged but static personality – for like many mid-Victorians he matured early and modified little in later years – which kept him for the remainder of his life unalterably in the public eye, as still the only surviving conqueror of the Matterhorn, still impersonating, as he came and went, the historic catastrophe.

For my generation, the familiar squared jowl and the unchanged idio-syncrasies in dress brought with them always into another century the sense of Zermatt in the '60s. His myth moved with him out of the past, isolating him as a legendary figure even in the company of greater nota-bilities. We did not expect him to behave quite like present-day men, and he never disappointed us. The grim mannerisms and the dry or bluff oracles were always consistently in the Whymper tradition: he was so aggressively himself as to give the close-up magnification of a film, and to seem to be looming a little larger than life. I remember him last, and best, in the Zermatt street, with courteous officials pressing him to attend and honour the opening ceremony of the Schönbühl hut. Impassive and dour he waited a dramatic moment, and then, the harsh growl anglicizing his accent effectively – '*Il faut avoir de la bière!*' We all smiled, and sighed happily – Whymper was still Whymper: the officials beamed, and flaunted a whole menu of wines, and Whymper rolled on imperturbably.

For a life story written upon a human face we can look at two portraits reproduced in Whymper's obituary notice in Volume 26 of the *Alpine Journal*. The first is of a young man of uplifted, resolute look and eyes full of inspiration: an expressive face, but one at war with itself, in which the wilful downward turn of the mouth and an obstinate set of the jaw are fighting to drag the eyes earthwards. Instinctively we wonder which will win. The second is of the Titan in age, with the leonine head, the granite jaw and the penetrating eyes. And we must decide for ourselves which had won, the eyes of the enthusiast or the mouth of the man.

Leslie Stephen has had imitators. Mountain writers have plundered his recipe book of everything but the unerring touch which made its proportions inimitable. Edward Whymper founded no school; no one has succeeded in copying anything but his egotism. Through the conventions of the contemporary prophets, the rococo, the Ruskinian, the jocund, the patronizing and the encyclopaedic, he crashed with a rude and well-directed vehemence that remains as individual as it was in his own day. If mountaineering owed its distinction to the good fortune of having been first proclaimed by the Victorian arbiters of thought, it owed its popularity to the fact that Whymper's *Scrambles* appeared in the same era. The dressing up, in public, of the novel sensations of mountaineering under many more correct guises might have limited its essential enjoyment to the experimental and the eccentric few. But Whymper's robust realism, his modernistic preference for banging a hard unfanciful head into hills and things from the bottom, rather than for looking them over with elegance from the top, drove in at a crucial moment, and scattered the new-graven tables of mountain stone to classes and strata of the populations at home and abroad whose participation in the realms of travel and gentlemanly adventure had never before been dreamed of.

With Whymper our authorized version of the major prophets was closed. There were other authors among the Olympians of our golden age, but their books have no claim to be classed as prophetic. Charles Edward Mathews wrote under a weight of contemporary convention which allowed little hint of his ornate personality to lighten the page. His great work for mountaineering was a personal one, in the rhetoric and sanity of his address, alive with the nobility of the Alps and with the depth of his feeling for them, and in his benevolence to all younger climbers. James Bryce, Frederic Harrison, Bishop Browne, Oscar Browning, like many others they did not write their memoirs until late in life: they assure us of the influence that mountains had upon their lives, but they do not attempt to make the spell live again for us. So many also of the really independent spirits never wrote more than occasional papers. I think of Kennedy, Middlemore, Whitwell, Gardiner, Anderson and the delightfully un-orthodox Stogdon. Bonney's sprightly and earnest humanity hugged itself, in what he wrote, deep under folds and anticlines of inseparable learning. All his books never said as much to me as one appearance of his at a Cambridge Alpine Dinner, when he was 85 or so, and, rumour said, keenly competitive with Dr. Liveing, his great Alpine rival in venerability, who was approaching his hundredth year. It was a bitter winter night, with iced pavements. The small figure in black cap and sweeping gown was very bent, and under his long beard he proceeded to hang a witchlike lantern. Mistakenly polite, I said something about both of us 'finding ice not so easy to walk upon as we used'. This was quite the wrong note. '*Not* at all, *not* at all!' he countered petulantly, 'I am *just* as active on ice as I *ever* was!' and literally skipped out into the falling snow. The manifold scholarship, the original personality and the immense range of travel of Douglas Freshfield set him high among our immortals. His love of moun-tains endured for his whole long adventurous span. His independence of mind took him out for his famous explorations of the Caucasus at a time when all others were still wrestling with the first opening of the Alps. He was generous, contentious and, in speech, witty and eloquent. He wrote prolifically. But, unless I am wrong, his contradictions kept him from ever becoming a very inspiriting or a disseminating force in mountaineering, and deprived his writings of much of their prophetic value. Although his feeling for hills was as profound as that of his fellow pioneers and the greater prophets, and his missionary work for distant ranges was as wide as that of the minor or later group, his books have not earned him full acceptance in either category; for the reason, I take it, of his attachment as an author to classic models and a period style, in his prose as well as his verse. His observance of an earlier and more stately convention in travel literature made him appear to write pontifically, and he rarely achieved the natural and urgent freshness which moves the common mind. It was again an instance of a mid-century convention partially perverting the mountain message; but an unusual one. For Freshfield's ironic, vigorous outlook, his resurgent enterprise and pungent speech could find no outlet in his chosen style – it did not admit even of Stephen's 'poetical or humorous turn' – any more than he himself could ever tolerate asso-ciation with any one school, or even any one generation, of mountaineers for long enough to be recognized as the leading spirit he ought to have become. In our former hall at Savile Row, I watched him on the platform steps, tall and head-tossing, and overlooking us with his genial aquiline sneer. He hurried down, caught me by the elbow, and 'Let's sit at the back – there's only these ancient bald and white heads to the fore!' He himself was then well over eighty; but he still revelled in all the intolerant privileges of youth.

After a very different manner, W. A. B. Coolidge has also failed to find a right prophetic niche. A mountain haunter and pundit in grain, and a potentially courteous and able consultant in correspondence as I found for many years, there was an evil fairy that dipped his pen in the juice of unkindness, and kept his great knowledge from ever freeing him from littleness. It could make him write at times his rich yield of the Alps into the dryness of a desert, or turn a dissent about a trifle into a quarrel rankling down the years, on his side with gleeful acerbity. He heaped Alpine lore into books and pamphlets with scrupulous devotion, and spread it out in guidebooks with good will; but to his accumulations he never once managed to set the torch of sacred mountain fire which could make of them beacons to oncoming climbers.

Clinton Dent had an influential and an enigmatic personality; but as a writer he stands aside from the great procession. His large accomplishment and his advantages and the range of his observation find only inadequate expression in *Above the Snowline*, which should have been his Alpine testament. It dates, as we say now, in some of its humour and its sentiment, and in passages of a certain facetious condescension which served to shelter the shy insular kindliness of travelling Englishmen, quite acceptably in the last century, but which has lost our sympathy in print, and with time. Dent was not among the prophets, even as a Jeremiah, but he served us well as high priest. In the *Badminton* on *Mountaineering* he codified admirably the inchoate climbing technique, and fixed our mountaineering rubric and our high tradition for the next half-century. It was a masterly compilation; and H. G. Willink's irresistible drawings, in themselves a climbing commentary, gave the book a value beyond its text-book order. Dent's genius was didactic: he loved directing and giving sovereign guidance, on or behind the scenes. He was not one who tolerated the future gladly, or indulged himself or others with the idea that the good past and the well-ordered present could ever be improved upon. He has often been quoted as saying that the Alps were exhausted as far back as in the 1880s, and he once wrote me a friendly warning not to attempt new Alpine ways, 'since there is really nothing left worth risking much for'. He and Willink were fine fencers, among their many talents, and when I was introducing fencing into Eton at the end of the century, I used to get them down for exhibition bouts. Afterwards we went to tea at Provost Hornby's, I with the unquenchable hope that, this time at last, their presence might lure him down from his starry drifting, to talk about the great 'Hornby and Philpott' partnership in the Oberland. Dent, on a lucky day, might become sonorous about the Dru, or caustic about an alleged rival to Burgener; but the Provost – the most adroit speaker I ever heard – would glide in some evasive allusion to art, or to skating, in which all three were adepts, and as the talk swerved in full pursuit, he would lean back and cross his legs, with a faint smile at me too remote to be malicious, but shadowing his secret relish in having once again eluded the obvious – apparently the single purpose of his later years. Once as we came away, Willink's trenchant optimism predicted that I might some day have to write a sequel to their work in the *Badminton*; and I answered truthfully that, to go beyond *that*, I should have to invent hitherto unattempted standards of difficulty, and imagine fresh climbing devices to overcome them – which is in fact what I did in parts of *Mountain Craft*, although truth has some time since overtaken my encouraging figments. But Dent's vast dark eye only slanted sideways and sardonically at me out of his long chiselled profile: 'In that too – I shall have anticipated you!' he intoned.

In a sense Dent's pessimism had the right of it. During the years of his ascendancy our Alpine enterprise was stagnating: their pristine inspiration was dying from the well-trodden ways. Except on occasional eastern summits, continental climbers were all to seek, and our own Alpine men were most in evidence as centrists, following traditional routes and historic guides, or ruling amiably as mutually appointed kings over hotels patronized by our countrymen. The very few of us who began at this time to venture youthfully upon new ascents outside the convention, felt solitary and even slightly censurable. It seemed only vanity to record difficult new ascents, when everything indicated that there would never be anyone wanting to repeat them. During the same ebb tide, Alpine writing ran out upon shallows of repetition, old jokes and comfortable clichés. The only lively shoot, in climbing literature, was strictly factual and expository, bidding us place a hand here and a bootnail there, in unportable volumes, with conscientious panoramas and nerve tremors at measured intervals. No wonder we grew uneasy, and a doubt began to grow whether the Victorian repressions familiar in our own youth might not also have deprived the mountain message, when transmitted by our prophets, of some of its lifegiving and enduring quality, so that it was already languishing into a pretty Swiss ritual, and threatening to end as the dry bones of acrobatics.

It was not ungracious, that we should have paused to scan critically the sources which had fed our own mountaineering enthusiasm. It did not imply a lessening of our veneration for the men or their works. My father had told me that no one who had not seen him ride past could ever understand the feeling of England for the Duke of Wellington, that set him at the end of his life as a man above all other men. I understood it, I thought, because I recognized that we felt something the same for our great Alpine predecessors. When I went as a young guest to Dent's Alpine Dining Club, figure after figure, with a blazoned name that I had thought to belong only in some prehistoric saga, seemed to materialize mistily out of the dark arras round the walls, step down into the candle light and sit godlike at the table. But just because there were still deities in our midst, and because we then lived out our mountaineering lives with a glittering absorption and seriousness, we could not but look to them, and question their authorized texts, if we were to find out how to set right some deflection in mountaineering development. Among other protestants and revivalists I wrote, I remember, in the *Independent Review*, upon Modern Climbing, stigmatizing technomania and 'Binks's Stomach-traverse', and being threatened with a libel action by one who was neither called Binks nor perhaps could stomach the cap fitting. But the appeal that will be remembered, and that has often since been quoted, was in the paper upon Alpine Humour in this *Journal*, by Charles Donald Robertson, a man of genius and of charm, whose death shortly afterwards upon Glyder Fach cut short a career of extraordinary promise for the country and for mountain climbing and literature. It was the fruit of many long talks, on glacier descents and by mountain camp fires, and it cannot be too often recalled: 'The matters of common knowledge in mountaineering are the emotions which form its very flesh and blood . . . But until men are found to say, and say with seriousness, what they pluck from danger and discomfort, to say and say in full, what they have found of beauty and delight, we shall not have an account of a climb which those who have shared the experience will acknowledge to be no more and no less than the truth, and those who have not will accept as a worthy vindication of our creed.'

Our attitude was a phase in the history of mountaineering as definite as that of the pioneers. If it dwelt – as I have done also here in recalling them – more upon particular prophetic short-comings than upon their grateful and preponderating merits, no apology should be needed. It was an inevitable moment in the movement for a reform and a revival, such as every generation must initiate if its belief is to remain vital.

But that which we did not see, and which has only become clear to me looking back across many years, was that our small Alpine revolt which we thought restricted to our forlorn youthful few, formed in fact part of a far larger progress, a continuous mountaineering development or change, which had begun before we ourselves had become active, and was proceeding at the time all round us. Indeed, some of us were taking part in its localized manifestations, quite unaware of being contributors to it under a second guise. The spell cast by the Alps upon the first mountaineers had been so magical that it held succeeding generations inexorably to the belief that the Alps *were* mountaineering. All other climbing was inconceivable as anything but a preparation for them. Our own Club, by the distinction and consistency of its members, its strong social tradition and high repute, contributed to this fixation. Thus, the pioneer cliff climbing upon the fells and in Wales, and the first Scottish winter and summer penetrations, were never looked upon, or designated, as anything but a preparation for the Alps, by the Alpine experts who began them. Those of us who joined in soon after, engaged upon the serious invasion of northern, western and Cornish precipices, never used the word mountaineering of such holiday escapading. Among ourselves we took, perforce, the hazards of the new practice seriously enough; but it still retained its primary character as training for greater mountaineering, and we took for granted that its mention in senior company might earn at best the half smile bestowed on some one 'who should know better' being caught pillow-fighting in the nursery. Similarly, when I originated roof and wall climbing as a sport, at Cambridge, I never conceived of it as a legitimate climbing variant, with its own specialized technique. It was to me, as to others, a pert and ingratiating parody upon our revered creed, and I gave it in serio-comic vein the parodied terminology of Alpine craft. We were quite unaware of whither all this was really tending. In the evolution, principally upon the Welsh slabs, of the new technique to which I gave the name in *Mountain Craft* of 'balance' climbing, and in the rapid uprising of our several schools of localized experts, we were contributing our share as an active element in an accelerating and general climbing process; as an element also in an extension of climbing principle which was in process of revolutionizing all our first standards of mountaineering, and which, as we were to learn later, was advancing on lines parallel to our own upon the pinnacles of the Eastern, and, among a small group of amateurs and Swiss guides in the Western, Alps. Mountaineering, in a word, which had made its first beginnings upon certain combinations of difficulty and opportunity to be found at their best in the Alps, and which had become associated in men's minds with them, and subsequently stereotyped for a time as appropriate and orthodox only when practised upon them, was breaking loose from its leading strings. It was discovering itself to be that which it is, an art and a craft or skill, which can be exercised upon an infinite variety of irregular surfaces, and which, like all other creative arts, contains within itself, and apart from any one local school or manifestation, the power of almost unrestricted technical development and geographical enlargement.

From the '80s onward, some of the master mountaineers of the generation between ours and the dynasty of the Alpine pioneers, were seen to be breaking away individually from the Alps where they had learned their craft, and to be returning to us from foreign parts with books of mountain revelation inciting to strange enterprises. We did not look upon them, however, as a movement. We saw them as fortunate individual adventurers; and it marked them as still more individual and eccentric in their goings, that most of them had fallen at one time or another under orthodox criticism for some audacious disregard of the already sacro-sanct Alpine code. But, looking back, I see them now as something very different: as the crests of a broad new tide of mountaineering, a second inspired group of mountain prophets, hardly less significant in our history than the first prophets themselves. I do not hold that great movements are derived only from the great men who led them. But the great man plays an indispensable part, in focusing the ideas out of a general awareness and in transmuting them by his genius into effective action. There was an awareness, general among us, of an arrest in Alpine adventure, and at the same time progress in climbing technique was proceeding restlessly and apace. The younger of us were chafing under the one, and experimenting with the other. But the great men, our elder friends and climbing counsellors, had already taken action.

Conway, Slingsby, Collie, Mummery, were men of wholly dissimilar type and surrounding; but they were associated in friendship by their equal passion for beauty and by their enduring chase through widely separated mountain regions in pursuit of it. Together they constituted a new prophetic brotherhood, representing a fresh approach to mountaineering and incorporating a body of novel doctrine in their writings. The two main elements of this teaching were, first, the enlargement of mountaineering idea to cover all distant ranges and the development of suitable climbing techniques; and secondly, the energetic implanting and promotion of climbing in our own islands, so as to provide for our mountaineering that local root and native nurture without which no British institution or interest can survive. There had been mountaineers before them in both these fields; but in their activities as a group, and in their writings, the two movements first came to a collective consciousness, and found effective expression.

Martin Conway's was a personality appropriate to a renaissance, of scintillating contrasts: a romantic, a sociologist, an art connoisseur, a worldling, an omniscient lecturer and compiler, a busy public character, and a completely casual will-o'-the-wisp. It used to seem to me oddly suitable that the only two people ever to receive titles for climbing should be Conway and Santa Christina the Wonderful; for certainly no two human beings ever pursued such widely divorced ideals by the same strenuous and fantastic means. Conway's butterfly flittings, artistically publicized, threw open the gates upon new worlds for ambitious younger mountaineers. On the other hand, his passion for orderly presentment led him to invent the idea of the first Climbers' Guides, which became the model for all such guides to all later time. And by thus being the first to draw attention to what had not been climbed, in the Alps, he was responsible for launching the 'new route' movement, and in this way, although himself rather an explorer than a climber, he contributed incalculably to the raising of the whole standard of climbing. Similarly, his *Alps from End to End* formed a deliberate challenge to our encroaching Alpine centrism and stagnation. I can recall how it shattered through certain Chamonix and Zermatt cobwebs. At his best, Conway's descriptive writing is as perfect as Leslie Stephen's, and we can climb our storied heights with him without fear of bumping our heads against the low ceiling of last-century emotional repressionism. Racily and charmingly, his unconventional mountain fervour gives us back our own experiences of wonder, and awe, and unsatisfied aspiration. His last book, *A Pilgrim's Quest for the Divine*, the spiritual aspect of his volatile chase after beauty, exemplifies how far he travelled from the conventions of his Victorian youth, and what a transition his writing covered. He valued it as his philosophic testament, and when threatened at the last by illness, asked me to see it through the press for him in the final event. By a coincidence, I had already 'read' it for a publisher, and had advised that the impersonal form, with a fictional 'hero', which he had adopted to observe the proprieties of fifty years before, made it impossible of modern digestion. Conway restored the autobiographical character, the book breathed again, and he himself lived to enjoy the celebrations contrived for its first, and his own eightieth, birthday. His mountaineering versatility was, possibly, too great and his colour and change too Protean for an enduring impression, and many of us may now regret that climbing guidebooks were ever invented at all; but Conway was only second to Whymper in bringing mountaineering home to our larger public, and among climbers themselves he undoubtedly gave an invaluable impetus to novel enterprise and its corollary technical improvement.

Cecil Slingsby's influence was as concentrated and personal as Conway's was artistic and diffused. It too had a dual character, in its contribution to mountaineering progress. But the methods were as different as the men. Where Conway flashed from Himalaya to Andes, Slingsby explored deeply into the possibilities of a single new mountain region, that of Norway, and he devoted his joyous northern energy to revealing its glories year after year, not only to all other mountaineers, but to the Norwegians themselves. By this, he endowed climbing with its first great, and near, alternative to the Alps. Again, he first brought ski to Switzerland, and reintroduced the practice as a sport to its parent Norway, and in this way he helped to double mountaineering opportunity, by adding a winter to our short summer season. Slingsby effaced himself in the very brightness of the enthusiasms which he was the first to set alight, and his buoyant book *The Northern Playground* was all too little known, until recently. That, however, mattered little to his enduring effect. A superb mountaineer – not improbably the finest of his accomplished generation – he had an unusual power of sympathy, and as adviser and friend his heartening inspiration radiated to every climbing nucleus as it was formed in our country. Indeed, the second of his dual functions as a prophet, was to become the best-known disseminator of a love of climbing among our countrymen and the principal promoter of our home climbing clubs and associations. I was myself an opponent of Clubs-and-more-Clubs in the early days, being a Cambridge individualist like my father before me, whose letter to *The Times*, in the '60s, emphatically disclaiming membership of the Alpine Club, I came upon with amusement just after I myself was elected. But I have come lately to see their merit, in that they give occasion for those friendly contacts between older and younger climbers which pass on our great unwritten traditions, and which meant so very much to me and to those happy enough to profit by the personal talk and example of the Alpine pioneers. It was due to Slingsby, and those of his Alpine-trained contemporaries who co-operated with him in the right inauguration of climbing and climbing clubs in our country, that the high and severe standards which he, in particular, sternly upheld and taught, in mountain craft, in comradeship and in mountain chivalry, were implanted in our home traditions; so that our modern climbing has been armoured to defend itself against the pernicious fascistic infections of over-competitiveness and spectacular stunting.

Under this heading, too, of our island prophets, one name cannot be omitted, the only name I am citing of a mountaineer who is still with us: Haskett Smith. In fulfilling that double role which distinguished our innovators, he became one of the first to proclaim the possibilities of the Pyrenees. But it was his bold pioneer work as a home climber for which he became famous; and to which he brought the skilled experience of a trained athlete and a witty and scholarly habit of mind. Haskett Smith wrote only two small sybilline books, of agreeable introduction to the potentialities of English and Irish cliffs. But they were to many of us the first notice that such a domestic fairyland existed, and the first authoritative acknowledgement that such climbing deserved to be, and must be, taken seriously. I shall not forget with what exultation I read them, and annotated them – mountain revelations, with (for the first time) kindly and homely names that kept them comfortably beside the pillow at night. Or how we bore them wetly with us on our tentative wanderings into those then rarely trodden, wild hill recesses. They told us not too much: they left us our imaginings. Would that all guidebooks had copied their restrained artistry!

Norman Collie was as different from the others of his group as it would seem inevitable that all great mountaineers should be from one another; and his exceptional gifts were almost more sharply contrasted. He combined the first-rate scientist and the first-rate artist, with all their attendant opposing talents in support; and he was fortunate to be able to find a harmonizing outlet for them all in his exploratory mountaineering. He was a master in both the prophetic spheres: on the one hand, a hardy and dauntless pioneer of new mountain regions, in the Rockies, the Arctic circle, the Himalaya; and on the other, the first and often the solitary explorer of remote Scottish, English and Irish precipices and of the magnificent sea cliffs on all our western and northern coasts. Of both these mountain worlds he wrote with all the poetry of a Celt, and all the knowledge of a faultless mountaineer, explorer and climber, in passages often of bard-like beauty. It is indeed an outstanding characteristic of the long lives of these men, and it gives a sense of a never-ending adventure to their prophetic books, that, after their very unlike fashions, they all continued to the close still as actively, and outspokenly, intent upon the pursuit of beauty; still seeking it, or returning to seek it at the end as they had at the beginning, among mountains, and behind the semblance of their surface loveliness and changing mystery.

With A. F. Mummery we have the satisfaction of returning to the Alps, and of tracing out how the new movement was simultaneously realizing itself in this first home of our climbing, in the progressive performances of a few exceptional guides and of a few unorthodox amateurs. For this reason I am considering him last among the later prophets, as I did Whymper among his contemporaries. There were other resemblances: both were dominant and individualistic mountain climbers, each of a new forward school; both wrote epoch-making books about their climbs; and each became the hero of a 'myth'. Fame balances its accounts drolly. Mummery's revolutionary economic theories, which I am told have now become accepted doctrine, earned him none of the fame they deserved; but fame is now crediting him with legendary qualities, as a universal mountaineering innovator and the founder of a new climbing technique, which formed no part of his considerable genius. Good climbing needs no bush of rumour: Mummery's record of ascents, even in the Alps, was relatively small, and he was not himself the author of any new route; his mountain judgement his letters show to have been defective, and the route designing and finding of his famous partnerships was done in the earlier years by his great guides and in the later by two of his great colleagues. The immense services Mummery rendered mountaineering can stand on their own feet without such manufactured pedestals. As a climber he was unsurpassed in his day: a supreme ice-man – the equal at least, as Norman Collie wrote to me last year, of the best professionals – a first-rate rock climber, of the new order of rock climbing, and, moreover, gifted with a dynamic personality, at once detached, original and electrifying, which rose above the challenge of difficulty or danger with serene humour. It

was this personal magnetism which led his expert parties to trust un-
questioningly to his tactical leadership upon any ascent or in any crisis,
and which – as happens more easily in cases where mystery surrounds a
heroic end – has survived him as a dazzling memory and enveloped his
achievement with an aura of always widening extent and multiplying
colours. It is, however, upon his fascinating book that the legend is chiefly
based, and upon which also his deserved reputation as a prophet rests.
The easy and masterful relationship it pictures between the climber and a
higher order of climbing difficulty, and with the *terribilità* of great peaks,
the emotional moments of beauty and suspense, such as we ourselves had
experienced in hard climbing but had found so seldom described and
rarely if ever with such intimacy, gave *My Climbs in the Alps* an immediate
and powerful appeal. Our generation had been uneasily waiting for a new
mountain revelation: it took time for the messages from the Himalaya,
Norway, home climbing, to filter into its consciousness: the Alps stood
always nearest its heart. Suddenly, in this stirring epic, and through the
clear glass of its style, we were seeing all the advance in technique of which
we were dimly conscious, and all the heightening of mountaineering
standards and the enlargement of mountaineering ideas, towards which
we were vaguely aspiring, being realized in practice and eloquently proclaimed – and actually in the classic world and on the historic peaks of
the Alps themselves. I remember myself the glorious excitement of that
first reading, and the veils it rent; and how I bombarded the Honorary
Secretary behind the then sealed portals of the Alpine Club, until he would
sell me a copy of the *Journal* containing 'Two Days on an Ice Slope', which
I still think to form an essential part of the saga. As I have said above, the
dramatic power of Whymper's *Scrambles amongst the Alps* brought it
about that we unconsciously identified him with the greatness of the
Matterhorn itself, confusing him personally with its mysterious forces, as
the hero of a sun-myth is confused with the nature forces from which the
myth derives. In the same way, the modern climbing generations are ready
to attribute to Mummery alone all the improvement in technique and the
new standards of performance for which his guides and friends and, in
fact, the whole accumulating wave of new mountain interest and exploration in which he shared, were all equally responsible. His just fame rests
upon his admirably written adventure stories, in which he portrays how
the general renaissance which was taking place in mountain climbing
manifested itself among an advanced section of Alpine climbers, professional and amateur. It was the first, and a most inspiring account of a big
stride forward in the progress of greater mountaineering; and it established
Mummery as *par excellence* the prophet of the Alps, in the confraternity
of the later prophets.

I have had to limit the term 'prophet' to those whose published books and whose sustained efforts to promote climbing by clubs, and personal leadership and encouragement, we can see to have had lasting effect upon the history of mountaineering in our own country, from which the mountaineering movement emanated. For, as soon as the spark was kindled on any part of the globe which had its own mountain range, regional prophets at once arose, on the Continent, in Canada, New Zealand, South Africa, India, the United States, and even among our own local hills. But these belong to a later historical stage. In considering only the limited number who seem to me without doubt to deserve a place in our own later group of prophets, I have been unexpectedly impressed by the worldwide variety of the mountain climbing these few men covered by their enterprise and opened up for us by their books. Collectively regarded, the range of achievement of this group of friends, alike only in their climbing enthusiasm, is astonishing: I had not myself realized before the magnitude of their missionary contributions, both at home and abroad.

With the turn of the century the face of the world changed, and all our social and group relationships were in solution. The motor car and electric intercommunication were dissipating local and social differences, and the intimacy and separatism of cult and caste and even of family life were melting steadily away. With them went much of the private freemasonry which had united all mountaineers irrespective of their nationality, and which had brought it about that all active climbers in our own hills knew, or could know one another. When every man began to have facility of approach to every hill, climbers ceased to be a close corporation or a happy family of initiates, united in the face of a censorious public even if squabbling at times admiringly among themselves. The challenge that hills make to all temperaments of a certain subtle blend, could now appeal directly to the infinity of separate individuals moving in dispersion over the face of the earth. Sibylline books and the prophetic voice were no longer needed, or able, to trumpet the message to fresh circles or to summon new crusades, and the secrets of the climbing craft were no longer attainable only by way of the guild. Books of specific information, as to the ranges to be climbed and the techniques to be mastered, and current and recurrent chronicles of expeditions completed or still in progress, took precedence of prophetic values. The authorized version of the minor no less than the major prophets was closed, even before the social precipitation of the last war.

And yet, as I look back across the long recession of great mountaineers, not only across the two groups of them I have defined, but a score of others whom I have excluded – and possibly wrongly – because they were not authors, one figure stands out in obstinate salience, over-riding any book-work qualifications, and wearing the mantle of the prophets with an upright distinction and an *insouciance* all his own. Percy Farrar was probably the strongest single influence which modern mountaineering has known. He wrote no book. But, as editor of the *Alpine Journal* for many years, and especially during the last war, he raised and kept it at a level of literary and scholarly excellence that could challenge comparison with any more celebrated quarterly. His own writing in it was always in character, virile, brusque, eloquent, strict in censure, but all of a sudden aflame with admiration and generous praise: his farewell apostrophe to his old guide, Daniel Maquignaz, is as noble as it is unconventional. But his influence was even more potent where it was exercised personally. Educated abroad, and successful in a South African career, and in its war, he combined the characteristics of a soldierly and sporting English countryman with the impetuous independence of a pioneer, the mental energy of a student, and a cosmopolitan social instinct and training. For a number of years, after we had captured him back into our mountaineering world from that of the Continent, by sheer good sense and goodwill he held together in sympathy the mountaineering elements over all Europe, the Dominions and the United States. I know nothing comparable with the affection and respect in which Farrar was held by the climbers, young and old, of nearly every land. During the troubled interlude following the last war, his tireless work in promoting international understanding through a common mountaineering interest, seemed to me – when engaged upon parallel lines – the most successful undertaking of the kind in Europe. Among ourselves, protesting fierce prejudices, he encouraged or shared in every new form of adventure with vigorous indulgence. His catholic sympathies embraced every age and variety of climber, and his finger was upon the mountaineering pulse of every country. With ageing or afflicted mountaineers, wherever he could trace them, he would start a mountaineering correspondence about the past with a charming deference that in itself consoled; and with the young and enterprising – if any man or boy had the mountaineer's faith in him and the courage to practise it, for Farrar he could do no wrong. It was a heroic effort, and an all-pervading presence, which for some years held together the loosening strings. But it could not survive him. He did not live to fight the new virus which poisoned so much of continental climbing and threatened our own; but I do not believe that even he could have done much against its evil trend. His was the last influence upon our mountain world which we can call in any sense universal, and the last which gave to it any sense of unity. With Farrar we may say with some certainty that even the revised version of the later prophets was finally closed.

❊ (Vol. LIV.)

T. S. Blakeney

15 ❋ Whymper and Mummery

The Alpine Club has received an interesting acquisition in the form of
Whymper's own copy of Mummery's *My Climbs in the Alps and Caucasus*.
The book was sent to Whymper for review, and the MS. of the review is
with the book. In addition, Whymper embellished the volume with MS.
notes expressing his views on Mummery.

It is needless to list all the marginalia in the volume, but two are worth
quoting, as giving a key to Whymper's outlook. On page xvii of J. A.
Hobson's 'Appreciation', against the statement that Mummery had a
disposition for seeking difficulties for the joy of overcoming them, Whymper makes the comment: 'In an ordinary life there are quite sufficient
difficulties without seeking more.' On page xxv, where Mrs. Mummery
quotes D. W. Freshfield's tribute in the Alpine Club on December 16,
1895, ending with the words (which Whymper underlines), 'His untimely
death is a grievous loss to the Club,' there is a single, pungent entry: 'I do
not agree.'

We are thus prepared for a distinctly original review, nor are we disappointed. Since this has been published in *The Sphere*, it is unnecessary
to reproduce it again; but some of its more striking phrases may be noted.
Whymper opens by calling it a 'vicious' book and prophesies that it will
sell well: those who read it, he thinks, will benefit from it. This apparent
inconsistency would seem, from the later comments, to mean that readers
will benefit by noting what not to do, in much the same fashion as Sherlock
Holmes told Watson that he had sometimes been helped by the latter's
deductions, and when it became necessary to be more explicit, explained
that what he meant was that, by noting Watson's fallacies, he was
occasionally guided towards the truth.

Whymper's prejudice against Mummery rather interfered with his
powers as a reviewer. He considered that because Llewellyn Davies had
made no 'fuss' over the first ascent of the Täschhorn, there was no need
for the account of the Teufelsgrat. A memorandum pasted inside the
volume shows that in the event of any remarks being called forth by his
Sphere review, Whymper intended to try and belittle Mummery by quoting
'my times across the Col Dolent against his across the Col des Courtes,

and my times on the Aig. Verte against his times'. No allowance is made for comparative standards of difficulty or for the possible advantages of a guided against a guideless party.

The review ends with the reiteration that, though the book is vicious, it will do no harm if Mummery's fate is remembered. Then follows a passage a little surprising even in days of more trenchant reviewing than we are apt to see today, when one remembers that Mrs. Mummery was alive to read it. Whymper proceeds to speculate on the condition Mummery's body is likely to be in, should traces of it ever be discovered below Nanga Parbat. 'It will be,' he says, 'in the shape of a dislocated skeleton, one bone here and another there, scattered over a considerable area. The stomach and heart will be nowhere.'

He concludes the review by postulating that, in certain important matters, Mummery was insane!

It is probable that, in allowing himself to dwell on the gruesome details likely to be attendant on Mummery's death, Whymper was drawing upon his own recollections of the condition of his companions killed on the Matterhorn in 1865. In *Scrambles*, he merely says that as they came in sight of the scene of death 'we saw one weather-beaten man after another raise the telescope, turn deadly pale, and pass it on without a word to the next . . .' But in a letter dated May 20, 1911, to Sir Edward Davidson, Whymper writes in greater detail:

> . . . When we recovered the remains of this grand man [Croz] he was, like the others, completely smashed. All were naked and it was difficult to distinguish one from another. I could only identify Croz by his beard. Part of the lower jaw remained, but the upper part of the head had disappeared.

Whymper's point is clear enough; Mummery is held up as an awful example of what will befall a rash climber; his imitators may expect to meet the same sort of end.

❉ (Abridged from Vol. LVII.)

PART TWO
MIDDLE YEARS

R. L. G. Irving

16 ❄ Five Years with Recruits

Five years with recruits may sound an odd subject for a short paper, but I promise you we shall gallop through them. And as you find yourselves being taken along well-known paths, you must let your memories talk to you; for it is your share and not mine in treading out the way that can invest my pictures with a living interest tonight.

Naturally the five years have not been spent in making new conquests, but in fitting the recruits for service in the great and growing army of mountaineers, the army in which the Alpine Club is the Imperial Guard. I dare say I was not qualified for the post of trainer; to some of you it may seem sheer impudence to usurp the functions of the professional experts of Meiringen and Zermatt. It may even be that I shall be accused of corrupting the youth; but my present business is to describe, and not to apologize for my actions.

Let me explain quite shortly how I came to take upon myself the duties of a recruiting sergeant. The only friend with whom I had done any guide-less climbing died five years ago, and in the summer of 1904 I found myself without a companion to share my Alpine holiday. I was in the position of a man who has sampled three kinds of mountaineering, and has to choose between them. I had climbed with guides, I had climbed alone, and I had climbed with a friend. The expense alone of the first was enough to deter me from returning to it; the second I had sampled far too freely already, but it had such an influence in persuading me to choose the third that I am going to call your attention to it for a few moments. The condemnation of solitary climbing has been very sweeping, too sweeping I think, because its generalities leave the novice unconvinced. The dangers have been greatly exaggerated, and the real drawbacks not sufficiently emphasized. There are routes up many peaks in the Alps, Mont Blanc and the Matterhorn being conspicuous examples, on which a solitary climber risks little more than a man who wanders alone on a wild Yorkshire moor. I am speaking of course of men who have learnt to move freely when unroped on snow or rock. But the rules of solitary climbing are terribly strict and hard to observe. Sooner or later they will be broken. First small patches of névé, and then quite considerable glaciers will be traversed by the luckless one to whom glissading and the delights of an easy descent over snow are forbidden fruit. The finest and quickest approaches to the big peaks are usually barred to him, and if he falls from grace and ventures on the snowfields, the constant anxiety robs the day of its restfulness and recreative power. If you climb for novelty and excitement solitary climbing is the kind to satisfy you; but if you climb for recreation of mind and body it is a failure. It is hard to estimate the strain a particular climb puts upon a man, but the kind of night that follows it is a good rough indication. The evidence in my own case has been astonishing. Time after time a solitary climb has caused me to lie awake for hours, or, worse still, to become just sufficiently unconscious of my surroundings to be pursued by persistent visions of the most sensational episodes of the day. Whereas the presence of a companion, even on the longest and most arduous climbs, has been an unfailing soporific.

And then so many of the pleasures of mountaineering are incomplete if we haven't a sympathetic friend to share them. Left to ourselves we can best feel the solemnity of the hills, but if we remain too long alone in their presence the lights grow dim, and the shadows over-long. Our mountain pictures need correcting from other points of view; there is generally some fresh touch suggested by the presence of others, some little patch of 'mountain gloom' to be brightened into 'mountain glory'.

But the solitary climber is severely handicapped when he begins to seek companions; he has got so used to following his own sweet will in the manner of his climbing, that his society may be a doubtful blessing to climbers of his own age and experience. He has been his own leader every-where, and murmurs, not always silently, at being tied fore and aft to men whose method of attaining the desired summit differs from his own. And even in moments of expansion he fears that the messages of the mountains, which he has treasured secretly for years, may sound mere platitudes in ears that have listened as long and as carefully as his own.

It was natural, then, that the idea of training my own companions should attract me. By imperceptible stages I should fall back from the position of first to that of second on the rope; and when there I should be hardly more jealous of my leader than a father of his son. My edition of 'Plain Tales from the Hills' would be good enough for those that had none, and the telling of the tales would be delightful. I think the need of having someone to talk to about mountains is quite as great as the need of having someone to climb with: starvation in either respect is terrible; and when I came back from a last solitary campaign in the Sierra Nevada at Easter 1904, I was determined somehow or other to secure a proper supply of both. It wasn't hard to do so; living in rooms almost adjoining mine were the very persons I wanted. The enlistment of my first recruit took place on the occasion of my finding him developing photographs during illicit hours. A tactful remark of his about a Swiss photograph led to an amicable discussion. He had seen the Alps, and had once stood on the summit of the Cima di Jazzi; so in his case the sacred fire needed no kindling, but only replenishing. A second recruit, a special friend of the first, was soon enlisted, and the planning of the campaign began.

Mountain nostalgia in the young is not a complicated disease; and the cure is simple, if somewhat expensive. We took it in the form of a ticket to Martigny. Arriving there tired, but too excited to be sleepy, we went straight on to Bourg St. Pierre, and were mad enough to try the Vélan the very next day. If you have played golf you will know what happens if you tear up to the club-house on your bicycle, and rush at once on to the first tee. It is not quite so bad in mountaineering, for as a rule if one man gives up the hole the others follow suit; and there is no unruffled partner, who has lunched comfortably at the club-house, to jeer at your failure. Both my recruits succumbed to acute 'mal de montagne', and in spite of their most gallant efforts we had to stop within 600 ft. of the top of the Vélan. They were dreadfully cast down about it; if this peak of 12,000 ft. were too high for them, what was to become of the Combin or Monte Rosa, whose names had been starred on the programme. The descent was a trying one, but the moraine was reached at last, and the two sufferers sank down and fell asleep upon it, as if its angular blocks had been the downiest of cushions. They awoke new men, and we returned to Bourg St. Pierre fresh and full of hope. This 'atra dies' with which the season began is well remembered among us; and the name of Vélanitis has been given to the mysterious disease which robbed us of our peak.

But the day was not so black to me as to my recruits. As far as the actual climbing was concerned, they had more than fulfilled my expectations; they had found the rocks very easy, and though there was not much snow to test them they were perfectly steady during the passage of their first bergschrund, in spite of the fact that their heads were aching violently at the time.

We did not renew our attack on the Vélan, but feeling that a defeat by the Combin would be an honourable one, we started the next afternoon for the refuge built by the Balleys below the Col des Maisons Blanches. We did not find it, but found the new Valsorey hut instead, a very pleasant mistake to make. In the morning it was my turn to be indisposed, and we stayed at the hut all day. A party of twenty-four Frenchmen came up in the evening, but we slept long and soundly notwithstanding, and did not stir from our beds till the last of them had left. Our intention was to climb the Combin and descend the same way to the Col des Maisons Blanches, so as to avoid the ice-slope and the avalanche-swept part of the ordinary route. The rocks leading up to the W. ridge of the Combin de Valsorey were very steep, but the recruits were quite at their ease. Symptoms of 'Vélanitis' appeared on the Combin de Valsorey, but a brew of hot cocoa kept off the attack, and we reached the top of the Grand Combin in another three-quarters of an hour. We could not resist the excellent tracks which led down towards the corridor. On the short ice-slope the steps were admirable, and my companions never gave me a moment's anxiety. Thanks to some delicious soup given us at the Panossière hut by the aforesaid party of Frenchmen, we reached Mauvoisin that night, and I am sure three happier men never went to bed in Switzerland. The Vélan was forgotten; its gloom had been swallowed up in the sunshine of the Combin. In dealing with rock, snow, and even ice, my recruits had performed wonders; they had won their spurs, and the great world above the snow-line was ours to conquer and enjoy.

Our next expedition was intended to provide some practice in glacier work. We walked up to Chanrion, and next day followed the high-level route to Zermatt over the Col de L'Evêque and the Col de Valpelline. I know of no expedition better worth repeating on a fine day than this one; we had perfect weather, good snow, and a succession of the small mishaps which are the spice of guideless climbing. First, I walked into a small lake near Chanrion, mistaking it in the dark for a snow-patch; then I fell into a crevasse near the Col de Collon far enough to make myself ridiculous and nobody anxious; and, finally, I quite failed to hit the N. Col du Mont Brûlé, and crossed the ridge at a depression much further to the N. – a mistake which delayed us more than 2 hrs. All through the day my two followers walked splendidly, and managed the rope well. Naturally we were all tired at the end; in fact when they told us at the Staffel Alp that an omnibus was all that Zermatt was likely to give us by way of bedroom we were only too glad to believe it, and stayed where we were.

When we did get down to Zermatt my recruits had plenty to see; there must be a twist in the mind of a climber who doesn't enjoy his first few days at Zermatt. A natural desire to be considered up to date calls forth loud lamentations over its departed simplicity; but his first thoughts are not of the crowd, the band or the bazaars, but of what has remained unchanged by these; he must learn to love what is still lovely at Zermatt before he can really feel the extent of the desecration committed there. We had only a few days at our disposal, but the weather was kind to us. We had a grand day on Monte Rosa; up by the rock rib from the Grenz glacier, then along the ridge to the Zumsteinspitze, which had baffled me with guides two years before, and down over the Lysjoch. Slight 'Vélanitis' decreased our pace, and it was quite dark before we reached Gressoney.

The following day we toiled up to spend a few miserable hours at the Sella hut. Our imaginations, unfettered by accurate information, had supplied it with a caretaker, and all that was necessary for a nice hot supper. What we found was a wrecked stove and some boards to lie on, quite bare, save for a few damp blankets and some stone pillows. By good luck we had a boiler with us, and managed to make ourselves some thin porridge; but the night was sheer misery. Jacob must have had a wonderful faculty of sleep. Our consciences did not trouble us for having robbed the guides of their birthright, yet we saw no bright visions; as it was, a nightmare would have been welcome. We stood it as long as we could, and then crept out on to the glacier just before dawn, and crossed the Felikjoch in a famished condition. We breakfasted at the Riffelhaus earlier than a good many of its inmates, and then went down to Zermatt to pack our things.

The same evening we took train to Martigny, where our small company was split up. I went up to Champex with the remaining recruit, where we spent a day of complete idleness, and then set out for Chamonix. While enjoying a cosy supper at the Cabane D'Orny, the route by the Fenêtre de Saleinaz and the Col du Chardonnet seemed hardly good enough for us. But in the morning we found we had reckoned without the weather, and were very lucky to reach Chamonix that evening by the Col du Trient and the Col de Balme, our passage of the former being far from orthodox.

A traverse of the Col du Géant and a very belated return over Mont Blanc ended our climbing for that year. I have taken you over a lot of very familiar ground, but I wanted you to know what my recruits were capable of their first year. I don't wish to imply that our expeditions were justified merely by their successful issue, but the fact remains that the climbs were accomplished, and that without the slightest accident and without excessive fatigue; and I attribute this to some extent to my knowledge of what I could or could not safely do, but chiefly to the aptitude of my young companions. In January 1905 I spent a week at Pen-y-Gwryd with some new recruits, one of whom had done some small climbs in the Alps and in Norway. We did not get very far into Mr. Abraham's list, but we enjoyed ourselves prodigiously, and learnt something about rock climbing.

Arolla was our headquarters for the following summer. Our party was a large one, and included some lady recruits. Our behaviour soon attracted the notice of the censors of mountaineering morals. It was hardly to be expected that a mother should allow her only son, and his sisters too, to pursue an apparently suicidal career, and escape criticism. One evening it leaked out that several of us were preparing to start for the Collon next morning. The alarmists were roused to action; they chose as their spokesman a well-known member of the Alpine Club, with a special knowledge of the district. It wasn't an easy job for him; but if ever a similar duty should fall to me, I should be well satisfied to perform it with as great courtesy and tact. The attack fell, not on me, but on the aforesaid mother of one of the party; she sustained it in a heroic manner, and allowed her son to go. But we agreed that under the circumstances it was better that two of the less experienced should not start. She spent the day with the late warnings ringing in her ears, but the worst was still to come. Owing to a disastrous short cut over a small col near the Col de Pièce we did not reach the N.W. arête of the Collon till mid-day. Through the telescope at the hotel we were seen on the top at eleven, but as a matter of fact we did not get there till two, when nobody was looking for us. Seven o'clock arrived, and still no sign of us. Down at the hotel the remnant of our party, concealing their anxiety, bravely sat down to an uncomfortable dinner. At half-past seven whispered consultations were held, and significant glances were cast at the empty places round our table; search parties were in the air, when our advanced guard arrived a little before eight. Half an hour later we were all in, and assisting at the joys of the réunion. There was a feeble repetition of the alarms when I started with my two best recruits for the Dent Blanche. The weather was perfect, but there was still a good deal of snow on the mountain, and we had it to ourselves. Not once were we in serious diffi- culties, and I felt as safe as if I had been with guides. From that day the alarmists let us alone. At the time I was foolish enough to show some resentment at their interference; but I have come to perceive their action was kindly and quite justified; and I wish I could let them know that I respect them for what they did, and regret my own attitude in the matter.

To those who are learning to climb, failure to attain the summit brings no shame and little disappointment, an advantage which has once or twice enabled us to achieve success on days which older climbers might devote to writing letters. The most notable instance I remember was the day we climbed the Perroc. It was raining when we started, and continued to do so all day; but the wind was warm and the rocks were not glazed. A thick pall hung over all the mountains, and the most sanguine of our friends at the hotel expected us back for breakfast. It was tea-time when we did get back after climbing the Perroc, and traversing the ridge over the Grande Dent de Veisivi to the Col de Zarmine. Our party of three included my youngest recruit, and I think this shows how quickly rock-climbing of ordinary difficulty can be picked up. This youngest recruit was only seventeen, and the other nineteen.

At Easter, 1906, three of us mobilized at Fort William, where we accomplished one rash and several very good climbs on the N. face of Ben Nevis.

The following season in the Alps was the biggest we have had. The peaks round Zinal and Zermatt were in wonderful condition, and there were not many of them we did not visit during the six weeks that we spent among them. Towards the end of our time my recruits had become so proficient that the ladies of the party were included in some of our most important expeditions. One day the Nord-End and Dufourspitze, and another day the Lyskamm, were visited by a large company of both sexes. The Lys- kamm was defended by a rather difficult bergschrund, and afforded a striking instance of the long apprenticeship necessary for snow and ice work. The ladies showed what a lot can be done by pluck and steadiness, but they naturally needed assistance in places, and I must confess that only one of my male recruits gave proof of sufficient steadiness and care on the descent. I do not mean that we narrowly escaped an accident, but that after two long seasons in Switzerland men may feel uncomfortable on the snow and ice met with on the ordinary routes.

We were surprised at seeing no one on the Lyskamm, for it can seldom be in better condition than it was then. And it may be worth while to mention a slight variation we made from the ordinary way of reaching the upper plateau of the Grenz glacier. We had dined at the Riffelhaus and started by moonlight at 10 P.M. By so doing we reached at 2 A.M. the upper ice-fall that cuts the Grenz glacier across at the height of about 12,000 ft. It is usually turned close to the great buttress of Monte Rosa, but at this early hour it was possible to go straight up through the séracs. I should be sorry for anyone who followed our tracks in the day-time. It was like approaching the palace of a great magician, when all the lions and dragons that ought to have been guarding it were asleep. For half an hour we wound in and out among great ghostly towers and over crazy-looking bridges, and once we had to cut up a delicate flying buttress of blue ice. It was the most fascinating bit of glacier I have ever seen, and when we emerged from it I longed for more. It was as bad as being wakened up out of a dream of fairyland. Some of the great pendant icicles must have been astonished to see our tracks under their very noses when the sun woke them up, and I expect they were all demolished long before the evening. We tried the same plan of starting after dinner again on the Matterhorn, and so got a long start of the ten other parties that followed us up the peak, and through having no one to set us right, we descended the highest rocks on the S. face by a long-discarded route, instead of by the comfortable ropes and ladder now provided.

I don't want to become entangled in details, but I can't leave the season of 1906 without referring to one crime we committed, which might have resulted in a serious accident. In the course of a short tour between Zinal and Zermatt we found ourselves on the W. face of the Za. The previous day we had all gone up to the Berthol hut; there some of the party spent the night, while three of us returned to Arolla, intending to traverse the Za and pick up the others on our way over the Col d'Hérens. We were called three-quarters of an hour late, and lost another three-quarters of an hour in the stony wastes of the hillside below the Glacier de la Za. Just as we reached the rocks we came up with five other climbers, an Englishman with two guides in front, and a German with a single guide following close behind. We were most anxious to get to the Berthol hut early, and, thinking that we should go quicker than a party of five, we went ahead of them. The guides naturally resented this, and when I tried to explain the reasons for our haste they did not seem to appreciate them. We got up a chimney above them as quickly as we could, and then, wishing to clear out of their way as soon as possible, forsook the boot-scratches and tried to traverse the S. face higher up. We entered another chimney, whose walls were of loose rock. My companions closed up, and I was waiting at the top for the second man to join me, when he took hold of a huge loose block that came away with him. I was well placed and stopped him, but the boulder, after removing some skin from his cheek, started off on a wild career down the slope. Our third man was quite close and a little to one side of the second, and the boulder did not touch him; but it was frightful to think of what it might do to the men below. We yelled with all our might, and prayed that they were under cover. The boulder burst above where they were, and we waited breathless for a few seconds. Then welcome voices came: they were far too loud and maledictory to come from men who had been badly hit. Whatever they said was fully justified, but one of the threats was truly awful: '*Nous vous aurions mangés, si vous nous aviez tués.*' The strain relaxed, we prepared to grovel to any extent. We had put ourselves so hopelessly in the wrong that there was no spirit left in us. When all the other five had passed below us we descended into the ordinary route, and soon came up with them. The anger of the guides abated before our penitent attitude, and they gave us an almost friendly farewell when we left the summit. I believe the Englishman was the same that had had such a narrow escape on the Aiguilles Rouges some days before; at the end of his description of that thrilling episode is a mention of this climb on the face of the Za, and he refers to some feature of the climb near the top which was shirked. I don't know what this was, but I think he showed wonderful generosity in not referring to this nefarious attempt on his life by three irresponsible youths.

A happy inspiration took us to Ried in 1907. It was ideal for a family party like ours; simple, homely, and rich in climbs of all grades of difficulty. We did most of the ordinary climbs there, and one which was in part new on the Breitlauihorn. But our ascent of the Bietschhorn appeared to impress the hotel staff more than anything else. Both the mountain and ourselves were in excellent condition, and we had to race a thunderstorm at the end, with the result that we got back to the hotel in time for *déjeuner*. We took just 4½ hrs.' actual climbing from the hut to the S. summit – a proof that our rock-climbing had progressed.

The last ten days of our holiday were spent at Chamonix. One of the recruits got a chill the first day, possibly from eating Mr. Couttet's ices; but I managed to ascend the Blaitière with the remaining one, though it took us nearly 20 hrs. to do so. We spent an awful half-hour fighting our way in the dark through some nut trees about a thousand feet above the

9. *Irving's recruits in action on Tower Ridge, Ben Nevis –*
Mallory as a schoolboy climber.

↑ *10. Nanga Parbat.*

→ *11. The Eigerwand,*
the highest face in the Alps and the scene of many dramatic climbing feats.

←12. *The final ridge of Everest.*
The picture was taken during the successful British ascent of 1975
and shows the late Dougal Haston climbing the Hillary Step –
there was much less snow on it when Hillary and Tenzing made the first ascent.

↑ 13. *On the North East Face of Badile.*

14. *The tremendous West Face of the Dru.*

15. *On the North Face of the Matterhorn.*

16. A modern British ice climb – Astronomy, Ben Nevis.

valley, and we gave ourselves two hours superfluous step-cutting by ascending the W. side of the Nantillons glacier, instead of the E. side where the tracks were. It was mid-day when we reached the Col des Nantillons. A stout wooden peg helped us over an awkward drop in the ridge leading up from the col. Another three-quarters of an hour was wasted cutting steps across an ice-slope to the col between the central and northern peaks. We meant to return to the latter, but as a matter of fact we inadvertently traversed beyond the central and climbed the southern peak first, and when we had come back and climbed the central peak it was far too late to think of the northern peak. It was six o'clock when we got back to the Col des Nantillons, and eleven when we reached Chamonix.

For some reason or other I have never been badly bitten by Aiguille climbing, and what working days were left to us were spent on Mont Blanc. I visited it first with a single recruit in whose progress I was specially interested, and the same week three of us traversed it from the Col de Miage over the Aiguille de Bionnassay. The sharp ridge descending to the Col de Bionnassay took us far less time than I had expected, for it was in perfect condition. Even so we were very pleased with ourselves, for it was the finest snow expedition we had ever made.

I have little to say about the present year; my recruits are fast becoming veterans. Last August two of them traversed the Strahlegg Pass, the Grünerhorn, and the passes leading from the Oberaar hut to the Lötschenthal, besides doing some climbing on their own account during our stay at the Fafler Alp.

Our two most difficult expeditions were the traverse of the Grosshorn by the S. and N.E. arêtes, and the traverse of the Mittaghorn from Obersteinberg to the Lötschenlücke, the upper portion of this last climb being of too hazardous a nature for my liking. Two days that I enjoyed quite as much were those devoted to the Nesthorn and the Aletschhorn. On the latter peak my youngest recruit led all the way up, thus proving he had learnt all he could learn from me.

Let me close my paper with a few general observations on the five years' climbing.

I am quite sure that with good recruits there is little risk while they are in the learning stage of mountaineering, and boys who are good at outdoor games learn wonderfully quickly. It does not follow that a man who is good at cricket or football will make a better mountaineer in the end than a man who has never played those games, but he starts with an advantage. He has a good eye, which means that his muscles readily act in concert with the eye and the brain. Kicking a football teaches a man to place his feet accurately and quickly on a given spot; and being able to hit a half-volley in the middle of the bat will help him to strike the ice with his axe exactly where he wants. Curiously enough gymnastics, while they are extremely useful in special places, do not seem to produce the same general ease of movement as outdoor games; but in combination they are excellent. It is extraordinary how little idea of grip people sometimes have if they have never handled the bat or the parallel bars. I have watched men of three or four years' experience climbing who were far behind some of my recruits in their first year, both in skill and in steadiness. Of course when it comes to leading and making independent expeditions, experience is essential. As a rule the all-important question for a leader is: Can I safely climb this place? not Can I get up further than anyone else? On routes which are followed because of their special difficulty the case is different; but hitherto we have got on well without these. My recruits have never urged me to undertake an expedition which I regarded as too ambitious for us; but they are very young still, and I dread their becoming infected with the spirit of competition that pervades a good deal of the climbing literature of the present day.

I suppose the public would think our love of mountains was dead if we did not occasionally commit some follies over them; but I really think we have done our duty already in this respect. Bad weather, bad conditions, and aberrations from the right way, will provide a guideless party with as many exciting and trying situations as they ought to wish for. Some of my companions on the rope have lately developed a thirst for very difficult routes; but I regard it as a good sign that the two most skilful climbers among them are also the most careful. Occasionally they have broken loose, and crawled along gutter-pipes and window-ledges.

And if one of them has the mortification of seeing us go off to Switzerland while he has to stay behind, he may well be excused for displaying greed over exceptionally severe climbs in Cumberland or Wales. In Switzerland they have been wonderfully modest, and have quite appreciated the need of experience. They have shown unfailing steadiness in dangerous places; and no physical discomforts such as cold, wet, and fatigue can induce them to turn back when it is safe to go on.

I have said very little about our climbing in Wales. For my own part, I heartily wish that the climbs there were unnamed. But there are hundreds of men who have little chance of going to the Alps, and for whom rock-climbing is a sport in itself; and if it helps them to have a graduated course that they can work through, and to have every ridge and gully labelled, we more fortunate ones must not grumble. Yet I do sometimes wish I could put the clock back, and return to the days when there was said to be good climbing on Lliwedd.

The young climber has now many inducements to try a large number of difficult climbs; and the accomplishment of these brings his standard of what is safe nearer to the limit of what is possible. The effect of a single week's climbing has been quite noticeable: increased pace and confidence on all sorts of rock; but with it a decrease of care in places that call for little muscular effort, but on which, nevertheless, a slip would be fatal. I cannot help thinking that the man who habitually and by preference does difficult climbs, is perpetually taking risks, which may be very small, but which will eventually catch him unawares. No doubt it is a fine thing to be able to delight in extremely difficult climbs, but the pleasure is dearly purchased with the loss of carefulness at other times. And if you tell me this loss of carefulness is not a necessary consequence, I will try to believe you, but the longer I climb, the harder I find it to do so.

Climbing, like other branches of art and education, is going through a phase in which it is demanded of them before all else that they be interesting. The beauty of a subject and the sort of thoughts it suggests are less considered than the evidence it affords of clever handling. The usual method of exciting interest in a climb is to introduce difficulties beyond those provided by nature, and in some cases the practice has been carried beyond reasonable limits. There are ridges and cliffs in the British Isles which resemble over-annotated editions of interesting classics, in which the conscientious reader is constantly having his attention distracted from the main thread of the story to some unnecessary and highly obscure note. I must admit that whenever I have had the temerity to attack the sort of rocks the modern expert calls interesting I have never failed to find them so. But with me the interest in finding an ingenious way up is often absorbed by the interest in what would happen to the party if I slipped. I do not deny this latter contingency has a high interest for all climbers, but I find a little of it goes a very long way, and repeated doses of such strong stimulants spoil the delicacy of the palate and render tasteless what was once a savoury dish.

Every man must seek the pleasures of mountaineering in his own way. There is no fixed rule for obtaining the joys that elude analysis. But each season as it passes leaves us some fresh indications of how to make a wise selection from our many sources of delight. And I have settled to my own satisfaction that mere novelty possesses but faded charms in the Alps. I cannot deceive myself into thinking I am an explorer when I succeed in scaling a few hundred feet of rock which have been known to climbers before I was born. There is a feeling of artificiality about such new climbs that robs them of the romantic mystery which surrounds the very name of the Himalaya and other unclimbed ranges. And so far is novelty from being necessary to me in my Swiss expeditions, that whenever I have been wise enough to make a second ascent of a peak, I have enjoyed it more than the first, and likewise with a third and even a fourth. Nevertheless, until we have followed one fairly difficult route upon a mountain we do not properly know it. A Swiss youth once remarked to John Addington Symonds, 'You only learn to love men whose bodies you have touched and handled,' and the same is strangely true of mountains. One aspect of them we may see when walking over their snowfields on a fine day, but before we have come to grips with them we are mere acquaintances. There is an overpowering sense of personality about a peak when we feel its broad snowy chest almost touching our own, when his great rocky shoulders rub against ours, and our hands clutch at his hard, rough skin to get a hold. Some sort of struggle, what the French call a *corps à corps*, is an excellent beginning to a lasting friendship.

We soon learn to value mountains by other standards than that of fighting power. And it often rests with us to decide whether they shall restore or exhaust our energies, whether they shall develop or test our powers of endurance, whether they shall deepen or disturb the current of our lives. Occasions constantly arise when we under-estimate the difficulties, or the weather plays us false. And then we can enjoy what is better than any self-imposed struggle; for the satisfaction of accomplishing a climb of catalogued severity is nothing to the joy of fighting a way out of difficulties and dangers that were unforeseen. The heroes of mountaineering are not those who have fallen in an attempt on some almost inaccessible pinnacle, but those who have perished like Carrel on the Grand Staircase. The long roll of Alpine fatalities shows that the most frequently trodden routes are not devoid of danger to the best of guides and amateurs. And the thought must occur to us, that the respect due to even the simplest-looking of the great peaks is lessened to a dangerous extent by frequent indulgence in very difficult climbs. To some men, I suppose, climbing really does become insipid unless it is strongly spiced with danger; but I hope that neither I nor my recruits will ever be of the number. We desire no more 'Golden Age' of climbing than that which began five years ago, and I cannot believe that the discoverers of the old routes got a much keener pleasure out of them than ourselves. Many of these routes are no more vulgarized than the naves of our great cathedrals. Everyone dislikes to see them strewn with orange-peel and sandwich-papers, or to hear their solemn stillness broken by cat-calls. But they are not vulgarized because other men have worshipped there before us. And judging by our own experience, the probability of being crowded off one's seat on the summit is much less than is supposed. You would be surprised if I were to tell you the number of well-known peaks of which we have enjoyed undisturbed possession for a day. And with so many less-frequented districts of the Alps still unvisited, we can look forward to the same privacy on many future days.

Perhaps my recruits will not be content with doing what becomes each year more easily within their powers. But I am hopeful; and when I read through the simple story of our climbs – it has reached its fourth volume – there is nothing that gives me more satisfaction than to find that we can still appreciate as of old the simple snow climb. Of course we do a few audacious things, we should not be young if we didn't; but we have tried to live up to our belief that there is an influence more purifying than danger in the beauty of the snows; and that among the countless ridges and recesses of the Alps, we shall find an outlet for the energies of youth without having constantly before our eyes immediate prospects of dissolution.

❄ (Vol. XXIV.)

17 ❄ *Condemnation*

Mr. R. L. G. Irving read a paper entitled 'Five Years with Recruits', which was illustrated by lantern slides.

Mr. C. Pilkington congratulated Mr. Irving, and thought that the paper spoke well for Winchester. He thought it doubtful whether a boy of fourteen to sixteen years should take long expeditions; in fact, he would consider it dangerous. The youths Mr. Irving had taken were from seventeen to eighteen years of age, but he thought that one ought to wait till well over eighteen before attempting long and difficult climbs.

Mr. Willink thought that perhaps it would be wiser to take such expeditions as had been described with other people's sons rather than with one's own; he should not have liked to go with his sons on the expeditions Mr. Irving had taken boys. It was true that in climbing with young people you were entirely master of what was to be done, and could therefore enjoy a day and make it enjoyable to others. It was delightful to climb with young people, who approached climbing in the right spirit. Young people must be taught not only gymnastics, but also to see the beauty of things.

Mr. Yeld did not know what it was to go with other people's sons, but he had several times gone with his own and found the experience very pleasant.

Mr. Corry mentioned the expeditions of a young German who climbed without guides.

Mr. Prothero did not wish to protest against such climbing, but thought that there was a considerable element of danger in it. He should be sorry to take young people up difficult places, especially on ice slopes, without practice or without a second man at least. If one took boys one incurred a responsibility that he should be sorry to incur. Though Mr. Irving's expeditions had been very enjoyable, and no harm had been done, he had hinted that they were dangerous and that there had been narrow escapes, which might have developed into serious accidents to the party or to other people. He would hope, if he might venture to say so much, that this example would not be followed, or at any rate not without the utmost caution and having a second man to help.

The Rev. G. Broke wished to endorse what the last speaker had said, as for fifteen years he had been doing much the same on a small scale. He had introduced eleven recruits to climbing. The ominous thing that struck him in the paper was the speed at which the boys moved for recruits. To study safety entirely the normal time taken by a party with guides must at any difficulty be doubled. He had more than once found that with every pre-caution climbing with recruits meant coming home late. It meant choosing peaks with great care and having a second man. Mr. Irving's nerves must have been exceptional if he had no anxious moments and slept after an expedition was over. He had known himself twice quite collapse on getting back to grass after greater difficulties than he had expected.

Dr. Longstaff thanked Mr. Irving for his paper, chiefly because it was controversial. He had raised some interesting questions. He did not think members would agree with him about the advisability of such expeditions.

Mr. C. Schuster was personally interested in the matter as a commoner of Winchester. He hoped that in future recruits would not be provided in this way. It would be sad for the Club if it were taken to be their view that expeditions such as that on the Grand Combin, which had been described in the paper, were expeditions fit for boys.* He did not think it less than his duty to say a few words of protest against such a form of mountaineering as had been presented to them in the paper.

The President proposed a vote of thanks to Mr. Irving for his paper, which was heartily passed.

Mr. Irving, in reply, remarked that the Grand Combin had offered good snow, not an ice-slope, and that on the Dent Perroc there had been no sensational climbing, though it was not dull.

* It was obvious that any slip on the ice-slope would have resulted in disaster to the party, and that a slip was more than likely.

CORRESPONDENCE

'FIVE YEARS WITH RECRUITS'

A DISCLAIMER.

We, the undersigned members of the Alpine Club, desire to place on record that we disclaim responsibility for any encouragement which the publication of Mr. Irving's paper may give to expeditions undertaken after the manner therein described:–

G. W. PROTHERO.	E. H. F. BRADBY.
C. H. R. WOLLASTON.	EDW. A. BROOME.
CLAUD SCHUSTER.	W. E. DAVIDSON.
G. WINTHROP YOUNG.	A. W. LLOYD.
C. W. NETTLETON.	GEORGE L. STEWART.
TOM G. LONGSTAFF.	SYDNEY SPENCER.
W. P. HASKETT SMITH.	DOUGLAS W. FRESHFIELD.

The College, Winchester: February 4.

To the Hon. Secretary of the Alpine Club.

Dear Sir, – I should like to express my gratitude for the courtesy which permitted me to see Mr. Prothero's communication before my paper went to press.

When Mr. Yeld offered to have it printed in the *Alpine Journal* I accepted willingly, and I can see no reason whatever for altering my decision. At the same time I should like to add my name to the list of gentlemen who 'disclaim responsibility for any encouragement which the publication of my paper may give to expeditions undertaken after the manner therein described'. I regret very much the lengths to which the discussion has been carried. The reasons for my choosing such a subject were, firstly, that it *was* a controversial one; secondly, that the method of my climbing was the only aspect of it that appeared to be either novel or adventurous. My paper is a record of my climbs, and the impressions I have received from them during the last five years, and therefore seems to me very legitimate material for the *Journal*. In no sense whatever do I wish to pose as a general advocate of my methods. But, while admitting the greatest respect for the opinion of the climbers whose names accompany Mr. Prothero's protest, I maintain that the risks attached to climbing, whether with novices or with experienced men, can only be correctly estimated by an accurate knowledge of the ground covered, of the conditions prevailing at the time, and, above all, of the capabilities of the individuals. We have been fortunate, and we have been at times indiscreet, but the pages of the *Alpine Journal* itself tell me that the signatories themselves have been in Fortune's debt. And I must state my conviction that there is hardly a single member of the Club who has spent several years in making first-class expeditions who has not found himself in positions of greater peril than myself and my recruits the first two years. I know men of many years' experience whom I should refuse to accompany without guides on the same expeditions which we undertook in those years. Experience counts for much, but it is not – and never will be – a *sufficient* criterion of a climber's value on the rope.

Lastly, let me add, in answer to a very reasonable objection to my 'methods', my firm belief that on every one of our early expeditions my 'recruits' would have been able to retrace their steps, had it been necessary, without my assistance.

I remain, Sir, very truly yours,

R. L. G. Irving.

✤ (From 'Proceedings of the Alpine Club and Correspondence', Vol. XXIV.)

G. L. Mallory

18 ✲ *Pages from a Journal*

France, Autumn 1916.

Dreariness, Monotony, Sloth! These I suppose should be the headings of
the new chapter. Truly the rains have come and the season of opaque mists;
the spells of long, damp waiting and cold inaction. An adjustment is
necessary. Perhaps G.H.Q. will oblige with a pamphlet, 'Rules for the
sober fortitude of those who prefer excitement'. How *do* men exist, I
wonder, the zest of action almost extinguished? 'Boredom', that odious
and too common word! do they go back simply to that? Thank God, I'm
not bored. Perhaps men only pretend to be bored because they think it
unmanly to be childishly amused; secretly perhaps they indulge visions of
delight. In any case I'll be nothing but grateful for my visions – grateful for
the supreme good fortune of Alpine memories. I can look long at my
mountains without being bored. And yet it is not wholly satisfying merely
to look at them. However sharply I distinguish those mountain-scenes a
certain vagueness remains to be dispersed. And why not clear it up – see
one vision clearly in its true perspective of deeper suggestion? I will record
for my own intenser light, one splendid day, all the facts and thoughts, as I
remember them now, completely and exactly. Facts and thoughts! a mere
jumble at first sight as I look back. Do the facts exist for me independently?
If I view them detachedly, as historically happening to historical people,
the Graham, the Harry and the me of five years ago, they seem to lose
their significance, to have no interest for me, no meaning. I can bring myself
with an effort to think about them like that, but it is not so that I remember
them. They passed into my mind, not as things that I witnessed, but as
thoughts that came to me. What more after all are the events of life than
moments in the stream of thought, which is experience? It is the experience,
in this sense, of an Alpine expedition that I want to recall. But can I recall
it? As the day even now begins to take more definite shape before me, I find
not only reasoned thoughts such as may easily be expressed in words, but
thought less tangible, less precise, thought that would rather be called
feeling. A stream of feeling I seem to recall. But am I feeling now what I
felt then? I can't be sure of that. Perhaps, through the strange contrast
between those scenes and this world about me, my present emotion is

further from the cold light of reason; I am troubled by the marvellous reappearance of so much lost beauty, so many loved shapes. And then, being human, I am subject to change; each day the sum of experience adds up to a different total. Decidedly the total of today is not that of five years ago; probably an emotion can never be exactly repeated or reproduced; the same chords may be struck, the music has altered tones. And yet there is ultimate truth in experience recalled – if not quite recaptured. It is only from what was originally thought and felt that any present emotion exists. The past may live again – with a difference; and what lives is true. And if I am condemned, in spite of all my remembrance, to see that day through the more travelled eyes of now, it can only live for me again through those other eyes – the eyes of one who stood in the sun and looked upwards with fear and hope, and who sat in the shade of rocks with half a world beneath his feet; I must stand where *he* stood in the sun, sit where *he* sat in the shade; inhabit the places where he most intently thought and felt and there look through his eyes.

Up and beyond a great tower of rock, not long after mid-day, he surveyed the first stage of the expedition duly accomplished. The efforts of climbing had been exhausting; now his limbs were folded restfully against the rocks where he lay niched beneath a granite wall; their dragging weight no longer counted. An unconsciousness almost of sleep had all his tired body and his spirit had the freedom of dreams.

The hewn forms on every side defined themselves insistently, there was pain in seeing them so acutely, like seeing suddenly into a man's soul, full of strange beauty and sorrow. The walls of a vast couloir guarding this side of the Brenva; the Brenva glacier itself, and beyond; the Péteret – all this world of white and black and blue loomed more and more fantastic. He seemed to hear the hiss of a monster steam-saw cutting the titanic members for a world of ice and rocks. Then came utter riot and chaos. He opened his eyes again and saw things normally. A spirit of insolence took him. Those straight-cut rocks beyond the basin of snow, how smooth and steep! probably vertical! They meant to be terrible. Yet men existed, he would wager, able to conquer them, who would, perhaps, scale them . . . And the Brenva (he noted the exact curve with which the ice arête hit the slope) . . . what was it? A staircase for men to walk up and down. Lies, all lies! To think at all of mountains in such terms was a lie. The whole mood was a lie, mean, vaunting, blasphemous . . . The dignity and peace of mountains from height to depth, from sunlight to shadow! The still glory of such a host, unmasked and beautiful! All the patience and wisdom of the ages seemed to be graven here, all the courage and endurance and all the travail. These forms had listened to the jar of terrible discords and the music of gentle voices; had seen the hard strokes of cruelty and the for-giving gesture of pity. They could be greatly troubled yet splendidly serene, they could threaten but also smile. These faces hid the depths of doubt and faith, of hate and love. They knew the energy of doing and the calm of repose; the stormy tossing of endeavour and the even keel of achievement; they knew the shades of care and the frank way of kindly laughter; anxiety and the quiet reaches of thought; slow pain and swift delight. They knew, changing with snow and wind and sun, the flicker of quick response to a thousand moods, and, with all this complex heart, had the strength of great resolves unchanging; a constant spirit immutably clean and true – and friendly. Here tortured pride, perhaps, would find the 'infinite wrath and infinite despair'; but here, too, among the mountains would be found infinite hope and steps for children's feet . . . Unchanging, and so still! Had the great heart stopped beating? Were the eternal whisperings silent? He saw three figures on a mountain's limb, flies on the carved thigh of a giant, waiting. Would they move again? It seemed more fitting that they should stay there always, himself in his rocky niche and the others perched just so. He became aware of a companion close at hand – Graham, preparing some soup. There was a purpose here; they would be going forward again presently and up. Was it this man's will – his own seemed to have no part in the matter – or was it a kind of destiny, something which they all obeyed necessarily?

Go on? Yes, perhaps; granted for the moment the possibility of that. But by what sort of miracle had he got so far? He went back to the ideas of yesterday. From more than one point of view Graham and he had gazed upon this limb of Mont Maudit, on the very place where they now were most intently; for wasn't it the knot of the whole expedition? They had prophesied no great difficulties below the tower, and that could surely be circumvented one way or another; the most formidable obstacle, as it appeared from below, was the steep rock wall above; but it ought to 'go' – this wonderful granite was always split somewhere; they would find a way. So they had talked; but for him, and for Graham too no doubt, the features of this expedition had taken tremendous shapes in the unspoken mind. Had he not gone to bed with toes and fingers tingling, tremulous, expectant, half-afraid, yet filled with the thought of a great hope to be realized! And how dismay had followed his first sensations of the early morning! The cause of the trouble lay in that innocent-looking meal over-night – pleasant meal, eaten in high spirits and with little jests that sparkled in the mirror of mountain friendships. Sour wine or dirty water? it had been a difficult choice after a dry day. He didn't blame himself for choosing wine, and decidedly not for immoderate potations of that discouraging beverage. Nevertheless, disaster came of the sour wine, new wine it was said to be. Damn new wine! What a shadow had fallen on his dreams when he woke in the morning and knew that his stomach was upset. He had made a start as a matter of course, not that he thought it anywise possible to go far that day, but it was necessary to demonstrate the impossibility. They had started punctually in the first light, about four o'clock. He was very glad of that; he wouldn't easily forgive himself for delaying a start. But in the very first steps over the almost level snow of the Col du Géant how heavily his legs had dragged, and what a weak, incompetent performance since. And yet what an ideal start! No track-hunting by lantern light, not a step of troublesome moraine, not even a dry glacier – not that such things hadn't their places too, but they belonged to a less elevated order. Today a splendid field of snow had led them from the outset to this great world of wonders; only one other start in his memory, for the grandeur of the scene and for pure physical joy, ought to be compared to that – when two of the same party had started for the Dent Blanche from the Col de Bertol. But that glorious snow-field was an Alpine highway. Today, from the moment when they had turned over the lip and down into the deep basin below the Col de la Tour Ronde, had been distinguished by their seeming to have severed themselves even from the haunts of climbers. He had noticed these sensations rather than enjoyed them. Not much physical delight had come to him. As they mounted towards the col it had seemed impossible even to climb so far. While still on the gentle snow, before they had begun seriously to ascend, it had come to him bitterly how different from the living dreams of yesterday was the dead reality. Hopes! there was no room for hope. It was degrading to be the slave of mere physical conditions; he hated as a personal enemy the domination of the material. And yet he had succeeded in thinking only of how to struggle on and how not to be sick.

So it had been with almost unbroken continuity up to the time of their first halt. The choice of route had come up among them and afforded a passing interest. Their ideas had seemed rather hazy as to where exactly was the Col de la Tour Ronde; but what did it matter? The arête leading to their desired buttress seemed accessible at many points on that side, and the obvious line was the nearest to their objective; there had been no great difficulty in reaching a shallow couloir, and once attained this simple channel had brought them out on the buttress well above the arête. A short discussion about falling stones had condemned the couloir for the purpose of retreat; even that small flutter of interest had served to break the spell and been strangely exhilarating – as though there were really a question of playing today that old game with the mountains. But the time had been long – nearly three hours from the start – for what seemed no great achievement, and when they disposed themselves at last for breakfast he had still no thoughts beyond his heart-breaking sensations – of lifting bars of lead and tugging bags of ore a long way up over snow and rocks.

Breakfast had been a lengthy meal – or rather it had provided a long halt, an hour and a quarter instead of the usual forty minutes – prolonged by a misadventure, if misadventure it was; a stone inadvertently dislodged had upset the seething mess of porridge. Graham, notorious the Alps over for an irrepressible passion for brewing things, had been distinctly annoyed though not very expressively – as indeed he had every right to be, since he, evidently, was to bear the brunt of whatever might turn up – and had at once re-established the pot with additions of snow and oats. Harry, however, had shown much sympathy for the author of the delay; perhaps he had experienced a spasm of not quite regretting it; and his attitude had contrived to establish or at all events to foreshadow an alliance of weakness, not that Harry had any need for such, but he had a way of staking out a claim in advance, a sort of insurance against the frailty of human nature; so here would be an ear open in the last resort. It was a comfortable feeling.

But there was more comfort than that. There was rest, not the least of the rewards. And there was beauty. He didn't precisely feel that these places were more beautiful than others. What use in comparing absolutes except to appreciate quality? This was conspicuously unlike many of the most beautiful mountain scenes, which are often dominated by the sheer lyrical force or the rugged magnificence of a single peak – so that one *must* look at the Weisshorn, it may be, or the Matterhorn, or the Dent Blanche. Here an enchanted host surrounded him. Probably every one who knew them had a place apart, as he had, in the imagination for the great members of Mont Blanc; their spell captured and held his mind during the first halt; not only the impression of what he immediately saw, beautiful as it was, but the sense of all that was suggested and could be said actually to be present because there seemed to be no limits. Therefore, so long as he had stayed just looking and wondering, feeling breadth and height and space, the personal question had been put aside. The end was still unthinkable; he had banished all agitating speculation on that head, not caring to be perplexed. To be there! nothing else mattered. And though no hope of the expedition had been born then, he had received an assurance of the day. The great thing had happened; the spirit had its flight; and the rest must take care of itself.

The problems of action, however, had their whole alarming value when the party moved on again. Breakfast, so far as he was concerned, had not been a success. He cast no aspersions upon the victuals; but with him they had been unfortunate. He had acquired no strength for what lay ahead. Graham went in front as before, and himself next on the rope. Rocks and snow were in good condition, and they were helped by the fierce little points of their crampons. For a long distance no big cause of delay kept them back. For him it had been chiefly a matter of keeping up – easier on rocks where his arms could help. Occasionally a more difficult passage had allowed him to wait while the leader went on alone and while Harry came up after him. But neither of them wasted time. He had moments of wishing that these men of steel could show some signs of fatigue, but their attitude discouraged weariness. It had been a relief to come upon a narrow arête; the angle was less steep and it was not a place to hurry.

Then they had been confronted by the great tower. It was a climax; a blessed climax! The old mountain was showing fight. Graham had invited his counsel; he had taken heart of that grace; to be consulted fitted in with his formulae for himself. He had a passion for projecting possible routes and always held a view about the best line. It had been evident almost at first sight that they could turn this obstacle on the left. Graham had pointed out that way. But it would take time to cut steps round there and they would still have to regain the crest beyond; which might prove difficult. To Graham's deliberations he had therefore suggested an alternative plan. From their position they might climb on to a conspicuous shoulder on the right side of the gendarme; and from there they would be able to judge whether it was possible to make a way along that side, or even, conceivably, to climb over the top. Half an hour might be wasted, but they stood to save much more than that if an easy alternative was found. This suggestion had been adopted; but the half-hour had slipped away with no good result. They had then proceeded to turn the tower on its left side – a matter quite happily accomplished, though not without a struggle up a steep little chimney before they had gained access to their present halting-place. It was while Graham was cutting steps for the traverse that an unheard-of and almost unthinkable thing had happened. The second man, planted on a ledge, and hugging the rock round which he was belaying the rope, had fallen asleep. He had been woken by the sound of Harry's voice (Harry was round a corner) warning him to pay out the leader's rope. How long had he slept? Perhaps only for a few seconds – not longer in any case than since the rope was last paid out. Harry had been amused and sympathetic, and Graham had made light of the incident. But that didn't alter the fact. He had slept at his post – a responsible post too. So far as concerned the rope, he was inclined to think that, if a pull *had* come, he would have worked the belay instinctively: but if he had fallen . . .

He was going over all this in his mind as he lay in his niche facing the great tower. It had been a tale of incompetence all along. He had just let slip the handle of the boiler which was now, presumably, lying at the bottom of the black shaft between his feet – if there was a bottom to it. He was particularly annoyed by this act of folly. 'No care,' he was saying to himself, 'no care.' But in this mood another question had to be decided. That lapsed half-hour! It was clear enough as he saw it that the right side of the gendarme (left side as he looked back at it now) was impassable – a sheer, slippery precipice. Had that suggestion of his been as foolish as it looked? Had his judgement as a mountaineer been at fault? It had not been an occasion to throw away half an hour lightly. He confessed that it had been a chimerical sort of hope that entertained at all the idea of climbing over the top; it was in too icy a state just where one wanted it clean. And mightn't he have inferred those steep walls from the structure of the crest? He became convinced that in his suggestion had lurked a personal motive. The sequel proved it. Why had exhaustion overcome him exactly there and then? True, it had seemed to him a very strenuous half-hour: but it wasn't only that; it wasn't merely a physical fact that he had succumbed to sleep; it must be interpreted as the collapse of 'moral'. And it came just then quite naturally as a reaction. He had wanted a supreme exhilaration; it was for that he had harboured the hope of a steeper way, more sensational. Such a way might possibly have been found; and the stimulus of such to the imagination and to the nerves would, he felt sure, have kept him going.

But what was to keep him going now? – since evidently he was fated to go on. The course of these reflections brought him sharply back to face that problem, the immediate problem which must be resolved. He couldn't any longer proceed like an automaton; that way had been tried and failed. A change of mind, or rather a change of heart, was wanted. The day, if it were to be saved, must save him; he must feel its full Alpine significance. Somehow he must be strung up afresh to the task; emphatically some stimulus was required. But stimulus he felt was not to be had for the asking; one must proceed delicately to net that bird and feign indifference to his approach. His mood was still dominated by that strange incident on the traverse and the sense of his guilt. At all events nothing of that sort must occur again. He must establish a different state of being – for Graham and Harry if not for himself. His companions – what was their attitude in these circumstances? How were they looking at the whole expedition? How did they stand as a party?

It was a critical situation seen whole – not that they had yet met with anything like a reverse; the conditions had been singularly favourable – perfect weather; rocks and snow as one would wish to find them. It was proving an easier course than might have been expected. One formidable difficulty mentioned in the scanty records of the previous party had been dealt with very happily. All had gone well so far, undoubtedly. But how far? So much lay in that question. They had all along to reckon with the salient facts that the one party before them had been obliged to sleep on the mountain. It was chiefly a matter of time. They had made about half the height from the Col de la Tour Ronde to the place where they expected to reach the true arête of Mont Maudit. Put down four hours for that; it hadn't taken less. How long would the next stage take? The steepest section lay immediately ahead of them, and therefore presumably the pace for a time would be slower. Put that against the big tower, which had taken time, and cancel the rest; it would be foolish to count less than four hours to the arête. They were not expecting difficulties once the arête was gained to the top of Mont Maudit; that part might take an hour or it might take two. Allow an hour and a half for it – five hours and a half so far. By this calculation they ought to find themselves on the summit of Mont Maudit about six o'clock. So far as safety went that was not one of the most alarming prospects; they could presumably get down by the corridor without much difficulty even in this year of open glaciers and join, so to speak, the high road to Chamonix; with the sort of tracks they expected to find after those weeks of fine weather they could make the Grand Mulets almost in the dark. True the two and a half hours that might be called daylight, from 6 to 8.30 P.M., were not a very large margin for that performance. He broached the subject of time to his companions – but they put it off, for the best of reasons; there could be no question yet of retreat; they had still two hours at least before they must go on or sleep out. They could postpone considering time till the crisis arrived. (Perhaps, he thought, they would postpone it even then.) They were going forward now, and for the present his calculation was beside the point. Blessed Mont Blanc was their object and no Maudit Mont.

This simple reflection, now that he felt its force, seemed to work a miracle. Suddenly the required stimulus came and the change of heart; the spell of a great Alpine adventure took and held him. At last his fluttering thoughts had spread their wings and flown strongly to the summit. Here the three of them were sitting in the knot of all their difficulties; there lay the goal, a queen among mountains; there the white dome-like top so remotely poised. The clear features of that wonderland came to his eyes again; the tumbling waves of ice and blue precipices, winding glaciers wide and narrow, large rolling seas of snow, mysterious shy peaks and overbold ones, firm limbs of glowing rock, great sawing crests 'gat-toothed'. He now regarded these amazing phenomena with a sort of spiritual greed. Perhaps since food still had done nothing for him he was looking to the mountains simply for strength. These hewn creatures of ice and rock could inspire the most 'dull of soul'; he began somehow to feel strong. He had very different feelings now from those of half an hour ago. Yet these emotions could hardly be understood except as added to those; for those had been rather like worship without praise and these perhaps were the complement. He had felt the universe before rather as one within its clutch than as one living in it; – if 'a pulse in the eternal mind', then a pulse that didn't beat. His mood had changed now. A place for the feet of children? Yes: but the children must bestir themselves; they may still be children. His perception of the Universe had led him to heroics; he had travelled that old, old road; for isn't the passionate pilgrim a hero? He was re-established now in purpose and confidence; he had ceased to be the mere mainspring of a grumbling machine, of legs and arms that seemed hardly to belong to him; he was a man again, one of a party. It was no longer a case of being the least of a fool one could; he was prepared to play a part and there was a part to be played. His praise was that of one who functions sweetly and well – at least in spirit.

The battle in fact was more than half won from the moment this purpose and hope inspired him. It may be harder to think oneself to the top of a mountain than to pull oneself so far. Their knot still remained to cut, and physical problems had to be resolved. But his imagination overrode the details; he argued serenely that if he had won so high he could win the rest – poor reasoning perhaps, but largely true and justified in the result. The rocks helped magnificently. Like the shell of a walnut pinched with exactly the correct strength the surface of the mountain, cracked delicately but firmly, presented convenient fissures. The tired man could have met nothing more suitable. So many muscles could be charged with the task! A method of heaving against the legs, like an oarsman, often helped him up surprisingly. In all it was exhilarating work. He had a sense of splendid combination; the rope was never in the way; the party was moving rhythmically; there was delight in the long reaching up and swift, eager advance. It was sufficiently swift; they had slightly overrated the distance perhaps, but they found themselves within hail of the crest in no more than an hour and a quarter and in half an hour more they were on it. The crest, however, was not gained without surmounting a difficult pitch – there was a climax, a pause, and, for him, a fresh crop of deliberations. He was standing in one of the final steps, hewn in the ice by Graham with infinite 'verve', which led up to a steep rock wall some twenty feet high. The wall presented itself in continuation of their stairway, so there was no gauging the obstacle till it was fairly reached. Would it go? And if not? The summit of Mont Blanc was a long way off; they still wanted all their time. An alternative might, and surely would, be found if necessary; but no other way had commended itself as simple and none was likely to be so short as this one. The issue would be decided by saving precious moments: there was every chance of wasting them in plenty. And was the party absolutely safe? The waiting strain emphasized his own exhaustion. His physical faith was staunch. But he experienced the conjectures that almost simulate doubt though the mind's trust too may be steadfast. He had no particle of doubt now; he stood absolutely for Graham with a crowd of recollections. Still, it was an uncomfortable place. The rocks, which came down just to his level, offered no belay, and not much holding for the one hand able to grasp them; and the ice-axe was no help. Not much chance, even for a strong man, of fielding the leader. And no better position offered unless a large platform were to be hewn up there from which to poke the first man into safety. It was nothing so very alarming or sensational after all – a tense moment, no more. But he came to see then, with peculiar clearness, what a fine ethic it was that bade him make a duty of these sombre conjectures and duly weigh them; put them alongside his trust for the leader and pass judgement. For the second man, besides ensuring the leader's safety in life and limb with every conceivable precaution, has also the party to defend, for the safety of all, against the leader's possible errors. Besides staking his uttermost farthing on that man he has positively to keep his conscience.

They paused on the arête – it can't be said that they halted – paused for a slackening of muscles and to gauge the situation. They looked up at the snow-slope rising in front of them to the summit of Mont Maudit, and saw that it was good – hard snow and not too steep; their crampons would easily deal with that surface. At three o'clock they were moving up again. For him the physical problem now presented a new form, and more disquieting. The difficulty had seemed chiefly to be in the weakness of his legs; he had been saved from utter disgrace before by the accommodating way of the mountain which had enabled him to use four limbs for hoisting. But now he could use only two. More than ever it had become a question of keeping up. Happily he remained supremely undepressed. A confidence that the day was won already dawned; the horizon had cleared. Moreover he derived comfort from observing his companions; they were beginning to lose that masterly air of being physically equal to everything. To his sharpened eye for such qualities it was remarkable that Graham lingered now and then in his step; and Harry had reached the stage of emitting significant sounds. Since his own trouble rapidly came to a point when the legs unaided refused categorically to make the required push, these signs (they were not omens) from his companions encouraged his pride and strengthened his faith that a way would be found. A way *was* found. The arms again came to the rescue. He drove in the axe's pick at a convenient height; and, with the inner hand pressing on the shaft, was able to pull himself up; the device succeeded beyond hope; it seemed as though an invisible machine were helping him; with each step at the moment of transferring the balance his hands were somehow caught and he was drawn quietly upwards. The monotonous machine seemed tired but worked sufficiently. Monotony was in the essence of this method; only he felt by a slow, repeated rhythm could he reach the summit.

They lay at last on the broad welcome spaces of the Col de la Brenva. It was a place of safety and enjoyment, wide and comfortable. Such noble amplitude was due from Mont Blanc. The divine sculptor, as Gibbon might have observed, after laboriously carving a multitude of gigantic shapes seemed in a moment of serene satisfaction to have designed a high imperial couch of purest snow. Here they must lie in delicious ease to stretch hard-worked muscles, to enjoy the high value of well-earned repose, and to drain the sunny cup of pleasure in contented peace. Much lay behind and beneath them. They had reached a brink of things – of all that lay, beyond sight, on the Brenva side falling into that steep Italian valley, and of the long slopes of snow and glacier stretching into France and into the lovely vale of Chamonix. Northwards lay all the spiky bed of aiguilles; to the S. the smooth white dome. How near they were to fulfilling all their hopes! They had but to put out their hands and take the crown offered. This pause, it might seem, had been given them to taste beforehand the final triumph in full confidence of anticipation; and to rejoice without restraint in the full measure of achievement. Any party that reaches the Col de la Brenva from Mont Maudit or still more from the Brenva Glacier must halt here with peculiar satisfaction. Perhaps, because thoughts of achievement would be scarce decent on the summit, one is presented with the opportunity of thinking them here. For his own part it was by no means wasted. However, in the course of pleasurable anticipation the white lump at some moments seemed alarmingly big. His companions did not pretend that it was small. But there remained with the party a certain sparkle of energy, a brightness of eye, a keenness of scent; they still were alert before action, quick, happy, present-minded; they ate to serve a practical need rather than any refinement of taste; and they had the buoyancy of fair prospects and noble promise – perhaps even the fine carelessness of assured winners when in the last lap sighting the goal.

They had halted on the col at 6.10 P.M. or a little later. Not too many hours remained to reach the summit and descend before dark. But enough, oh! yes, enough; they were well agreed on that point. If they kept going the result was not in question. And what doubt they would keep on? The alternative, however, was suggested among them – the descent by the Corridor; a prospect clearly of ignoble ease, but quite seriously suggested on account of the weakest member. Shame couldn't have allowed him to accept such a proposal. They had trusted him so much! He was proud to be there; he would be proud to the end. They must trust him for the rest.

After forty minutes they were moving on again towards the Mur de la Côte. The great dome of Mont Blanc was fairly fronting them at last, theirs to win with stout hearts in a fair white field. But he no longer felt as they went forward the full zest of struggle. The way was easy; and he was confident of strength now, for the poison had lost its power and he had eaten food. The end was too certain. He was calm and a little sceptical. He began to fear an anticlimax, a disappointment in things attained. Wasn't it like a slice of bread and jam, the last unjammed portion? Wasn't the adventure ended and this merely a depressing fatigue? But in the mere act of firmly planting the feet he found an answer to that last doubt; at each step upward and steeper there throbbed a dim faith refuting the heresy. The spirit didn't come so far to slip all down to nothing; all parts of such experience were significant; the dream stretched to the very end.

A breeze cool and bracing seemed to gather force as they plodded up the long slopes, more gentle now as they approached the final goal. He felt the wind about him with its old strange music. His thoughts became less conscious, less continuous. Rather than thinking or feeling he was simply listening – listening for distant voices scarcely articulate ... The solemn dome resting on those marvellous buttresses, fine and firm above all its chasms of ice, its towers and crags; a place where desires point and aspirations end; very, very high and lovely, long-suffering and wise ... *Experience,* slowly and wonderfully filtered; at the last a purged remainder ... And what is that? What more than the infinite knowledge that it is all worth while – all one strives for? ... How to get the best of it all? One must conquer, achieve, get to the top; one must know the end to be convinced that one can win the end – to know there's no dream that mustn't be dared ... Is this the summit, crowning the day? How cool and quiet! We're not exultant; but delighted, joyful; soberly astonished ... Have we vanquished an enemy? None but ourselves. Have we gained success? That word means nothing here. Have we won a kingdom? No ... and yes. We have achieved an ultimate satisfaction ... fulfilled a destiny ... To struggle and to understand – never this last without the other; such is the law ... We've only been obeying an old law then? Ah! but it's *the* law ... and we understand – a little more. So ancient, wise and terrible – and yet kind we see them; with steps for children's feet.

✻ (From 'Mont Blanc From The Col Du Géant By The Eastern Buttress Of Mont Maudit' by G. L. Mallory. Vol. XXXII.)

Frank Smythe

19 ❊ A Bad Day on the Schreckhorn

On July 30, 1925, Bell and I arose early from our beds in the comfortable
Strahlegg hut intending to attempt a previously planned route up the Klein
Fiescherhorn. A badly swollen ankle prevented Bell from starting. I
accordingly joined forces with Messrs. Douglas and Harrison in an assault
on the Schreckhorn. The morning was fine and calm as we trudged up the
easy rocks of Gagg and across the snow slopes to the Schreckfirn. Yet
there was a warmth in the air which boded ill. A wild, hurried dawn greeted
us on the Schreckfirn. Yet scarcely had the rays lit the snow wall of the
Fiescherhörner when it was superseded by a weird greenish glow. None of
us had seen such a sunrise. Far beyond the foothills of the Oberland the
plain of Berne was drowned in a green haze. Everywhere we looked the
green colour predominated. It was a portent, beautiful but evil. We were
foolish to disregard it. I have since spoken to Dr. A. Russell, the noted
expert on thunderstorms and their attendant phenomena. He told me that
these 'green ray' sunrises are not unknown to scientists, who do not,
however, understand their cause. One thing only is certain, and that is they
almost invariably precede exceptionally unpleasant weather; I can vouch
for it. It is a curious fact that the colour in question was identical with that
emitted by a Crookes' vacuum tube, though whether there is any connection it is as yet impossible to say. A few days later Bell and I were
crossing the Grünhornlücke en route to the Agassizjoch when we witnessed
a stormy sunrise with a distinct greenish tinge about it. Without argument,
we at once abandoned our plan and turned off to the Finsteraarhorn hut.
We were justified, for a thunderstorm and blizzard developed with extraordinary rapidity. It was this storm that killed a German on the easy slopes
of the Rottalsattel. On the present occasion, however, the weather appeared
reasonably good otherwise; only a few smooth, oily clouds, far detached
from the world, suggested evil, while away in the far south a massive range
of cumuli brooded over the Pennines.

   Our route up the Schreckhorn was by the S.W. arête. Bell and I had
ascended this arête two days previously on our traverse by the Schreck-
horn-Lauteraarhorn ridge. In my opinion it is much more interesting than
the ordinary way, but I should not hesitate to define it as a more difficult

climb. In my own case, however, it is difficult to judge. I climbed the Schreckhorn by the ordinary Schreckjoch route under exceptionally good conditions in 1923, whilst last year it was exactly the reverse.

To attain the crest of the S.W. arête it is necessary to climb a wide couloir that drops on the S. side of the arête to the Schreckfirn. Messrs. Wicks, Wilson, and Bradby who first climbed this ridge mention a red buttress by which they ascended. This buttress is formed by the rocks of the W. wall of the couloir. The couloir, however, appealed to us as being quicker. It is also in normal conditions probably the easier alternative and quite safe from falling stones.

Plodding across the Schreckfirn we crossed the bergschrund by a good bridge and attacked the ice slope above. Cutting across to the left we reached easy rocks which brought us without trouble into the couloir above the steep and icy rock wall over which it drops at its base.

Conditions had changed considerably during the two days since my previous ascent. Where we had found hard snow and dry rocks there was now ice and verglas. Progress over the icy slabs that formed the bed of the couloir was slow. It was a place not so much technically difficult as requiring great care. According to Douglas the work was not unlike that on the traverses below the Z'Mutt ridge on the Matterhorn. We mounted steadily to the foot of a long snow patch. This snow patch helped us considerably for a while. Higher up the snow thinned down to ice and impending rocks forced us to the left. The rocks at the head of the couloir were more pleasant than the smooth slabs lower down, but they were more difficult; and though there was far less verglas, what there was usually covered the best holds. At 7 A.M. we gained the crest of the arête and sat down to second breakfast. The weather did not look promising, the clouds in the S. were massing in ugly grey battalions; but over the Oberland the sun smiled kindly as yet. Bad weather was undoubtedly in the offing, but everything pointed to its holding off for some hours. By the time it did come we confidently expected to have traversed the mountain and be off all difficulties. The morning was still remarkably warm and windless.

We did not linger over breakfast and were soon off again. The S.W. arête of the Schreckhorn is composed of sound and rough rock. It is indeed a joy to climb. In places it is steep, but the holds are always there in bountiful profusion. Climbing quickly and for the most part all together, progress was enjoyable and rapid on this splendid arête.

The storm came with incredible rapidity. We were less than 500 ft. from the summit when we heard the first roll of thunder, and looking round saw a dark wall of cloud with leaden hail trailing at its skirts rushing up from the N.W. We at once looked round for shelter and were able to climb down to a small ledge partially protected by an overhanging rock a few feet below the crest of the ridge. Our ice-axes were left behind lying in a patch of snow.

Within ten minutes the storm was upon us. First we heard the bombardment as the storm-clouds reached the Eiger; without a pause they rushed across to wreak their fury on the Schreckhorn. They came with an insane squall of hail and tremendous cracks of thunder. Every few seconds the lightning struck the ridge above with a rending, tearing *bang*. After one particularly brilliant flash that seemed to flame all round us, accompanied by a terrific report, there was another crash and a mass of rock dislodged by the lightning fell to the left of us. We looked at each other. All we could do was to hope for the best. An appreciable time after the initial bang of the discharge would come the long roll of echoes from peak to peak, booming in tremendous waves of sound from the cliffs of the Lauteraarhorn. It was terrible, but it was also magnificent.

Meanwhile hail fell steadily. The air was full of it, we could see but a few yards. Our ledge afforded but slight protection, but the weather as yet was warm and we were reasonably comfortable.

The storm lasted for about an hour; when it had gone we climbed back to the ridge where we were greeted by a glimpse of blue sky and a wan fugitive sun. Our ice-axes we found uninjured, much to our relief.

On the ridge we held a short council of war. If we went on we should have an easier descent, but we should be on an exposed ridge for at least two to three hours. To be caught by another thunderstorm on or near the summit of the Schreckhorn, with the added possibility of really bad weather into the bargain, was not to be thought of. The rocks, moreover, were covered with the newly fallen hail and progress must of necessity be slow. To retreat by the way we had come would be the more difficult but shorter. In the circumstances we decided on retreat. We started down the ridge moving as fast as possible. Progress, however, was not rapid for the rocks were covered in half-melted hail.

We had nearly reached the point where it is necessary to turn down into the couloir when again storm-clouds blew up from the N.W. Like the first storm the second developed with extraordinary rapidity. We had barely turned off the ridge down the head of the couloir when it was on us in a blinding *tourmente* of snow and hail, snarling wind, and crashing thunder. There was no previous indication of the electrical tension. Ice-axes and metal objects did not hiss. The charged clouds were blown at great speed against the mountain and as soon as they were near enough discharged their electrical energy.

Douglas and Harrison were below me moving carefully over the difficult rocks when there was a blinding glare and a terrible explosion. I received a stunning blow on the head as if I had been sandbagged. For a second or so I was more or less completely knocked out, and but for the rope, which I had previously belayed securely round a rock, I might have fallen and dragged the party to disaster. When I recovered my wits sufficiently to move down, fits of trembling supervened. It was with difficulty that I could control my limbs. No doubt the nerve centres were affected. Considering the violence of the discharge and the terrific report which accompanied it, the shock I received was without doubt only the secondary effect of the flash. A direct hit must have been fatal. Even the secondary or 'corona' effects of a lightning discharge may be fatal to life. Dr. Russell tells me that had my clothes been dry I would in all probability not have survived such a powerful shock. Fortunately we had been well damped by the first storm and the electrical fluid naturally ran down my wet clothes in preference to the body. As is well known a high frequency current utilizes only the surface of a conductor. This peculiarity is known to electrical engineers as the 'skin effect'. In my case my 'skin' for electrical purposes was represented by my clothes.

For the next hour or so our progress was painfully slow, less on my account than owing to the ferocity of the storm which reached a pitch I had never before experienced in such a situation. We were in imminent danger of being blown off the mountain. For minutes at a time we could barely cling on while the wind roared by beating us with hail and snow until we were sheathed in ice from head to foot. Worst of all, the hail left by the first storm had partially melted, and now the bitter wind was freezing it on the rocks in sheets of ugly verglas which in turn was being covered by evil flour-like snow. The only alternative to the horrible icy slabs was the ridge and buttress forming the W. wall of the couloir, but this the lightning was hitting with unfailing regularity, and the wind would have blown us off like flies. No, the couloir was the sole way. There, at least, was a certain amount of shelter, though there was always the risk of falling stones dislodged by lightning. Once we were out of direct danger of being actually hit by lightning we gave up worrying over it. Yet never shall I forget the fearful rending bangs for all the world like Mills' bombs magnified many times just above or to the left of us. Suddenly above the howl of the *tourmente* came the sound of falling rocks. The fall occurred down the E. wall of the couloir, but we barely noticed it, though had we been 100 ft. lower we should have been wiped out.

A slip was not to be thought of; steadiness was essential. Never did Douglas or Harrison falter, their progress was mechanical rather than human in its certainty. It is only thus that a party caught by weather of this description on an exposed and difficult place can hope to get down in safety. Whether we could stick it out was not so much the question as whether the storm would *allow* us to stick it out.

Often we were dependent on the rope. Several times I could neither find a hold nor feel what I was hanging on to. On these occasions I was forced to let myself slide, braking with my axe on the icy slabs, an evolution known in climbing parlance by the expressive term 'scrabbling'; but always

Harrison was below, a tower of strength to gather me to his bosom in fatherly manner at the end of the 'scrabble'.

At length we were off the upper rocks and could cut across an ice slope to the long patch of snow. There we could kick steps and move all together. The exercise was more warming than crawling down the icy slabs. The storm, however, increased in fury. We were unable to see where we were going, or each other, owing to the blinding clouds of powdery snow that came pouring down from the cliffs above until they would be caught by the hurricane, and whirled furiously back in writhing, suffocating columns.

Knowing the route better than the others I undertook to go first. With faces to the slope and axes well driven home at every step we slowly struggled down to the safety that seemed so far away. So blinding was the drift that the holds kicked by me were immediately obliterated, and Harrison as next man had perforce to make his own. We were often unable to see each other, though separated by only a yard or so, and two or three times I felt Harrison's boot on my head as he moved down a step, quite unaware that I was immediately below.

We were not more than half-way down. In three hours we had not descended 500 ft. of the couloir. The storm was increasing rather than decreasing in fury. It was bitterly cold. Finally we could barely move at all, and for minutes at a time it was as much as we could do to prevent ourselves being blown from our holds. I remember well the weird noise made by the wind as it came rushing up the couloir. Sometimes it fell upon us with a furious demented screech. At others it approached with the roar of an express train in a tunnel. Now and again it struck with a boom like thunder. We began to realize that our chances of survival, if things went on as they did, were not very bright. The forced inaction was telling. Soon the wind would numb unless we could keep moving.

Then Providence intervened. The wind moderated. The mist swept away for a few moments. We could see the route down. Somebody suggested some chocolate. The effect was great. It brought warmth and renewed determination to get down, come what might. So on we went leaving the snow for the interminable ice-sheeted slabs where nearly every hold had to be hacked out with the axe.

Presently the storm came roaring back like a giant in anger, but not with the same fury as before. We were able to go on moving, albeit with difficulty. So for a total of six hours we fought our way down a couloir not more than 1,000 ft. high, reaching at last the easier rocks and the ice slope above the bergschrund. On the ice slope our steps had been obliterated and we had to cut them anew, but what a joy to be able to cut into good honest ice after the hours of hacking, scraping, and groping on the horrible slabs. Not worrying about finding the bridge over the bergschrund, we sat down and one by one slid down and over, subsiding ungracefully into the soft snow of the glacier. There, with nothing but easy ground separating us from the hut, we shook hands, not without feeling, for it had been a very close thing, and turned for a moment to listen to the wild orchestra of the storm in the great crags above.

We were soon at the hut where we found Bell anxiously awaiting us. Had we not returned he was fully prepared to organize a search party before nightfall. As it was he was able to turn his organizing abilities into the preparation of a truly superb stew.

We all went down to Grindelwald next day where together with a large and jovial party of the S.M.C. we forgot our troubles and the weather in a huge feast of *pâtisserie*.

✳ (From 'Thunderstorms in the Alps' by F. S. Smythe. Vol. XXXVIII.)

T. Graham Brown

20 ✻ Route Major

The great Brenva face of Mont Blanc de Courmayeur and Mont Blanc had not been climbed between the line of Güssfeldt's ascent of the Aiguille Blanche de Pétéret and the line of the Brenva route until Smythe and I had the good fortune to discover the 'Sentinel' route in 1927. From the Col de Pétéret round to the Col de la Brenva the length of the crest must be but little short of 3 kilometres. The face below it forms a great amphitheatre which tumbles down to the W. bay of the upper Brenva Glacier. It is an intricate face, broken by great ribs. On the S. there is the colossal buttress of rock running up to Point 4244 m. on the Pétéret arête. From the inmost recess of the W. bay of the Brenva Glacier two lines of rock run up; one, more to the S., leads up between hanging ice walls and is apparently difficult of access at its base; one, more to the N., prominent and well defined, forms the right bank of the Great Couloir which descends from under the summit of Mont Blanc itself. Immediately to the N.E. of this couloir lie the twisting ridge and intricate outcrops of rock up which the 'Sentinel' route leads; again to the N.E. of this is another ridge near the base of which stands the 'Red Sentinel', and the top of which disappears in the ice slopes below the sérac wall to the S.W. of the Brenva route. Finally, the arête of the Brenva route itself conveniently forms the N.E. boundary of the face.

Every mountain climber who has looked on this face from the E. must have ascended in thought by one or other of these routes; and the idea of making the attempt must often have been entertained, as it is said to have been by Preuss, and by Grunewald and Bickhoff. G. W. Young and George Mallory examined a route here; and of all these possible routes undoubtedly the most striking is that leading up the long and steep ridge immediately to the S. of the Great Couloir. As seen in face from the N.E., this ridge is fascinating but forbidding. As seen more in profile from the S.E., from the Val Veni (as Herbert and I saw it), or from Mont Chétif, it is distorted by perspective and slopes back a little too alluringly. From either direction it is prominent and obvious; and after we had climbed the 'Sentinel' route and while we were discussing the possibilities of this great ridge, Smythe told me that Blakeney had pointed it out to him on a photograph – a good instance of mountaineering vision.

But when Smythe and I set out last year to see if a new route could be made on the Brenva face of Mont Blanc, our ideas of that face were ill-defined, and it was not until we had examined the upper part of the face itself from the Torino Hut that we could form any clear plans. The route which then first fixed our attention was this same ridge lying to the S. of the Great Couloir. The ridge terminates above in a huge buttress of rock crowned by the ice wall below the final slopes. As far as we could see in the forenoon light, it was a matter of doubt whether this ice wall could be surmounted, supposing it were possible to reach the top of the buttress. We turned to examine the other two routes. Smythe's idea was to attack by the ridge on the Col de la Brenva side of the branch couloir, but as this would have necessitated an exposed (and probably unjustifiable) traverse under the great ice wall, we soon abandoned that plan and compromised on the twisting ridge lying to the N. of the Great Couloir and between it and the branch couloir. When the afternoon sun struck sideways across the other ridge to the S. of the Great Couloir, it threw the terminal sérac wall into high relief – and what we then *thought* we saw still further deterred us from an attempt on that route.

But when we rested for lunch at the top of the 'twisting rib' on the 'Sentinel' route we could examine the upper part of this other great ridge. We *then* saw that the sérac wall could almost certainly be surmounted at a tongue of ice which pushes down from the upper slopes on to the top of its final buttress. I sat there and, in imagination, climbed that final buttress. The way led horizontally across a very steep slope of ice on the side it presents to the Great Couloir; and this traverse was followed by an intricate ascent on the rocks of the buttress up to its tip. Again I traced the route with Smythe, but we were both agreed as to the exposure and steepness of that slope of ice. Nevertheless we then and there resolved that the route must be attempted; and, in the event, our way up the final buttress followed closely on the imaginary footsteps of 1927.

But although the final buttress was probably the most serious problem of the climb, we yet knew that it was not the only one. In particular, it seemed to us that there might be a question whether we could get on to the foot of the ridge at all.

When we set out from the Torino Hut at 8.15 on the morning of August 6 with the 'Red Sentinel' as our objective we were uncertain if the foot of the Great Couloir could be crossed. We carried heavy packs – perhaps 30 lbs. each – for we had added sleeping sacks to our equipment; and our route to the 'Red Sentinel' was almost the same as that of 1927. We traversed the S. face of the Tour Ronde as before.

The day was a glorious one, but as we crossed the central bay of the Brenva Glacier we saw that a fierce wind was working its will upon the summit of Mont Blanc. When we arrived on the crest of Col Moore, it was obvious that much of our further route to the 'Red Sentinel' would this year be over rock. But the second couloir was in much the same condition as before. We came to its deep avalanche run and at once realized that it presented a difficulty much more formidable than in the previous year. Its depth was at least 12 ft., and its near side was overhanging – this year completely undercut. The groove had however to be crossed. I lowered Smythe on the rope, round my deeply implanted ice-axe, to the bed of the groove. So deep was it that he had again to climb up a little way on the rope before he could grasp his ice-axe which I stretched down to him at the full length of my arm, he cut across the couloir, surmounted its other and comparatively easy side, and then ascended the snow slope on that side of the groove until he was almost the rope's length above me. I took my courage into my hands and dropped into the groove. As I bumped, slid a little down its ice, and then lay for a moment slightly shaken and held only by the rope, I had an awful feeling of being deserted by the world. But it took little time to scratch the not too hard ice sufficiently to hold crampons and then to cut a step or two up to the steps at which Smythe had crossed. Then the far wall of the groove was surmounted and no further difficulty lay between us and the 'Red Sentinel'.

We reached the 'Red Sentinel' at 6.50 P.M., and found a little place to the right of our old tilted slab which could be made into a more comfortable bivouac. Smythe lit the spirit-stove and I levelled the bivouac site. Soon we had simultaneously a level sleeping place ready and a good meal. We got into our sleeping sacks and enjoyed the meal and the glorious view. The sun set, and we saw the great shadow of Mont Blanc in the sky over Aosta crowned with a single black ray. Then everything became cold and grey. A keen wind blew on us from the S.E., but disturbed us little in the warmth of our sleeping sacks. Last year the intense cold of even a windless night had prevented us from sleeping at all. This year the warmth of Smythe's excellent eiderdown sleeping sacks enabled us to sleep – although fitfully – in spite of a cold wind. From time to time we were awakened by the coldness of the stones and snow upon which we lay, but soon turned round and got to sleep again. We were, however, both awake when the moon and Venus rose in the East – a beautiful unreality.

Next morning, after a brief breakfast, we selected a small store of food to be left at the 'Sentinel', put on our crampons, and set out at 4.55. After traversing the ice couloir on the far side of the 'Sentinel' we climbed round the base of the next ridge to the foot of the Great Couloir. Here it is perhaps 100 to 150 ft. in width and its angle eases a little. Smythe then took the lead across it; it presented little difficulty – for we could almost run across on our crampons. A high wind was blowing ice crystals off the summits, and these hissed in a continuous stream down the Great Couloir. Sometimes the stream swelled in volume, sometimes it diminished; and as

Smythe cut a couple of steps at the far edge of the couloir I stood in it – a queer experience, for the stream offered little resistance, and yet prevented you from seeing where you were going – it was like wading through foam. But the couloir was crossed in certainly less than ten minutes – perhaps scarcely five – and we had gained the foot of the great ridge with little difficulty.

This we ascended until forced again to the edge of the Great Couloir by a perpendicular step. We avoided it by ascending the edge of the couloir close to the rocks, and soon again regained the arête. As we now ascended there was a great fall of ice from the hanging glacier below the Pétéret arête. The fragments broke and cascaded down the steep Brenva face in a wonderful white torrent. At 7.30 we reached a short ice arête which was very narrow; but the snow on its left or S. side was in good condition. More rock led us at 8.45 to the foot of another and a longer ice arête just below which we found a rather precarious sitting place, where we rested and had a good breakfast. It was a silent meal, for the views made speech impossible. On our left hand to the N. was the Brenva face of Mont Blanc with its great sérac wall and the line of the 'Sentinel' route leading up towards it. To our right we looked at the Pétéret arête across the great perpendicular ice faces, and across the broken ribs of this colossal mountain side; but no words and no photograph can give an adequate description. The morning was calm and warm; as we sat in silence a rather ominous cigar-shaped cloud formed far in the East. A butterfly fluttered round us.

Above us lay three ice arêtes of which the nearest presented little difficulty; the two upper ones were formidable. We set out again at 9.50 A.M., not knowing that we were to have no further halt until after we had surmounted the final sérac wall more than 8½ hours later. The next ice arête went easily, and we were immediately faced with the two more formidable arêtes separated from each other by an outcrop of rock.

Of these two ice arêtes, the upper is the longer; but the two are very similar. Each commences at a point formed by two converging snow edges. From this point the arête runs along, slightly ascending for about half of its length. Then it ascends ever more steeply towards its terminal apex – the final angle being perhaps 45°. The arête is excessively narrow in its more level parts. Here some trick of wind and weather forms a narrow blade of ice along the crest. Its sharp edge acts as a convenient hand-rail. So narrow and clear is this ice that the strong southern sun shone dimly through it. In each case we found the snow on the S. slope of the arête to be in bad condition. We walked along the arête itself, and then on the right-hand side of the narrow blade of ice. Soon Smythe, who was leading, went on to the right-hand slope itself and cut up to the apex of the arête. The butterfly had followed us until the commencement of the step-cutting on the lower of these two arêtes – when the wind first caught us. The small cloud was dissolving; the views were grand beyond description.

Twenty minutes' rock-climbing took us to the foot of the last arête, which was surmounted in the same manner. Below its apex we wasted some time in a vain attempt to find lodgement on an outcrop of rock upon the right-hand slope. Then Smythe cut directly up to the apex of the ridge along the edge of this outcrop.

The final buttress is in two parts. It is like a pyramid set upon a low pedestal, the surface of which is not horizontal, but slopes sharply down to the N. – that is towards the Great Couloir. The apex of the highest ice arête ends at the foot of a 15-ft. chimney which led us up without difficulty over the wall of rock and on to the surface of the 'pedestal' at 1.40 P.M.

Here we resolved to try to ascend by the route planned in the previous year – that is, to traverse on our right across the steep ice slope above the Great Couloir – the slope which forms (as it were) the surface of the pedestal. I drove my axe deep into the snow while Smythe walked across the slope. Above us on our left was the overhanging N. face of the buttress. In front of us, a tongue of rock ran down from this at a right angle. There is a chimney in the recess thus formed. Soon the axe had to be used. The slope turned to ice, hard, brittle, and green – almost transparent, for its surface was covered by verglas. It became excessively steep and hand holds had to be cut. Smythe asked me what I thought of the chimney, and I replied truthfully and frankly – 'it looks beastly'. It appeared, however, that we were forced to try this way, and I must say that the alternative – a traverse round the descending tongue of rock – looked even beastlier than the chimney. Smythe cut up to the corner, where I joined him. There was a gap of a few inches between the top of the ice and the rock wall on our left, and we jammed the ice-axes and stood on the narrow top edge of a slope of hard ice which must have been at least 60°, perhaps 65°, in steepness. Smythe attempted the chimney without success, and then I tried it and similarly failed. Yet it looked as if this was the only way. Neither of us wished to retreat, and it was doubtful whether the S. side of the buttress could offer an easier way or if there was now sufficient time to get round and ascend by it. I must say that I shuddered at a suggestion of descending into the Great Couloir, crossing it and attempting the summit by way of the upper part of the 'Sentinel' route. It was this alternative, I think, which prompted me to offer Smythe my back in the recess. You may perhaps wonder why the offer was such a tardy one – but we were wearing crampons and could not take them off. Smythe accepted the offer; tried the chimney again, and again failed to overcome it. He came down on to my back with an unfortunate effect, for my side pocket was ripped open and I lost my pipe – a sad discovery only made later on at the Vallot Hut. Smythe then gallantly offered me similar aid. Again lodgement at the top of the chimney was found to be impossible. Above it was a slab covered with verglas and affording no trustworthy hold. I descended and, am thankful to say, with less destructive effects. There is advantage (sometimes) in a small and light build! Again the horrible alternatives presented themselves to us and drove me to suggest an attempt to get round the descending tongue of rock and traverse still farther to the right. At first the descent was down our old steps, but then led near the edge of the rock down the steep ice. Soon it was possible to get along under the rock; and as I rounded the corner I saw to my amazement that, on the other side of the rocks and some way above, the ice slope merged into a broad couloir set at an easier angle and filled with good snow. In a little while the snow was reached with not much rope in hand, a sound belay found, and Smythe rejoined me. We ascended the couloir until stopped at the foot of a wild rocky gully up which our path seemed to lie. Direct entrance was impossible, but there was a short and difficult 15-ft. chimney on our right, from the top of which a traverse might be made into the gully. The finish over the left wall of the chimney was a difficult one; however, it went. I hauled up the rucksacks and the party came together again. Smythe then led across into the gully which we ascended for perhaps about 50 ft., to a place where there appeared to be three possible routes. The direct ascent of the gully failed. I found that an exit to the left led up merely to a difficult rock face. Smythe tried the way to the right which had always looked the easiest but seemed to lead too much towards the sérac wall. As we went on, however, we found that the route was still entirely unexposed. Another slope of good snow led up to the foot of another gully, narrow but filled with snow; and we now knew that we were reaching the top of the buttress. In places ice necessitated step-cutting, but soon an exit by the rock on our left led us to the very top of the buttress.

As we stood here, the huge sérac wall ran on our right in the direction of Mont Blanc. Across the Great Couloir was the sérac wall above the 'Sentinel' route and nearly level with us. The 'Sentinel' route lay spread out like a map, while over on our left we looked down along the great Pétéret ridge on to the top of the Aiguille Blanche. To the rocks upon which we stood a tongue of ice, perhaps 20 ft. high, ran down from the final slope on to the top of the buttress. This tongue was irregular and broken up by a ledge of ice. We could see that our difficulties were over. In a few minutes we walked up the sérac wall and at 6.10 P.M. were on the final slopes below the summit of Mont Blanc de Courmayeur. We had perhaps lost more than two hours in our various attempts to find the proper route, while the climbing day was now far spent.

All day long a strong wind had blown across the summits. We had first met it – fierce and cold gusts accompanied by stinging ice crystals – on the ice arêtes. The wind was now bitter as we made up the slopes towards the first great horizontal crevasse which runs across far below the summit ridge. Here we arrived at 6.25 P.M., descended into the crevasse, and took shelter from the wind – our first deliberate halt since we had left the breakfast place at 9.50 A.M. Our plan had been to make this new ascent a route to the summit of Mont Blanc de Courmayeur, and, if we were to succeed in this, time was short. So we gave ourselves only fifteen minutes' rest before setting out again.

The final slopes on this side of the mountain present no great difficulty, but they are steep, and the crusted snow made their ascent laborious. The fierce wind struck at us as we zigzagged up and we were both blown about at different times, here and on the crest. Once, as I looked back, I saw far below us the summit of Mont Maudit, bright pink in the sunset light – a vivid contrast with the green-grey colours of the now darkened Brenva face of Mont Blanc. It was strange to look out of shadow *down* on to a peak lit by sunset glow. We arrived on the summit ridge at 7.30, turned to our left and in fifteen minutes – at 7.45 P.M. – were on the summit of Mont Blanc de Courmayeur.

As we reached the summit the sun was near the point of setting, but was now masked behind a bank of cloud. Everything about us was grey and sombre save for a deep red line in the West. The loneliness was almost terrible, but as we came on to the actual summit a miracle happened – we were suddenly joined by distant friends. For, as we faced East, there was a bright flash from the Torino Hut, and we knew that friends had seen us and were signalling their good wishes. It was not until later that we heard that Herr Alfred Zürcher and Joseph Knubel had come up that day to the Torino Hut, and that Knubel had flashed his lantern to us at the moment they had seen us reach the summit.

The wind was still blowing, but not so fiercely as before. We turned with scarcely a pause towards Mont Blanc and walked along the summit ridge. Once I glanced to the East: the sun at the moment of its setting was shining beneath the great bank of western cloud, and the cone-shadow of Mont Blanc now stood out high above the horizon over Mont Emilius. We went on, and when I again looked a few seconds later the cone had disappeared. On the summit of Mont Blanc the wind had fallen somewhat in strength, and now – thank goodness! – blew steadily. We reached the Vallot Hut at exactly 9 P.M., and descended next morning by the Grands Mulets and Pierre Pointue. Thence we walked across to the Montenvers. Happy and contented we lingered on the way.

❊ (From 'First Ascent of Mont Blanc de Courmayeur direct from the Brenva Glacier, and Other Climbs' by T. Graham Brown. Vol. XLI.)

Erwin Schneider

21 ❄ *Disaster on Nanga Parbat*

Nanga Parbat, the western corner-stone of the Himalaya and probably the tenth highest peak of the world, has a comparatively ancient history. In 1895 Mummery's party, composed of some of the best and most active mountaineers of the time, made the first attempt – an attack worthy of the party's reputation. Mummery, coming from the Rupal Nullah over the Mazeno Pass to the Diamirai Glacier with two Gurkhas, attained a height of over 20,000 ft. on the W. flank of the mountain. But passing over the Diama Pass to the N. face of the mountain, he disappeared there with his two companions.

Willy Welzenbach first, then Willy Merkl, began preparations for another assault many years later. In 1932 Merkl led a party of prominent German mountaineers to the peak. He tried to find a way over the N. flank from the Rakhiot Glacier. With his companions he succeeded, after overcoming great difficulties, in reaching a height of nearly 23,000 ft., the expedition failing through snowstorms and porter troubles. The party was nevertheless certain that Nanga Parbat was definitely accessible by this – in all probability the *sole* – route. In 1934 Merkl wished to complete his unfinished task, but fate was once more against him; the mountain has prevailed again.

The Sports Clubs of the German State Railways provided the necessary funds. Towards the scientific aims of the expedition the *Notgemeinschaft* of German science and the D. u. Œ.A.-V. contributed generously. After months of intensive labour Merkl completed the necessary preparations. The members of the expedition started for India in two parties at the end of March and beginning of April respectively. Merkl was, of course, the leader: as members of the climbing party came Peter Aschenbrenner, who on off-days in the Base Camp was able to supply us with ibex, thanks to his skill with the rifle; Fritz Bechtold was the official photographer; Alfred Drexel was in charge of the wireless for quick transmission of reports between the different high camps as far as Camp IV; Peter Müllritter was another photographer, while Willy Welzenbach was second in command of the party; Ulrich Wieland, together with myself, looked after the high-altitude porters. Dr. W. Bernard was medical officer and Hans Hieronimus commanded the Base. The two transport officers, Captain Frier – who had been in charge of the same in 1932 – and Captain Sangster, gave us great assistance, as did the Swiss,. Kuhn, who with the German Consul, Kapp, joined the Base Camp a month later, coming from Rawal Pindi. The scientific side, to study topographical, geological, and geographical questions concerning the region, was composed of Doctors Finsterwalder, Misch and Raechl. One of their most important functions was to produce a good map on photogrammetrical methods to illustrate the terrain traversed by the expedition. The map, moreover, should prove a basis for scientific study of the vast mountain range and the solution of all sorts of further problems. We trust that the far-reaching results in these respects – results obtained with great labour – will prove of scientific value.

Thanks to the co-operation and help of the British and Indian officials, as well as that of many friends, our work in India was completed speedily and, by May 2, a start with 500 loads could be made from Srinagar. Accompanying us were thirty-five of the best Sherpa and Bhutia porters, together with their *sirdar*, Lewa, from Darjeeling. These men had all proved their worth on many previous expeditions on difficult ground and at great heights.

Our route from Srinagar to the Base Camp in the Rakhiot glen was well over 100 miles in length. It leads over the Tragbal and Burzil Passes of 11,580 ft. and 13,775 ft. respectively. Both these passes at this season of the year were still lying deep under winter snow. It was not altogether easy, with our large party and in bad weather, to cross them without loss of time. After Astor, one of the smaller resorts on the way to Gilgit, we did not take, as in 1932, the weary route *via* the ridges, but, having the necessary permits, proceeded by the Indus valley to the Rakhiot. At Rakhiot bridge the Indus flows at a height of only 1,100 m; 7,000 metres of sheer height separated us from the summit of Nanga Parbat. Nowhere else in the world is there a similar difference of altitude. At the bridge we took in the Indus our last bathe for a long time, reached Tato after a long and steep climb, and attained our former camp in the high forest two days later; seventeen days after our departure from Srinagar we pitched our tents there. At this high altitude the thick snow carpet began; to reach the Base Camp, situated at the same spot as in 1932, we had to break a trail. We sent our Darjeeling and Balti porters, of whom we had collected twenty, up and down in succession with our kit and stores from the above-mentioned camp to the permanent Base. The latter, situated at 3,850 m, was now – middle of May – still buried under 7 ft. of snow, its appearance being anything but prepossessing. Camp was pitched in a scooped-out hollow in the snow; the luggage was piled alongside in sorted heaps. Later, on the snow melting, it was a wonderful experience to rest here on off-days; the camp gave the impression of a Middle-Ages town in the midst of modernity.

The first advance to the upper camps was made by Bechtold, Müllritter and Wieland, accompanied by some porters. Camp I was pitched behind the top of the great moraine at the base of Nanga Parbat's N. face, at a height of 4,200 m. The object of this reconnaissance was to ascertain snow conditions for a further advance and to enable Bechtold to film the great ice avalanches falling continuously day and night and sweeping the entire 13,000-ft. face. The party returned with the cheering information that snow conditions were very good. One day later Aschenbrenner, Drexel, Welzenbach and I, with sixteen porters, left the Base Camp with the intention of pushing on to Camp IV and inaugurating it. Our route was the same as in 1932, the weather being changeable and mostly bad. With intensive labour we forced our way up to Camp II, but on the first day had to pitch an intermediate camp in the icefall owing to deep snow and difficult terrain. Camp II was in the most magnificent situation amidst the wildest icefalls that we had ever seen. In the evening especially, the view towards the W. over the immeasurable chain of the Hindu Kush was of surpassing splendour. The quick movements of the glacier in this part made, however, life anything but pleasant in Camp II. As time went on, great crevasses formed under the tents, while during the night avalanches thundered and the ice burst all round in the vicinity. Finally the site was abandoned after some thousands of tons of ice had fallen one night just in front of the tents. The further route towards Camp III led also through icefalls; we were again compelled to pitch an intermediate camp owing to the difficulties. From this spot we tried vainly for half a day to find a route through the great, sheer walls of ice. Camp III was inaugurated on a névé ridge at the end of the difficulties: from this spot more or less gentle snow slopes led towards the watershed between the E. peak (of Nanga Parbat), the Rakhiot, and the Chongra peaks.

We had short light skis with us fitted with skins. They proved useful, and we had already employed them in the approach march over the snowy passes. On the mountain we took them to Camp IV, whence they lightened the labour of an ascent of the western Chongra peak. From Camp IV to the Base we accomplished most of the journey, even portions of the icefalls, with their aid. Quick descents were often possible with decent snow. Thus we once accomplished the 3,000-ft. descent from Camp IV to Camp II in ten minutes. The 'slalom' through the icefalls and over the narrow snow-bridges below Camp III was quite unique. Moreover, the employment of skis was justified since in the final stage they provided admirable fuel for camp fires!

Bechtold and Müllritter had arrived at Camp II and assured the upwards transport of kits. We were in wireless communication with the Base and could quickly transmit our observations and wishes. The small apparatus communicated only at short distances, while later on connection failed between Camp IV and the Base. Nevertheless, one afternoon Captain Sangster got into touch with a military instrument which informed him that various unknown British officers of the Indian Army had been granted leave. But what was the use of that when we could not even 'get' our own operator in the Base Camp? . . .

. . . Drexel was usually in charge of the wireless. In Camp III a violent storm was raging that day and Drexel's usually clear voice was difficult to understand in the Base camp. He seemed to have caught a chill. We called to him (by wireless) to descend to the base to recover his health there. Drexel went down with his porter Angtensin to Camp II. We three others went up higher to Camp IV. On the following morning a porter arrived with a letter from Bechtold in Camp II, saying that Drexel had arrived there in a collapsed condition and that Müllritter had left at once for the Base to fetch the doctor and help. During the day and night the condition of Drexel had grown so rapidly worse that he was incapable of descending further. Dr Bernard arrived in the afternoon with Müllritter, but Drexel died at 9 P.M. from pneumonia. During the night Wieland arrived through the savage icefall with two porters and oxygen, but it was now too late. We all returned to the Base camp and buried our comrade on a moraine pinnacle with his head facing the north wall of Nanga Parbat. This was our first great blow and the fourth victim that the mountain has claimed since Mummery and his two companions.

During the following days Camp IV was fitted out with equipment and food, Captain Frier making the arrangements. On June 22 Merkl, Bechtold, Müllritter, Welzenbach, Aschenbrenner and I went as the advance party to Camp IV. Captain Sangster, Wieland and Bernard followed three days later. From Camp IV nearly everyone climbed the Western Chongra peak. This camp, at a height of 5,950 m, served as a kind of advanced base and from it we went up and down twice with porters to Camp V conveying stores. The route is steep but can be accomplished with good snow and tracks in 3 hrs.; a long climb still separated us from the summit. Our intention was, from Camp V at the foot of the Rakhiot peak, to make our way to the great upper névé plateau by passing *over* this peak and the connecting ridge to the *Silbersattel* lying between the two eastern peaks: this rises gently from a height of 7,600 m over a distance of nearly 3 kilometres to the little lower top, whence the route continues, *via* a descent into the last depression and a steep shoulder in the ridge, upwards towards the summit. The route is mostly difficult and especially very long as it lies at an average height of 7,000 m (= 23,000 ft.). This constitutes the main difficulty and the solution to the attainment of the top. We considered our best plan was to overcome these troubles by a rapid assault and short pauses, thus not meeting with hindrances from lack of (atmospheric) oxygen. We wished to preserve our strength and powers for the final assault on the summit.

Camp V was situated at 6,700 m, just in front of the abrupt final step leading to the Rakhiot peak. This step we rendered secure by fixed ropes and the hewing of big footholds for the porters – a two days' job. On July 4 Merkl, Bechtold, Welzenbach, Wieland, Aschenbrenner and I, with eighteen porters, arrived at Camp VI. Camp V was the true take-off for the real assault on the summit of Nanga Parbat, for in this place it was possible to construct a 'strong point' fitted with sleeping-sacks, food and fuel. Müllritter returned from this point to Camp IV with a sick porter. His orders were to return later to Camps VI and VII and equip these in case of need with fuel and food, thus covering our retreat (from the top) to these camps.

From the jutting ridge-shoulder of the Rakhiot peak we turned on to the W. slope and avoided the summit. Afterwards, once more on the crest, we attained our Camp VI at a height of 6,900 m. It stood in the same place where Camp VII of the 1932 Expedition had been erected. In that year the party had attained the locality by the great hollow followed by a steep and fatiguing snow and ice gully. On this occasion, however, that route was blocked by an ice wall at the base of the gully, consequently we took the ridge route.

During this period, below at Camp IV, the weather was mostly bad. Higher up progress was *above* the clouds; these latter rising only towards nightfall and smothering the ridge. The wind, although violent, was not disagreeable. Progress along the snowy ridge was marvellous since everything below us was concealed by a sea of cloud from which Nanga Parbat – like an island – alone emerged. Below us fell the immense wall towards the Rupal Nulla; often the wind scooped a clearing in the clouds and we saw, 14,000 ft. below us, the level, débris-strewn glacier with its neighbouring green meadows. For us who had lived for so many weeks in snow and ice, it was like a vision of another world.

We dug out a camp site for our tents in a notch in the ridge just below the steep rise to the *Silbersattel* – Camp VII, 7,100 m. The clouds had met on the ridge, causing a snowstorm and making our labour severe. In the evening, however, it cleared, and once more on the following day we became inhabitants of a lonely isle far above the clouds. In this place we could still eat, but it consisted mostly of soup, in which we dumped a great mass of butter for increased nourishment. We slept in two tents with two in each sleeping-bag. Bechtold left us here in Camp VII with two sick porters; he had been taking films up to this spot. His instructions also were to follow up with Müllritter later and keep Camps VI and VII open. At

Camp VI four porters had had to fall out sick, so on July 6 we set out with eleven porters to Camp VIII – the last before the summit. We got away early, all were in good form, and progress was at the rate of 200 m (= 650 ft.) per hour. On the steep slopes leading to the *Silbersattel* we cut a series of steps for the porters. Above, sitting on the rocks of the E. peak, Aschenbrenner and I waited for the others following up with the porters, smoking cigarettes we had borrowed from the latter. The doctor had forbidden smoking for the party, consequently tobacco in Camp IV was very scarce. On the head of the column attaining the *Silbersattel* we proceeded, skirting the upper névés, as far as the first top (*Vorgipfel*). We then turned back, since we saw that the porters could not go farther, and Camp VIII, 7,600 m, was pitched close to the *Silbersattel*. It was still early when we turned back, the height was about 7,900 m, 50 m below the measured first top (= 25,800 ft.). A ridge some 900 m long and 240 m in height (*ca.* 800 ft.) still lay between us and the summit (26,620 ft.). We were full of confidence and never doubted about attaining the top next day.

That evening we were able to eat some soup and were quite carefree concerning the following day which was to consummate our victory. Fate, however, was against us. The night was still clear, but the wind raged – probably always the case. In the morning a tremendous snowstorm burst over the tents. The blizzard was so violent that it was almost impossible to breathe in the open; the driving snow was blown horizontally in broad sheets, while perpetual darkness seemed to gather about us. During the preceding night a pole of the larger tent was smashed, while a second went the same way on the following. It was impossible to dig out a cave in the level névé; the surface of the latter was wind-blown into an iron substance which even on the first night had but barely allowed us to scrape out a hollow for the tents. The small tent occupied by Aschenbrenner and myself was no longer sufficiently wind-proof against the elements; during the first night we lay in our sack amidst driving snow, but had managed to become almost accustomed to it. In spite of everything we decided to wait one more day, since according to the observations of 1932, a storm of this nature on Nanga Parbat hardly ever lasted more than a day. On this day we took nothing at all beyond half a cup of tea apiece. Food and fuel we possessed in sufficiency, but in the howling storm it proved impossible to melt snow or prepare any warm nourishment.

The second night was almost worse than the first. Yet another tent-pole broke during a squall, while at daybreak there was still no improvement. It was useless to wait yet another day and night; accordingly we decided to descend. Aschenbrenner and I led with three porters to break the trail, our companions intending to follow at once with the remaining natives. None of us was in bad condition and there were no complaints as to ailments. Our only sorrow was the thought of the long grind upwards again from Camp IV to VIII and of the valuable time lost. We thought ourselves certain to return in a few days when the weather had cleared.

On the *Silbersattel* an india-rubber mattress was torn off the back of a porter; this was immediately followed by a heavy sleeping-bag. The storm blew these horizontally and bodily into space – they vanished round a corner. The sleeping-bag was ours, the porters still possessed their own. On the steep traverse below the ridge we cut steps, while on the crest itself we forced our way through the snow masses. The storm drove countless snow particles into our eyes, so that we could see nothing; in fact, Aschenbrenner, 10 or 15 ft. away from me, became nothing but a greyish shadow.

We lost sight of our three porters near the tent of Camp VII. On the Rakhiot peak we followed the ridge over the top, turning down at the ropes towards Camp V. We dug the tents out of the snow and ate something. In the late afternoon we reached Camp IV, where Bechtold, Müllritter and Bernard were waiting. They had attempted vainly to mount on the preceding day, but were held up by masses of snow before reaching Camp V. We were of the opinion that the porters and our companions would soon follow us; when no one appeared we thought they had spent the night in Camp V. On the following day the storm continued, as it had in fact done in this spot for nearly a week. During the evening of the following day it cleared with a raging gale that swept the billowing clouds off the ridge. We perceived figures descending the Rakhiot peak and made towards them. They were four porters, Pasang, Kitar, Kikuli and Da Thondu; all were frost-bitten and completely exhausted. We rubbed them with snow and sent them down to the Base camp with Bernard on the following day. We attempted to go up and give help, but it proved impossible. Once we attained Camp V, three climbers and six porters, literally buried in bottomless snow up to our shoulders. Here another storm caught us; not a porter could move. We ourselves were too weak to go higher alone. On another occasion we even failed to reach Camp V; no porter then accompanied us – even they were exhausted utterly by the long high-altitude sojourn. On July 15 came the porter Angtsering from somewhere above Camp VI. From him we learnt of the tragedy above. Wieland had died near Camp VII; he appears to have sat down for a short rest and went to sleep without waking. Welzenbach died in Camp VII, while two porters, Nima Nurbu and Dakshi, perished higher up still. Merkl proceeded with Gay Lay and Angtsering some way towards Camp VI. About this place he sent on Angtsering to bring help; had it not been for this (? *i.e.* the previous presence of Merkl and his porter), the latter could hardly have possessed the strength to force his way down alone through the storm [sic]. Three porters, Nima Tashi, Pintzo Nurbu, and Nima Dorji, died shortly before Camp V. Gay Lay stayed with his Sahib – to die with him. May his memory be honoured for ever.

Meanwhile we sat almost within shouting distance and could do nothing. Always we tried to force our way up and ever we failed. Raechl and Misch came up to Camp IV to help; they failed equally to reach Camp V. It was dreadful, this continued effort, worse still to know that it was always vain and useless.

On July 18 we evacuated Camp IV and descended. The way was difficult, harder than on the way up, as we sorrowfully tracked through deep snow and the torn icefalls. Halfway down, between Camp II and III, we met Bechtold and Müllritter who had once more come up to help. It was far too late: our last hopes of being able to bury our dead friends and porters were extinguished in the drifts of new snow and continuous storms. Weary and worn out, we descended over the moraine pinnacles to the tents of the Base camp. Hieronimus and Kuhn came to meet us. Everything had been arranged at the Base, the sick porters looked after and much labour accomplished. The frost-bites of the porters healed well under the doctor's care . . .

Shall we be lucky enough to fight another round with Nanga Parbat? And shall we once more return there?

❖ (From 'The German Assault on Nanga Parbat (1934)', Vols. XLVI and XLVII.)

Angtsering

22 ❄ A Sherpa's Story

'On the morning of the 9th, after sleeping between Camps VIII and VII – on the descent – the party left: myself, Gay Lay and Dakshi. I was snow-blind and the other two weak. We three spent a further two nights without moving, after which my eyes improved. Dakshi was alive, but too weak to move, and so with Gay Lay I proceeded down, leaving Dakshi. Before reaching Camp VII we saw Wieland's body. At Camp VII we met Merkl and Welzenbach. Merkl said, "Stay with us until food and help arrive." The Europeans had no sleeping-bags and sheltered in the only two-man tent. We two porters had sleeping-bags and no tent. We all stayed at this camp for another two nights. On the second night Welzenbach died, after which I said to Merkl, "We must go on down, as no help will come up to us." So myself, carrying two sleeping-bags, Merkl's rucksack and ground-sheet, made the track down, Gay Lay and Merkl following. After covering three-quarters of the distance to Camp VI Merkl could not go on, and at this point we spent the night. The next morning, from our position above Camp VI, I saw three Europeans and four porters coming up from Camp III to Camp IV, but no movement was made upwards from Camp IV. I pressed the Sahib to continue on down. His hands and feet were very badly frost-bitten, also his face, and he was absolutely helpless. He then ordered Gay Lay down to Camp IV with orders to the Sahibs to bring up brandy, food and every assistance. Gay Lay was unable to proceed, and I under-took to go down carrying my ice-axe only and leaving at 5 A.M. As my hands and feet were frost-bitten, progress was very slow. Below Camp V I called out for assistance to Camp IV. It was a long time before anyone heard me. At last Pasang Dorji and Nurbu Sonam came out with tea laced with brandy, and assisted me in to Camp IV. I told Lewa that Merkl (and Gay Lay) were above Camp VI and wanted immediate help in the way of stimulants, food and porters to carry them down. A rescue party was fixed for the following day. This party was unable to venture upwards, as con-ditions were too bad. I had not eaten from the day we left Camp VIII. In Camp IV there were six Europeans and four porters, the former fit, but the latter unfit for further work.'

❄ (From 'The German Assault on Nanga Parbat (1934)', Vol. XLVII.)

E. L. Strutt

23 ❄ *Peepshow for the Proletariat*

The N. face of the Eiger consists, as is well known, of two halves separated by a great buttress or edge. The eastern half was climbed on August 20, 1932, by our Swiss members (the late) Dr. Hans Lauper and Herr Alfred Zürcher, with the Valaisan guides, Alexander Graven and Josef Knubel – one of the strongest combinations yet pitted together against a great face. This climb constituted the first ascent of the Eiger by the N. face. The western, or 'Eigerwand', portion of the face, the great precipice in which gapes the window of the Eigerwand station of the Jungfrau railway, was attempted with disastrous results by Herren Sedlmayr and Mehringer in 1935.

The following is a very brief summary of the events of July 1936, compiled from various sources and narratives. The line taken in the assault of the Eigerwand by the victims of 1936 lies somewhat to the right, W., of that attempted by those of 1935.

Several German parties were in position at the base of the face in July last, but with the exception of those to be mentioned, all had previously retired on account of the exceptionally bad weather and conditions prevalent throughout the Alps. The die-hards consisted of Herren Andreas Hinterstoisser of Reichenhall and Anton Kurz of Berchtesgaden, together with an Austrian combination, Herren Willy Angerer and Eduard Rainer, who had arranged to join forces. On July 7 an attempt by the two Germans had been repulsed at about 3,000 m, when during the descent one of the climbers fell heavily some 120 ft., his life being saved by luck and the fact that he pitched on to a patch of soft snow. Not much damage was caused.

On Saturday, July 18, during a momentary weather clearing, and in the teeth of every conceivable warning from the local guides and experts, the four climbers set out for the N. face of the Eiger, 3,974 m, at 02.00; Kl. Scheidegg being the point of departure. The ages of the united party varied between twenty-seven and twenty-three years. All – especially Kurz – are stated to have been competent rock-climbers with much Eastern Alps' experience; in fact, the Germans were qualified 'guides'. Their equipment was sadly deficient as regards clothing and food, although immense quantities of rope and metal were carried. The former comprised, per man, a small waterproof sheet, 1 lb. of bread, ½ lb. of bacon, a few sardines and a little sugar, tea and meta fuel: the latter included a total of 60 pitons, *Karabiner*, together with 400 ft. of rope besides line. All the members were stated to be competing for the Olympic medal to be awarded 'for the greatest mountaineering feat achieved in 1936', following the evil precedent of the said medal when presented for the conquest of the N. face of the Matterhorn in 1931. Shortly after the departure of the party, a telegram from the officer commanding the Germans' regiment arrived, forbidding any attempt by his subordinates on the Eigerwand. We commend the action of the said C.O., but fate intervened.

The party, watched through telescopes from Kl. Scheidegg and by spectators at Alpiglen, had gained by 08.00, thanks to the previous reconnaissance, a height of some 3,000 m, while at 08.30 the bivouac of July 7 was duly attained. Now began a comparatively short but most difficult and dangerous *descending* traverse to the left, E., towards the line attempted in 1935. This was accomplished, mechanically, by 09.25. The party now turned upwards and with immense labour attained the neighbourhood of the upper, 1935, bivouac at 16.30, retreat from this spot appearing quite hopeless. The advance continued up an often overhanging and 700-ft. boss, glazed with ice and swept by stones, called the *Rote Fluh*. The party bivouacked just above this spot. It was a veritable *tour de force*. Bad weather, thunder and lightning, came on, the face streaming with water and snowslides. The height attained was about 3,200 m, or some 2,500 ft. below the Eiger's summit.

At 06.45 on Sunday, July 19, during a momentary break in the storm, the party were observed to force their way up an ice slope, securing themselves to a piton. Then the clouds shut down definitely. On Monday, July 20, through swirling mists, a fresh start was observed at about 08.00. After some hours of exertion but little actual progress, it was noted that the party was now descending and that Angerer (? or perhaps Rainer) was apparently suffering from a head-wound. At 17.00 they were on the great snow slope above the *Rote Fluh* and still descending; visibility then became nil and it is surmised that they possibly re-attained the Saturday bivouac. The weather now became fearful, the entire face being swept by torrents of water, stones and avalanches.

At 09.00 on July 21 the party was again observed momentarily just above the great *Rote Fluh*, with its fearsome and previously described 150-ft. traverse. Attracted by the cries of a railway ganger, who, from a gallery leading to the open from the tunnel of the Jungfrau railway, situated to the W. of Eigerwand station, had observed the party in distress, a rescue party of guides now set out. Adolf and Christian Rubi, Hans Schlunegger of Wengen, together with Arnold Glatthard of Kl. Scheidegg, made up its members. Debouching from the same gallery, they contrived under terrible difficulties and danger to force their way eastwards across the face towards the line of descent of the Austro-Germans. These latter, all on one rope, endeavoured to accomplish the now *upwards* traverse to the *Rote Fluh*, but the latter proving utterly impracticable, nothing was left but to rope down direct over the overhanging precipice. With Angerer leading and the others respectively to right and left of the supporting piton, a desperate and prolonged effort was made. What then happened can never be known exactly, but the further narrative is compiled from the guides' statements, from telescope observations and from disjointed shouts exchanged between Kurz, the last survivor, and the Wengen guides.

Angerer endeavoured to rope down, but there being insufficient rope available, Hinterstoisser was compelled to detach himself from his loop to enable the former to descend. Hinterstoisser fell at this moment, while Angerer, making an effort to avert the fall, was caught by the swinging coils and instantly throttled to death where he stood, Hinterstoisser's body crashing to the base of the cliff. Meanwhile, Rainer, the last man, to the left of the *Karabiner*, was jammed by pressure against the piton, the wrench of the rope, together with (?) injuries and cold, causing death within a few moments. Kurz, still able to hold, called out to the guides below that he was now 'alone' and that the others were dead, his position being the third on the rope. Exhausted, with one arm and its corresponding fingers useless from frost-bite, nothing is more remarkable than the extraordinary fortitude and resource shown by this young soldier of twenty-three during the long-drawn struggle. Pitons, *Karabiner* – all were expended, while the climbing rope, swollen by wet to monstrous proportions, still bound Kurz to his dead companions. Stones and snow-slides dislodged by the struggles above descended ceaselessly on the heads of the still advancing guides, Glatthard narrowly escaping destruction. Night came on and exchanging shouts with Kurz, who stated that he could not hold out another day, the guides were compelled to retire. Their descent in the darkness and storm proved a nightmare.

On July 22, at 04.30, the guides recommenced the ascent: heroic efforts resulted in their attaining a spot some 150 ft. distant from Kurz, who had survived his fourth night out. It will be understood that the Austro-Germans having roped down into space, were well away to the E. of their, and the only possible, line of ascent. These 150 ft., vertical and entirely glazed with ice, proved insuperable even to the professionals. Shouts were exchanged with Kurz, still in the same position. He was bidden to cut the rope between himself and Angerer – this he finally contrived with his ice-axe, the body plunging into space and narrowly missing the guides. The rope thus freed, and the various ends knotted together, could then be lowered to the guides, an exhausting work accomplished by Kurz in more than three hours of labour. The rope thus lowered, some 150 ft. long, just reached the guides. To this they attached two further 60-ft. (British) ropes, together with two pitons and *Karabiner*. The whole was then drawn up by Kurz, passed through the fresh *Karabiner*, and a (sling) *rappel* contrived. It appears that the lowering manoeuvres could not be undertaken by the guides themselves owing to their own and Kurz's position, as also to the knotted ropes. Be that as it may, Kurz, slowly and with immense labour, began to rope down over the cliff. Hours passed, but during all this space of time the undaunted German, gasping for breath, was able to acquaint the men below of much that had happened above. A snow avalanche swished over the party, concealing Kurz for some minutes, yet he managed to reach a place where Glatthard, standing on Rubi's head and held against the cliff by the latter's outstretched arms, succeeded almost in touching Kurz's cramponed feet with extended axe. But the knots of the rope now jammed in the *Karabiner*; Kurz endeavoured to pull them through, but swaying gently in the wind some 20 ft. clear of the cliff, exhausted by the protracted struggle yet within a few feet of safety, at 11.30 quietly expired.

It was the end; in ceaseless danger the guides fell back once more. Most gallantly, they had achieved far more than their duty.

'. . . The Eiger had struck down three assailants and destroyed the fourth through cold, hunger and exhaustion. Four guides had during seven hours of ceaseless stonefall struggled to save the lives of desperadoes who driven forward fecklessly by irresponsible desire for notoriety had fought to place in the temple of fame of their false gods the mightiest of Alpine faces . . .'

On July 24 a party of eight Munichers, subsequently increased to fourteen, belonging to the Bergwacht and including Herren Franz Schmid and Rudolf Peters of Matterhorn and Grandes Jorasses fame, arrived at Kl. Scheidegg to search for the remains. The leader was named Siebenwurst. The German wireless brazenly informed the world that the rescue had been attempted by the Bergwacht, whereas this latter did not reach the vicinity of Alpiglen until *after* the death of the last survivor! Moreover, it is instructive to note that the Bergwacht took four hours to traverse from the tunnel-gallery to the place where Kurz's body was hanging, whereas the guides, under the worst conditions, accomplished the same distance in 45 minutes. Nevertheless the devotion of the former is worthy of the highest praise; in fact all risked their lives in what seems to us but a pious and useless quest. The result was the discovery at the base of the cliff of a few remains identified as those of Sedlmayr who perished in 1935 and of Angerer, and later of Rainer of this year's party. The body of Kurz was cut down by means of a knife fixed to a long pole and allowed to fall to the base, where it was recovered on August 25. The remains of the others have not yet been found. It is now (October) stated that some properties belonging to Mehringer, a victim of 1935, have been identified. It is assumed lately that Mehringer and Sedlmayr were killed by *falling* and did not perish from cold and starvation.

The Austrian victims were members of a refugee camp in Germany, while the Germans were soldiers. Their attitude towards the projected ascent may be summarized in a statement made to local guides previous to the attempt. '*Die Wand ist unser – oder wir bleiben in ihr.*' Surely a more honourable one than that attributed to one Teufel, killed on the Schneehorn while 'practising' for the Eigerwand, 'You Swiss are worthless, WE will accomplish the deed.'

The following are excerpts (*Neue Basler Zeitung*) from statements made by our member, Dr. Oskar Hug of Zürich, to the Swiss Press:

In reply to the question 'Is the ascent of the Eigerwand possible?' Dr. Hug answers: 'Nowadays nearly everything is possible, not even excluding this face. Regular siege tactics including assault sections and casualties are however obligatory. But the forcing of the Eigerwand is principally a matter of luck – at least 90 per cent of the latter is required. Extreme forms of technical development, a fanatical disregard of death, staying powers and bodily toughness are in this case details of mere secondary importance. The incalculable elements of fate, chance, the possibility of escape from objective dangers – stonefall, avalanches, etc. – are so overwhelmingly important that this face-climb lies completely outside the pale of mountaineering, belonging far more to a degenerate form of the Children's Crusade of the Middle Ages . . .'

'Technical equipment and food for a first ascent of this face were insufficient. The first attempt in 1935 had shown clearly that it is not a question of one or two days. The party began with a grave error: the members were accustomed to dry and low faces, they treated the Eiger on an Eastern Alps' scale. This reckoning was altogether false. On the other hand in such an assault an important role is played by the weight of the equipment. Rope coils, pitons, clothing, etc., grow so heavy that less food can be carried.'

Dr. Hug considers that foreigners attempting the Eigerwand should be forced to provide their own rescue parties. We would go further still and suggest that all extraneous search or rescue parties be forbidden, 'for why should the lives of good men be risked to save those individuals who, before starting, have made already the sacrifice of their own?' As regards the Olympic Medal for 'Alpine Valour' – for which the Austro-German party was ostensibly competing – our member states:

'An Olympic medal for mountaineering is to be deprecated at all costs. Mountaineering, as understood by Swiss and British climbers, is not an Olympic sport. Mountaineering contains some elements of sporting characteristics, but these are of a quite secondary nature. The form however fostered by Eastern Alps' scrambling smacks more of the Olympic stadium where publicity is not unwillingly sought. Swiss and British mountaineers will have no dealings with Olympic medals.'

The *Volkische Beobachter,* a well-known German national paper, remarks:

'A fresh and doubtful fight has arisen with the defences of the mighty face – in which the latter have remained triumphant. The critical opinions of the Swiss Press have however received too little attention from our youth. That is the lesson to be learnt from this second disaster in the great face, where a terrible mountain tragedy has just been enacted.'

With the concluding remarks of our Swiss contemporary, the *Journal* and British mountaineers concur entirely: 'We wish that the above statements (i.e. of the German paper) could be painted in red and taken to heart throughout the whole of Germany. Then might this destroying face lure no more unnecessary victims to their death, nor endanger the lives of heroic rescuers.' *

Perhaps the most disquieting result of this almost inevitable disaster is the fact that the Teutonic Press as a whole considers that harsh criticism of the insane deed has been meted out by the Swiss and European newspapers. In my opinion – repeated on several occasions in this *Journal* – modern German methods of what is misnamed 'mountaineering' in that country are, but too often, thoroughly unsound, and in every way destructive to the first principles of that pastime as known to every beginner throughout the remainder of Europe.

To the families of those who, worthlessly, have thrown away their valuable lives, we offer our sympathy; to the guides who generously risked their all, our sincere admiration.

❋ (From 'Accidents in 1936', Vol. XLVIII.)

The proletariat, herding round the base, awaited events with the same deplorable expectancy as in 1935–6.

A well-known mountaineer writes: 'The Swiss papers make a joke about the Eigerwand, pretending that the Teutons are going home saying, "It has lost its kick; the Bernese government has confiscated all the *Heldenbeobachtungsfernrohre.*" When I passed the Kleine Scheidegg on my way

* By a decree of the authorities at Interlaken an order has been issued forbidding access to the Eigerwand and threatening all manner of fines to transgressors – dated July 25, 1936. Doubtless the Swiss authorities are conversant with their own business, but such legislation seems to us absurd and impossible of enforcement. No law yet made can prevent suicide, still less intemperate and vicious attempts at the same.

down from the *Mittellegigrat* there were long queues of people waiting their turn at the telescopes for glimpses (at a price) of the Teutons on the Eigerwand.'

❈ (From 'Accidents in 1937', Vol. XLIX.)

The Eigerwand – still unscaled – continues to be an obsession for the mentally-deranged of almost every nation. He who first succeeds may rest assured that he has accomplished the most imbecile variant since mountaineering first began.

❈ (From Presidential Valedictory Address, 1938, Vol. L. The Eigerwand was climbed later that year.)

T. S. Blakeney

24 ❄ Two Editors

Edward Lisle Strutt (1874–1948). Colonel Strutt was Editor of the *AJ* from 1927 to 1937, and President of the AC from 1935–7. The Strutts were a Derbyshire family, notable as cotton spinners in collaboration with Arkwright, and E. L. Strutt's grandfather was created Lord Belper in 1856. Strutt's father died when the boy was only three years old and he was brought up as a Roman Catholic and educated at Beaumont College and Innsbruck University as well as Christ Church, Oxford. He developed strong Continental contacts and in particular enjoyed the freemasonry of titled and Catholic families abroad, especially in Austria. He became an expert French and German linguist.

Strutt joined the Army and served in the South African War in the Royal Scots, and in World War I, when he was badly wounded and mentioned four times in despatches, as well as winning the DSO and five foreign decorations. In 1919 he was made a CBE for his work in bringing the Austrian Royal Family safely out of Austria into Switzerland.*

Strutt early showed a bent for mountaineering, and a cousin of his, G. H. Strutt, had been a member of the AC since 1859. Education at Innsbruck naturally gave Edward Strutt a special interest in the Eastern Alps – Bavaria, Tyrol, Engadine, Bregaglia – which later found expression in his editing (1910) the two Bernina vols of the Conway–Coolidge Climbers' Guides.

He had been appointed High Commissioner of Danzig in 1920, but left following a clash with Lord Curzon, the Foreign Secretary. In 1922 he was made 2nd-in-command of the Everest Expedition, and as General Bruce did not go beyond Base Camp, it fell to Strutt to organize the work forward. Though a good deal older than most members, he acclimatized well enough and spent close on a fortnight at Camp 3. When Morshead had to be sent back frost-bitten to Darjeeling, under Longstaff's care,

---

* This episode and subsequent actions of Strutt in relation to the Austrian Emperor and Empress are chronicled in Gordon Brook-Shepherd's *The Last Habsburg* (1968). Strutt's diary of February to April 1919 is used, and exhibits his qualities of determination and resource, though coupled with evidence of how he could rile people.

Strutt, who by now was played out, returned with them and Finch. Longstaff's recorded opinion was that Strutt had done a very good job at the advanced base, but there is no doubt he felt the strain of the altitude and the wind and, never the most even-tempered of men, he became cantankerous and disagreeable, and the expedition was not sorry to see him go.

This illustrates a feature in Strutt's make-up; he was apt to be caustic in speech and minded little if he put up people's backs. John Morris, Transport Officer on Everest, 1922, in his book, *Hired to Kill*, writes of Strutt as the most complete snob he had ever met. Certainly Strutt was not a good mixer and this affected his relationships in the AC where, while he might be admired (for he was an able and courageous man and mountaineer), he was seldom liked.

As a mountaineer, Strutt was old-fashioned in the sense that he usually employed guides; but he was no mere passenger on a mountain and in particular was an outstanding iceman. He climbed (sometimes using skis or snowshoes) in winter as well as summer and had many acquaintances among leading continental mountaineers. His knowledge of the Alps was extensive and, in his favourite areas, deep.

On paper, Strutt should have been an excellent successor to Farrar as Editor – nor was it easy to follow Farrar. And in many ways Strutt was a successful Editor; the journals under his aegis are not less interesting than those that went before. He was well aware of the expansion of climbing, particularly in the Himalaya, that coincided with his editorship, and he did not shirk the tasks involved. Unfortunately, the qualities already hinted at too often detracted from his service as Editor; Strutt wielded a ready but abrasive pen, and he was apt to express violent disapproval of things novel or alien to his thinking.

This effect of Strutt's editorship has been dealt with by Longland in *A J* 62 (1957), and while keeping a foot in both camps, Longland does come down fairly heavily against Strutt for the latter's lack of sympathy with current developments in mountaineering practice during the period under review. And undoubtedly Strutt laid himself open to retort by his at times stupid antipathies to such things as crampons or other artificial aids.

It is necessary to remember, however, that the use of crampons was still not universal and a tradition existed that crampons were for experts only. Even relatively young climbers might hold those views, E. S. Herbert, for example; and Strutt was by no means alone among elders who had doubts – Raeburn and Rolleston, for example.* It was open to anyone to do without

---

* Even as late as 1949 a Committee dealing with the accident on the AC Meet of that year, chaired by G. I. Finch, virtually re-affirmed this old-fashioned outlook.

crampons if they wished, and to refrain from carrying pitons, but Strutt made himself absurd by the manner of expressing his dislikes.

In point of fact, the use of artificial aids to climbing, other than the traditional ice-axe, rope and nailed boots, had existed for a long time (fixed ropes or chains on mountains had often occasioned disapproval, as spoiling an otherwise good route). Clearly, once artificial 'steps' in the form of pitons were admitted, the same danger could be repeated – and often was. The prophets of doom, like Strutt, who denounced what they regarded as a sure degradation of mountaineering, were not, fundamentally, different from the young climbers who, at an A C symposium on the future of climbing, on 10 April 1973, admitted that things were getting out of hand; or the 'tigers' who, about the same time, on a T V programme about the excessive use of 'artificials' on Cerro Torre, pleaded that the abuses now in fashion ruined the sport, and that it ought to be allowed for a mountain (or a route) to 'win' at times.*

Longland's article was useful in reminding readers of the points made by Farrar in his Valedictory, viz. that young climbers went to the Alps far better prepared than their forefathers had been, and that if enterprise in climbing was not to flag, new routes, involving new techniques, must be expected. There was, however, a danger in the shift of interest away from the mountain to the climbers, so that, as a young climber of post-2nd War age expressed it, 'a climb becomes less a venture into the unknown than the performance of a more or less prescribed exercise'. It was here that people like Strutt, and not only he (Claude Wilson and Geoffrey Young were others), were to forecast a change in the character of mountaineering, as the wider and more humane approach to the sport was at first diluted and eventually swamped by the floodwaters of technique and personal expertise.

Other factors tended towards this change and were objects of Strutt's detestation. One was a diminished concern for the value of human life, and a readiness to accept risks that earlier generations rejected. If men, by their own assiduous practice and by virtue of specialized equipment, become capable of more formidable climbs than their forebears, they will attempt such climbs, and if they are prepared to risk life more readily than in the past, they can be certain of making climbs that an earlier generation would have ruled out. That lives may be lost in the process is true, and regrettable, but the new climbs are made nonetheless. One has only to

---

* The *American A J,* 1972, p. 1 seq, 'Preserving the Cracks', has a timely article on the over-doing of piton technique. In the Alps one has only to think of splendid rock climbs such as the Salbitschijen being overloaded with pitons, or even modest climbs like the Jägigrat above Saas – which surely does not need any pitons at all – to realize that the use of artificial aids all too easily leads to their abuse.

think of the perturbation in 1865 over the Matterhorn accident to realize that Frank Smythe was right in his book on Whymper when he said that human life in 1865 was more precious than in 1939. In deploring the accidents, Strutt had a legitimate point; but too often there crept into his comments a tone of arrogance that betrayed the fact that he had not sufficiently realized that a far more numerous and more varied type of climber was now in the field.

Another feature of the 1930s was the aggressive nationalism that had appeared in mountaineering, especially on the part of Nazi Germany. Strutt had no use for this, and Longland expresses agreement with him. Of course, rivalry between climbers was no new thing, but the substitution of national prestige for healthy maintaineering ambition was novel. It was during this period that mountaineering achievement came to be regarded as a proper means of enhancing a nation's fame, a defect far from dead now, and indeed aggravated by the commercialism that today infects climbing.

In terms of its day, it may be questioned how far Strutt's animadversions really had effect. Longland claims that young mountaineers felt frustrated,* but one's personal recollection is that one shrugged the fulminations aside: it was 'only old Strutt blowing off steam'. In some ways, people like Claude Wilson or W. N. Ling appear more reactionary than Strutt was; their contributions to the 'Accidents' symposium illustrates this, as do Wilson's passing remarks in the Ellis Carr obituary, or in his own Presidential Valedictory. Strutt, as Editor, had of course greater means of expression, but one should not allow his occasional explosive footnotes to damn the whole of his very considerable editorial contribution to the merits of the *A J.* If he was narrow and short-sighted over the new type of mountaineer to be found in the Alps or elsewhere, his fears that too much use of artificial aids would lead to a change for the worse in mountaineering outlook, could arguably be held to be more correct, judged by events of today, than were his critics. Could he have lived to hear Geoffrey Young's Centenary address to the A C on 10 December 1957, he would have found a speaker who echoed his own thoughts, though in less strident tones.

Thomas Graham Brown (1882–1965). Brown's term of office ran from 1949 to 1953, and they proved stormy years. By profession he was a physiologist, holding the chair of that science in the University of Wales from 1920 to 1947. He was elected F R S in 1927. He came to mountaineering relatively late in life, for he was in his forties before he embarked on larger Alpine climbs, though accustomed from earlier days to climbing in Great Britain. He was very tough and strong and notably tireless; but was a poor tech-

---

* It is difficult to think of Longland of all people being 'frustrated' by so small a cause!

nical performer. This made him unsuitable as a guideless companion. Fortunately, he had ample private means and could afford to pay for the best guides, leaving it to them to do the work and to get him along. Being able to spend many weeks in the Alps, he soon acquired a formidable array of climbs, to which was added his own profound study of the literature of mountaineering. His retirement in 1947 from his Chair of Physiology gave him the necessary leisure for editing the *A J*; his extensive climbing experience, which included the Himalaya and North America, and his wide knowledge, should have made him ideally fitted for the task of an Editor.

Unfortunately, it did not work out like that. Graham Brown was a man of strong likes and (more often) dislikes. He rather enjoyed controversy,* but if, like Coolidge before him, it could be said that he could do anything with a hatchet except bury it, unlike Coolidge, Graham Brown was never abusive in his writing. He was always suave and precise, though his pen might be caustic.

For certain people he developed a dislike that became obsessive; he had come to regard Geoffrey Winthrop Young as a humbug because of certain errors in his writings, errors seemingly due to vanity. As for Frank Smythe, with whom G-B had made the splendid Red Sentinel and Route Major climbs on Mont Blanc in 1927 and 1928, he lost all sense of proportion in his detestation. Lord Tangley discusses some of these points, which were the more remarkable because G-B might be friendly and generous of his great knowledge, though unfortunately he was so neglectful in answering letters that friend after friend dropped off, giving him up as hopeless.

Mountaineering was the outstanding interest of his life,† though in later years he revived a boyhood love of sailing and owned a small motor yacht. He was a meticulous planner of his climbs and very disinclined to alter them, as is pointed out in his obituary notice and Lord Tangley notes that Graham Brown even gave a false gloss to a climb rather than admit any error or inadequacy. This factor was very marked in his accounts of climbs made with F. S. Smythe, some of G-B's statements being quite grotesque, and it is well-known that his book *Brenva* in its published form was very different from the earlier drafts.

G-B's contentiousness soon found its way into the pages of the *A J* that he edited. Nor were the problems of his editorship restricted to his likes or dislikes for individuals; his unbusinesslike methods, and failure to deal with correspondence or with proofs, caused incessant delays in the appearance of the *Journal*. Assistant editors and printers were equally in despair; complaints in the Club mounted; eventually the A C Committee

---

* This was noticed in his scientific work and in his dealings with the authorities at Cardiff.

† The obituarist in the memoir of the Royal Society (Nov. 1966) notes how little scientific work he published once he had achieved his F R S.

had to grasp the nettle. As Lord Tangley relates, the occasion of Graham Brown's dismissal from the editorship coincided with his being in hospital; but nobody knew of the latter circumstance, and though he had been invited to give his views on the editorship to the Committee, he did not do so, as the letter did not reach him in time, since he had for a while managed to conceal his address from the hospital.

So much for one side of the picture: what of the journals themselves that appeared over G-B's name? As might be expected from so high an authority on climbing history in the Alps, more than one article of historical interest appeared such as the Innominata route on Mont Blanc; the Matterhorn accident; the Wetterhörner. But undoubtedly the outstanding event during these years was the successful ascent of Everest in 1953, and Graham Brown made good use of this opportunity. Indeed, the quality of the *A J*s during his editorship was high, though the fact that they appeared at all owed little to the Editor's efforts and much to those who assisted him.

It was a great pity, as Graham Brown had great gifts, had he chosen to use them well. As it was, he earned the unfortunate distinction of being the only Editor who has been sacked by the Committee – and a sigh of relief undoubtedly went up from those who had been connected with the journal under his regime.

❄ (From '*The Alpine Journal* and its Editors' by T. S. Blakeney. Vols. LXXIX–LXXXI.)

PART THREE
MATURITY

Kurt Diemberger

25 ✻ *My Finest Route in the Alps*

The hours one enjoys most are always the hardest to describe. They come and are gone, leaving one groping for words in which to clothe their shining image. In the end, all we can find to say is how lovely they were and how serene their enjoyment . . .

For me the Peuterey ridge was more than a climb.

How often had I looked up at it, studying its every mood. I had learned to know it when the dark clouds of an approaching storm were closing in; when the soft raiment of newly-fallen snow covered it far down on to the Brenva glacier; and again when its brown rocks, white-crested, leaned sharp against the faultless blue of the heavens. Morning and night, I knew it now; and on many a late return from some climb or other I had come to know it too under the star-studded sky.

For years I had longed to traverse it in its entireity; it had become for me the grandest and most desirable of all Alpine routes. Nor has familiarity since caused me to change my mind.

It was not only the immense triple upward sweep of the great ridge which continually excited my imagination; there was more to it than that. What face in the Alps can rival the wide prospect opened by this route? What a magical progression it offers. First, the green slopes above Peuterey, then the slabby rocks, followed in tremendous succession by the South ridge of the Noire, flinging its towers to the sky; the ensuing upward sweep to the icy comb of the Blanche; the broad col before the last, steep 3,000 ft.; and, finally, the gentle finish leading to Mont Blanc's lofty dome. Hadn't such a route got everything? And doesn't a climber's progress follow the self-same rhythm all through his life?

What a unique experience such a climb must offer – a climb which in a threefold sweep leads him from the flower-starred meadows at valley level to the summit of the Monarch himself, with its prospect out into illimitable distances and downwards on to all other summits in the Alps!

Even when I had gained actual experience of some of its separate sectors, the ridge as a single entity still fascinated me; but whenever I made plans to do it, something always seemed to turn up to thwart my overwhelming urge. When, later, a propitious summer had granted me success on the last of the three great North faces of the Alps, a still, small voice came sounding through the retrospective-reflective mood which set in after the successful completion of that climb. 'How lucky you are!' it seemed to say; 'you still have the grandest and finest route in the Alps waiting for you.'

Then I was grateful that my luck had always robbed me of it. Looking across at the mighty surge of the Peuterey ridge, I suddenly felt that this time it must at last come my way.

IN THE VAL VENI

Autumn had come, with its short but brilliant days. The air was clear and the sky was a quiet cloth of blue, drawn taut above Mont Blanc. The Val Veni meadows were gay with meadow-saffron; the grass and ferns of the foothill slopes had turned ochre, brown and red. Here and there grew a few solitary flowers, altogether foreign to this season of the year, doubtless under the impression that it was already spring-time, so long had the weather been fine and warm. And yet, wherever there was shade, there lingered little patches of snow, which had fallen a few days earlier and was only slowly vanishing. The first September days were here.

A wide meadow dotted with a few sparse trees stretches in front of the Peuterey alp; for some years it has served as a camping-site in summer. Now it was empty and silent except for the tinkling of a few cow-bells. A careful scrutiny would have revealed a single small tent nestling under a great pine, and outside it two unshaven and somewhat scruffy figures, sitting on the grass, surrounded by a variety of gaily-coloured objects and delving deeply into the pages of a book.

The tent belonged to me and my friend Franz Lindner from Krems. We were busily discussing a photograph of the Noire and a report in a C.A.F. *Journal*, with a view to making adequate preparations for the 1,700 ft. abseil down the Northern arête – itself a mere detail in the five miles of ridge we were proposing to cover (weather permitting, of course) in the next few days. The weather didn't really worry us – it is usually good in September – and in any case we were prepared to meet all eventualities; we were pretty optimistic. Of course we remembered that the climb had only been done twice, first in 1953, when Dr. Richard Hechtel and his party did the whole ridge, including the mighty South ridge of the Noire; then not again till 1957, when a Polish team repeated the climb, like their predecessors taking three days over it.

Now, in 1958, we were allowing anything from four days to a week, for the following reasons. Franz and I were both convinced that the climb on which we were embarking would provide an experience never to be repeated, at any rate not in our Alpine days. And, since not many others were likely to follow in our footsteps on this immense route, we were determined that everyone who loves mountains should be able to share in the wonderful sights and scenes that lay before us. So we had decided to capture at least some part of that great experience for their eyes, as well as for our own permanent record, on 16 mm film. True, the most we could bring back from those long days spent on the ridge would be a film running for three-quarters of an hour or so – but it would mean taking much longer over the climb, for all that. To start with, we would be carrying a much heavier load – the camera itself weighed 5 lb. and that was the least of the equipment we would need. We were very fit and our heavy rucksacks wouldn't lower our morale; but our speed would almost certainly be affected. Then again, because of our film project, we intended to reject the outlook of climbers storming upwards over all obstacles at top speed, and to substitute for it, so far as possible, the contemplative mental attitude of a wayfarer, delighting to rest for an hour by the roadside, to watch some particularly lovely cloud effect, to savour, in peace and quiet, every beauty encountered as he travels his long road, equally content to reach journey's end after two or twelve hours on the way. We were ourselves a little surprised that this conscious and almost total elimination of the time-concept could lend a fantastic sense of beauty to our undertaking. But what more attractive adventure could one want than to go as wanderers go in places where wandering is not the normal form?

The traverse of the entire Peuterey ridge without the provision of at least one small depot is, security-wise, of doubtful wisdom; for the savage blizzards which suddenly break over the Mont Blanc range could make it impossible to get off the ridge for a week at a time. Where then to site our depot?

We knew that Dr. Hechtel had dumped some of his equipment and provisions on the summit of the Noire before starting up the South ridge, thus enabling him to move both unencumbered and quickly on the ridge. As neither of these considerations affected us, and because in my view only a depot sited beyond the Noire could ensure the safety and success of our climb, we decided to place it in the Brèche Nord behind the Dames Anglaises, where there is already a bivouac box and where the normal 'short' Peuterey ridge-climb starts.

After careful consideration of the contents of our depot, we packed everything up, including the equipment for the ice-ridge. Down in the village we had managed to borrow two ancient and immensely long 'ancestral' ice-axes for our return journey, promising by all that is holy to bring them back in good condition. With these and our fairly heavy rucksacks we set out, hoping fervently that the lovely weather would last for many more days . . .

THE FIRST MOVE

It was dark when we reached the bivouac box in the Brèche Noire at about 11,500 ft.

Before I fell asleep in that comfortable little shelter, I lay thinking what a long way it was up from the valley. The Fresnay glacier had in the course of the last few years lost none of its reputation for disruption, its tottering séracs none of their hostility; the couloir up to the Brèche was as steep as ever and today the upper part had even been hard, smooth ice.

I had been up here some years before with my friend Wolfgang Stefan, intending to do the Peuterey 'short'. It had come to nothing, for a sudden break in the weather overtook us long before the Aiguille Blanche. The next day we managed to get down with the greatest difficulty, as the first avalanches were pouring down the couloir and new snow building up almost to our knees. We had been heartily glad to get down again in safety that time.

Now, when morning came, we soon found a good site for our depot, in a rocky crack below an overhang. We carefully stowed in it two pairs of crampons, two ice-mallets, some ice-pitons, a litre of petrol, spare batteries and bivouac torches, film equipment and, last but not least, a heavy canister containing food enough for a whole week. Nothing whatever was to be allowed to chase us off the ridge, once we had reached this point – even if it chose to snow us in for several days on end.

Unfortunately one of my crampons had become unserviceable. In the darkness on the previous day I had got a point of one wedged in a crack in the rocks; as I freed myself, off came the point. There was nothing for it but to go down to Courmayeur and fetch a new crampon, a crampon fit for the South ridge.

We were just going to start down when we noticed someone coming up the couloir from the Fresnay glacier; we could hear their voices quite clearly and every now and then we recognized rope instructions. We were very surprised that anyone should be coming up so late in the year. It turned out that the three Italians who presently put in an appearance had only come to check the condition of the bivouac box. And one of them, who had a long kind of contraption in his hand, was looking – believe it or not – for uranium.

'Luckily he won't find any,' I said to Franz, 'and let's hope no one ever will stumble on that kind of hidden treasure among these hills.' He nodded in agreement and gave the uranium hunter a rather dirty look. Shades of the mighty Peuterey ridge! We were glad when, in due course, the party started down again.

We followed close on their heels, for every hour was adding to the danger of bombardment by falling stones in the couloir. Thanks to those reliable old ice-axes, the Fresnay glacier proved amenable without cram-pons. Finding a much better route between the crevasses and ice-towers, we soon reached the prominent notch of the Col de l'Innominata and hurried down the slopes of old snow to the scree-chutes and the meadows below. And as we made haste down to the valley, we kept on glancing up at the red towers of the Noire. Up there was our South ridge and now we would soon be on it.

By the afternoon we were back at our tent on the alp, with the first move completed.

A JACOB'S LADDER OF GRANITE

Dusk was falling as we climbed, over slabs and slopes covered with green-ery, into the great half-circle of the Fauteuil des Allemands. Soon we could see a tiny hut at the base of a rock-cliff, the Noire Hut. It is an old-fashioned type of refuge, without a guardian and boasting few sleeping places. One has to fetch water from the stream beyond a great patch of boulders, the stove smokes horribly and you get your wood from where you can find it. In brief, it is just what is meant by a 'good old comfortable climber's refuge'.

We got everything ready for the morning, took a last look at the weather and fell asleep, wondering where the next two nights would find us . . .

It was still dark when I woke up, worrying about the time. There were definite signs of a new day, but my luminous watch showed only two o'clock. The weather was still fine and there was a moon. Franz said it was too early. I agreed that a little more sleep would do no harm and rolled myself up again in my corner.

Next thing, it was four o'clock and high time to get a move on. We were up in a moment and all our surmises about the day to come were shed in an instant. Today had arrived and nothing else counted. We opened the door to let in the keen cold morning air. Soon the rice-crisps were crackling in the oven and the soup was heating up. Not that we were exactly hungry, but we swallowed what we could – at least our backs would be that much lighter.

We went across to the stream in the half-light and, as we slowly mounted the endless slopes of rubble to reach the base of the South ridge, the gentle fingers of the morning sun touched the rocky towers high overhead. They glowed brownish red and we thrilled at the thought of the climbing awaiting us up there.

We were on the South ridge of the Noire, with gorgeously rough rock under our fingers and hand-holds true as steel. Up it went, up and up, slab after slab, cliff upon cliff, tower after tower, all of it steep, and always above the sheer abyss on either side. Mists came drifting up from the séracs of the Fresnay glacier, to dance around the pinnacles and about us as we climbed on, drinking in the fresh, clean autumn air.

All around us lay sunlight and valley and vast distances; the banks of cloud building slowly in the sky, the turquoise eye of the little Checrouit lake far below and the warm scent of autumn rising from the foothill meadows; the grey rubble-stream of the Miage glacier, snaking deep down into the valley, right into the green of the forests and the fields; the tiny houses along the Dora's banks – all far, far below.

The rock was beautifully varied. We met slabs whose rounded surfaces were covered with greyish-green lichens; white felspar crystals stuck out here and there, asking to be pocketed. There were ledges, offering firm foothold for a groping boot, wrinkles in the rock inviting one to entrust the whole of one's body weight to them and heave it up with one's arms. We came to a huge overhang and used each other's shoulders to overcome it. Then we were over the second tower and on our way to the next, the massive Pointe Welzenbach. We traversed out on to the right-hand face over ledges and slabs.

So we went on and up along the granite Jacob's ladder of the South ridge. And while our arms and legs were busy with the mechanics of climbing and our eyes engaged in searching out the way ahead, our thoughts went out over all the depths and distances around and about us. It goes without saying that we were happy beyond measure on our South ridge.

By the afternoon we were on the summit of the Pointe Welzenbach. There we sat down to rest and eat and looked down on the way we had come. The first tower, the Pointe Gamba, looked like a small tooth, the pinnacles of the second lay far below us, and here we were, sitting on the third. Willo Welzenbach once got as far as this; it was some time after that before a way was found to the summit over the Pointe Brendel and the Bich. Looking up at the yellow and rust-coloured walls, we rated them at fully V – perhaps a bit more than that, though there is only one short traverse on the vertical face of the Bich which is supposed to be from V to VI.

We were at a little flat place with a bivouac wall all round it, a reminder that not everyone can do the South ridge in a single day and that we would probably find quite a few more 'parapets' higher up.

We wondered whether we could still get to the top of the Pointe Brendel before nightfall. We thought it worth trying, so we started off on the abseil which follows. We soon found a suitable block, the rope went whistling down and we followed comfortably enough in our 'Dülfer' seats. There followed a gently sloping step and a traverse to the left before we were at the foot of the Brendel's severe upthrust.

We craned our heads backwards to look up at it, and spotted the route up the almost perpendicular slabs to the left, leading to the overhang above. This was another of the many things we wanted to film, but the difficulty was how to look after the rope at the same time? 'Leave it to me,' said Franz, taking the camera, and off I went. After a slightly overhanging start, I reached the first piton and could see the second, ahead of me. Of course the rope had to jam plumb in between the two, just when I was not exactly comfortably placed. 'What's up?' I shouted down to Franz. 'Give me some rope!' 'Lovely shooting,' he replied calmly and put the camera away. 'Now you'll have to wait a bit while I get the knot undone.' It didn't really take very long but, getting my breath back at the second piton, I thought to myself: 'No more safety knots in the rope, thank you. It's better just to rely on climbing carefully!'

Unfortunately the sun chose that moment to disappear behind a big cloud, so I had to wait. Not that it mattered, for we didn't care how far we got that day; but as the blessed light of the sun seemed to have gone for good I decided to get on with the traverse. The moment I was across, of course the sun came out again. Up came Franz's voice; 'Get back again!' I couldn't very well refuse, and in any case, it was a nice traverse; so back I went and did it again. It all took ages, but I had to chuckle at the thought that we didn't mind about time, and what huge fun it was not to have to. Our journey up the great ridge would go on for days – just as many days as it needed – all of them glorious days, as we simply climbed higher and higher up it.

We climbed the second pitch of the Brendel in the dusk. Presently it was quite dark, as we felt our way over easier rock to the spacious summit. There we found a splendid place for a bivouac overnight, in a hollow, where we could lie down and stretch full length side by side; once again it was equipped with a protecting wall to break the wind. There was only one fly in the ointment; we were dreadfully thirsty. Naturally there isn't any water laid on on the South ridge, and nowhere on the way had we seen so much as a spot of snow. There was nothing to be done about it, and one can't have everything; perhaps we would find some tomorrow, on the summit.

The night was still, with only an occasional feeble stirring of the air about the peak, born only to die away almost at once. We were very happy with the day's work and looked forward to a night in the open worth remembering. It was very clear and a thousand stars shone down on us with a rare brilliance. Soon I was welcoming my old friend Orion, as he came up over the horizon.

Then I suddenly noticed a patch of light shimmering between the rocks. I switched my torch on and there, miraculously, in autumn-time, up here, was some old snow. It must have been the only fragment of snow on the whole South ridge. We took it in turns without more ado to lie on our stomachs sucking in the little trickle of melting water from the old snow, repeating the performance again and again. It was bliss, and now our happiness was complete. The only thing missing had been water.

It was a lovely night. We slept full length on our rocky bed, wrapped warmly in our fleece-bags, covered by the tent-sack. Every now and then I woke up to look up at the stars, to the glittering scarf of the Milky Way, and to watch the leisurely progress of Orion; happy in the knowledge that we would be continuing our journey up this great ridge for many another similar day.

Being autumn, it got a little chilly towards dawn. Slowly the sky lightened, yellow at first then blue to eastwards; then the sun shot up and it was day again. The granite towers of our ridge were swathed in mists, turning our little summit to an island in the monotony of grey, through which the sun glimmered from time to time. At times the wind parted the curtains and we looked up to Mont Blanc, still remote and high above us. Down below, the cloud shadows were chasing across the crevassed surface of the Fresnay glacier. We made breakfast and did some filming, before we realized it was eleven o'clock and time to be on the move.

Ahead of us lay the hardest sector on the whole climb, the precipitous surge up to the Pointe Bich, whose arête and the ensuing traverse had moved even Hermann Buhl to respectful utterance. We wondered a little how we would fare on it with all our baggage. The passage of a few pinnacles in the next col brought us to the foot of the pitch. Baggage and all, it went better than we had expected; admittedly, we were reaping the fruits of an unbroken summer's climbing, and that helped a lot. Once up the steep arête, we tackled the traverse, which goes off to the right along a short airy rock-ledge above an overhang, offering only tiny finger holds and forcing one's body out over nothingness. Short as it is, it made extreme demands on our fingers, while our packs did their best to pull us outwards off the mountain. It was soon over and we stopped for a breather before continuing for quite a time over easier ground. Now it would not be long before we were on the Noire's subsidiary summit. Then came another difficult rope's length, involving slabs and a small overhang. While Franz worked his way up from piton to piton, I filmed him and looked after his rope. Then we decided to put the camera away for a while, for it was time to be getting on to the summit of the Noire. On we went, over easy rock, to the subsidiary summit and looked across to the true summit, on which the metal statue of the Madonna was reflecting the light of the setting sun.

Below it blazed the gigantic slabs of the West face; and there, far down behind the Noire, where it was now getting dark, we thought we could make out the bivouac box, and wondered if we would get there tomorrow. We only stopped long enough to glance at the vast panorama spread about us, then roped down into the next gap. Soon we were climbing over easy boulders, sometimes on the ridge, sometimes on the face, towards the summit.

A red sunset was flushing the sky as we reached the Madonna. There were isolated clouds floating above the mountain-tops, shaped like big fishes, raising sudden misgivings in our minds. What would we do if the weather chose this moment to turn sour on us? Ahead lay the tremendous abseil down the Northern arête of the Noire, an undertaking to be treated with the greatest respect. It would be a serious blow if the weather broke here and now. We could only hope it would hold till the day after tomorrow and that we would be able to reach our provisions at the bivouac box first. We found a sheltered place just below the summit, with plenty of room to lie full-length, and made everything snug for our second night out. The lights of Courmayeur twinkled up from the valley as the night passed slowly by.

A BREAK IN THE WEATHER

The summit of the Noire put on a halo of gold. A sky of unusual beauty, shot with every imaginable colour, heralded the rising of the sun. And the weather was still good.

We breakfasted on porridge and packed up. We knew that very few parties had roped down the North arête, so we had brought plenty of pitons in case we went wrong. The abseil facilities at the summit did not look very safe to us, so we banged a heavy ring-piton into the rock just below it on the northern side; as it went in more firmly at every stroke, my grateful thoughts went out to Wolfgang Stefan, my companion through years of climbing, who had given it to me for this very purpose. We had climbed the South ridge several years earlier up to this point, but no further, thinking ourselves not yet ripe for the whole Peuterey ridge ...

The piton was home, down went our two 130-ft. ropes, and I was soon on my way down over sloping slabs, and straight into thick fog, a not very helpful feature, which would make route-finding very much harder. However, the weather was still fine, even if things seemed to counsel greater speed than before. At the bottom of the rope I found some more pitons in the rock, and made myself fast, leaving the rope free for Franz's descent. We were soon heaving the ropes out into a white emptiness again and listening for them to 'slap' down below. For a few moments we caught a glimpse of the inclined slabs which would be our next landing ground;

then we tested the pitons and followed one another down through thin air. We were delighted to find the next launching platform, after swinging to and fro a little in our chairs; there were three differently-coloured loops of rope hanging there. All we had to do was to retrieve our own rope, thread it and go on down.

We could have done without the fog, though. Finding the right place for the next stage in the descent at the end of each rope's length was becoming quite a problem.

After another 'air-lift' we found ourselves jammed together on an exiguous stance on the crest of the arête. We could see a shelf 30 ft. below us, with pitons and wooden pegs coming up to us, new ones; so we must be bang on Jean Couzy's direct route. We heaved the ropes over the edge; they disappeared silently, drew taut, without so much as a 'slap'. All the indications were that we would be sitting suspended over the void at the end of our 130 ft. We dropped a stone and – after a longish time – could barely hear the sound of its impact; so there must be 200 to 250 ft. of vertical and partly undercut rock beneath us. We had better go down the 30 ft. to the shelf. We reached it soon enough and when I pushed myself along it, still in my sling, at last I came upon an abseil-piton, from which our ropes would touch bottom.

That airy descent landed us on the great shoulder of the Noire's North arête. From there we were left with the same distance down a chimney in the West face as we had already come from the summit. The first thing to do was to retrieve the rope. We tugged with all our strength; it wouldn't budge. It had stuck somewhere up there.

Stupid! We changed position and tugged some more. Both of us, with might and main. All in vain, the rope just hung there, hopelessly stuck up above – 130 ft. up above, right at the top, of course. A nice kettle of fish, to be sure. The only solution was to climb all the way up in Prusik-slings and straighten things out.

Franz volunteered for that thankless job, saying he had been practising the technique only a little while ago. To some purpose, I had to admit, when I saw him get up in under a quarter of an hour. Meanwhile, it had started to snow. The weather had broken. Franz arranged the ropes in a different direction, tested their mobility and came down again. We both hauled anxiously on the rope, this time with better results than before. Cheers – the thing was moving!

The gigantic chimney, with its thousand feet of roping-down, was barely discernible in the mist but when, at the end of our first abseil, we came upon a chock-stone with a rope-ring, we knew we were on the right road. Rope after rope, down and down we went. At times stones whistled past, dangerously near. After a time it stopped snowing again. The chimney became a steep groove which we only left almost at its bottom, traversing out to the right between abseil stages every now and then, so as to lose height as quickly as possible and at the same time land up in the rift which falls from the Brèche Sud to the Fresnay glacier.

It was halfway through the afternoon before we finally got into the rift. There was no time to waste if we were still to get to the bivouac box in the Brèche Nord. We packed up the ropes and climbed up over slabby débris to the Brèche Sud. There we had to turn the pinnacles of the Dames Anglaises, rising in an irregular cluster ahead of us, on their left flank. We climbed a little way, then traversed slightly downwards, with frequent changes of direction, dictated by the nature of the ground. We had to go very carefully, for the rock, while not difficult, was unreliable, and there were snow patches in between. After much up and down and to and fro on the unstable stuff, we were very glad to reach the couloir leading up to the Brèche Nord. All that lay between us and the bivouac box now was the upper arm of the couloir consisting, unfortunately, of sheer, smooth ice.

So near and yet so far! We were dog-tired, hungry and it was getting dark. Otherwise we were perfectly happy. In spite of a day of bad weather we had managed to traverse the Noire and reach our objective. The rest of the ridge was practically in the bag, for with enough provisions up there in the bivouac box to enable us to face even a prolonged spell of bad weather, what could now prevent our going on, to the top of Mont Blanc?

I led, using the only crampon we had with us, while Franz belayed me with due care. While I was beating step on step in the smooth surface with my ice-hammer, it was suddenly pitch-dark. At long last we got off the ice and reached the shabby saddle of the Brèche Nord, with the bivouac box close at hand. Outside, the snow-flakes were whirling down, as we lay down there and then to sleep. How long, we wondered drowsily, before it turns fine again?

Our fourth day on the ridge dawned. We snuggled closer in our blankets with only one resolution in our minds – to have an off-day. All the same, we took a look at the weather through the door of the box; fresh snow was lying outside, but the sun was shining, newly risen. The fine weather was back again after the break. We would certainly have to wait a day for the layer of snow to settle. So we fetched everything out of the depot and had a good tuck-in after our days of scanty fare. We reconnoitred the next day's route for a short way and took a few feet of film. Our load for the following day was hugely inflated by provisions, ice equipment, extra film gear, a tripod and all the rest, but we felt very fit. Still, if we were going to climb from 11,500 ft. where we stood, over the Aiguille Blanche and on to Mont Blanc's 15,782 ft. summit, we should have to make an early start. A fine day gave way to a clear evening. We knew then that we could be sure of fine weather for the last stage of our long trek.

THE FINAL DAY

Autumn, in tune with our most secret desires, gave us, for our last day, her most perfect of all perfect days. As we climbed the Aiguille Blanche, our eyes ranged far and wide over innumerable peaks, in the warmth of the morning sun, under an immaculate blue sky. Down in the green valleys the houses of Entrèves and Courmayeur were small beyond belief. It was sheer bliss to be alive.

Behind us the Noire diminished rapidly. We kept on thinking about its South ridge, the nights we had spent out on it, the exciting endless abseil down its Northern arête, till at last the traverse of the triple-headed Blanche began to demand all our care and attention. From the summit we looked down on the huge saddle of the Col de Peuterey, lying nearly 1,000 ft. below us – another long abseil. Once down, we jumped the bergschrund and tramped across the broad, smooth saddle; up over the opposing schrund, and then a short rest. The sun was already slanting down, so short are these September days. On we went, up the long, long 3,000 ft. which separate the col from Mont Blanc's summit. Once on the ridge again, we were met by an icy blast, though the view and the sky remained clear. We made slow progress, taking care that the bitter gusts didn't un-balance us on that narrow white edge. Suddenly the great white mountains about us glowed red and Mont Blanc's monstrous shadow streamed out across the world. It was an overwhelming sight, even if the gale called for all our attention and our fingers had grown numb.

Presently there was nothing except a livid twilight. Moving together, we worked our way up without a pause. We did not belay, but each of us was on the alert, knowing that a slip on that narrow ladder to the sky could hardly be held. Then it was night. The abyss fell away beneath us, impalpable, illimitable, invisible. We only knew it was there below us. Neither of us could see the other, obliterated by the uncanny darkness. And so we climbed, endlessly, onwards. Endlessly, straight up – up into the vague, dark nothingness overhead; but now we were belaying one another, rope after rope. The ridge gave way to a rounded slope, a kind of broad rib, getting steeper and steeper. The gigantic cornice of Mont Blanc de Courmayeur never seemed to want to put in an appearance.

We could see a sharp silhouette against the stars. It was the cornice and soon we had found a way through a breach in it. We sat down thankfully in the snow. We had done it. We were up. What was left to do would be nothing by contrast with the last few hours.

We moved on again, through the marvellous night. This was the last stage on the long journey from the valley to Mont Blanc's summit; and as we went, our thoughts were centred on the days behind us.

The rest of the route, to Mont Blanc's own slightly higher summit, is easy; all we had to do was to check our direction occasionally. It was 10.0 P.M. when we sat down to rest on the highest point of the Monarch's snowy dome. The icy wind had almost died away, but it was still very cold. We didn't intend to stay long before making downhill for the Vallot Refuge. We shook hands – there was no need for words. We were utterly weary and utterly content.

This much we knew, that the days we had spent on Mont Blanc's great and glorious ridge, to say nothing of the precious minutes on his summit under the immense star-encrusted vault of the heavens, would never pass away from our memories.

❄ (*A description of the third ascent of the whole Peuterey ridge, including the South ridge of the Aiguille Noire*, Vol. LXVI.)

Sir Edmund Hillary

26 ❄ The Last Lap

Gregory, Lowe and Ang Nyima left almost immediately after they had put down their loads. We took off our oxygen and started clearing a platform, on the sloping ground, on which to put our tent for the night. We had to hack away stones from the ice, and when we had finished the platform was in two layers – one about 6 inches above the other. We found that it was difficult to anchor the tent and had to fix our guys to the oxygen bottles, as there were no convenient rocks to which to tie them. We spent a cold and uncomfortable night – myself sitting on the upper shelf and Tenzing half lying on the lower. We had enough oxygen for two periods of an hour each and during this time we dozed fitfully.

At about 4 A.M. I looked out of the tent door and saw that it was obviously going to be a fine day. Just before we finally started, I looked at the thermometer and saw that it registered −27° C. We brewed up some tea, ate a few biscuits and left at about 6.30 A.M. after putting on our oxygen apparatus.

Soon we were on the ridge; we kicked our way up the slopes beyond, and at first it was not very steep but it was narrow and demanded every care. We moved continuously and came eventually to the long 400-ft. snow slope leading to the South Summit. This was a very steep section and dangerous, and whilst we were on it I thought that it might avalanche at any moment. I made the steps, carefully packing the snow at each step. About halfway up I turned to Tenzing and said: 'What do you think of it, Tenzing?' He replied that it was very difficult and dangerous. I asked him again, 'Shall we go on?' and he replied – he is a very polite fellow – 'Just as you wish.' I decided to continue. Soon, to our great relief, we reached the South Summit. We were now at about 28,700 ft. and were at the point reached by Bourdillon and Evans two days before. We sat down, had a drink from our water bottle, and I calculated that we had sufficient oxygen to continue. We then looked in the direction in which we had to go.

The summit ridge certainly looked difficult. The first portion of it was a gradually rising snow ridge with large cornices overhanging the Kangshung face on the right. To the left, the South-west face of Everest fell steeply to the Western Cwm. Beyond this initial section I could see the steep rock step which we had thought all along would be the crux of the climb. I started cutting steps along the ridge between the rocks on the left and the snow on the right. The snow was firm, and two or three blows of the ice-axe made a satisfactory step. We moved one at a time, myself cutting all the steps.

Suddenly I noticed that Tenzing was lagging and that he was gasping for breath. I examined his oxygen set and found that his outlet tube was blocked with ice. However, I was able to free this and give him immediate relief. Soon we reached the foot of the big black rock step. It looked very formidable and perhaps impossible to climb at this height. Then I noticed a long vertical crack between the rock and the ice of the cornices on the right. This crack was about 40 ft. high and large enough to take the human body. I crawled into it and started forcing and jamming my way up it; my crampons on the ice behind me and my face towards the rock. It was very hard work, but finally I dragged myself out on to a little ledge at the top and lay there gasping like a fish for several minutes. When I had recovered sufficiently I signalled Tenzing to start. He entered the crack and forced his way laboriously up and finally landed, as I had done, gasping for breath on the ledge. After a short rest we continued slowly on.

We were now both feeling very tired, but felt that it would take a lot to stop us. I cut steps round the back of one steep snow hump after another. They seemed to continue endlessly. Then I noticed suddenly that the ridge dropped away steeply in front of me and in the distance I could see the barren plateau of Tibet. I looked up to my right and 40 ft. above me was a rounded snow cone. A few blows of the ice-axe, a few weary steps, and I was on the top. My first reaction was that of relief. I then took off my oxygen apparatus and photographed Tenzing as he stood on the top. He had the flags of the United Nations, Great Britain, Nepal and India unfurled from his ice-axe, and these fluttered in the fresh breeze that was blowing. I then took photos looking down all the main ridges of the mountain and in several directions.

To the east Makalu stood out prominently. I automatically looked to see if there was a route up it; the visibility was very good. About eighty miles away, beyond Makalu, was Kangchenjunga, standing up clearly. Over to the west I could see Cho Oyu, our adversary of 1952, and in the distance was Gosainthan. Looking down the north side I could see the North Col, the North Peak and the East Rongbuk Glacier clearly.

I had now had my oxygen mask off for nearly eight minutes and was becoming rather clumsy-fingered. In the meantime Tenzing had buried some lollies and biscuits as an offering to his gods and I left a crucifix given to me by John Hunt. We put on our oxygen masks and set off from the top down the way we had come.

We moved quickly but cautiously along to the top of the rock step, slid down the difficult chimney and then made our way back to the South Summit. We then descended the steep snow slope which was so dangerous on the way up, and our old fears returned as we felt it was going to avalanche. The hour we spent on this slope was one of the worst that I have ever experienced. It was a great relief when we reached the ridge again and moved down it, very weary, and at last reached Camp IX.

Here we stopped for a little and brewed up some tea and lemonade, and then started off down the remaining ridge to the top of the couloir. We were extremely tired, and when we reached the couloir I saw with dismay that we would have to cut steps down it, as all our tracks of the day before had been removed by the wind. However, there was nothing for it but to start. I slowly but carefully cut steps down for one or two rope lengths and then Tenzing took over the lead and found some deep snow in which he could kick steps, and by this means we came down the remaining part of the couloir. As we descended slowly, we could see tiny figures come out from the South Col camp. We finally got to the Col itself and walked over its glistening and slippery surface to be met by George Lowe who had brought out some hot drinks. We told him our news.

He helped us back to the tents, and there we saw Wilfrid Noyce who was looking very fresh and strong. For the next hour or so we told them about our climb and answered their questions. Then darkness fell, and we spent a most miserable and uncomfortable night. We were cold and exhausted, and the continuous flapping of the tents in the tearing wind made sleep nearly impossible.

At last dawn came, and we staggered out of our sleeping-bags, ate a most distasteful meal and packed up our things. We left the tents on the South Col, and as we walked up the 200-ft. snow slope to the top of the Eperon we could see the wind tugging hungrily at the guys, as though impatient to sweep away the last traces of our expedition from the Col. It was a weary grind up those 200 feet, but at last we could start going down and we went slowly but reasonably safely across the great traverse to the top of the Lhotse Face and Camp VII. We were moving extremely slowly, as Tenzing and I were very tired. However, after a few hours we got to Camp VII and there Charles Wylie was waiting for us with more food and hot drinks. We decided, after a short rest there, to move on down to Camp IV and this we did, going slowly but steadily. The way down the Lhotse Face seemed to take an age. Nevertheless, soon we were past the site of Camp VI, and as we reached the bottom of the Lhotse Face and were approaching Camp V, Tom Stobart and some Sherpas were there to meet us.

After another short rest at Camp V we pushed on down to Camp IV, and as we neared Camp IV we could see the other members of the party coming out to meet us. They started to run towards us, and finally George

Lowe put them out of their suspense and gave a thumbs-up sign. Soon we were shaking hands and talking, and when we got to the tents there was James Morris to take down the story immediately and get it off to London. It was a great moment for us all.

❊ (From 'Everest, 1953' by various members of the expedition. Vol. LIX.)

George Band

27 ❄ *Kangchenjunga Climbed*

While I got the sleeping oxygen ready, Joe Brown lit the primus and began melting snow for drinks. We were determined not to let ourselves get dehydrated. We made lemonade from crystals and then a mug of tea each, with lots of sugar. Supper consisted of asparagus soup from a packet, a tin of lambs' tongues with mashed potatoes, and a nightcap of drinking chocolate. I think that's a better meal than most summit parties have had. Then we crawled into our sleeping-bags, keeping on every scrap of clothing – even our boots. We didn't want to risk ours getting frozen hard like Hillary's on Everest. I wore my boots solidly for three days and nights during the assault.

We shared a yellow 1,600-litre cylinder of oxygen between us. Being not quite full, it gave us nine hours' supply at one litre per minute each. I didn't sleep as well with it as usual. Perhaps it was the excitement. As we lay side by side, fragments of snow kept skittering down the slope and hitting the tent. Sometimes I thought it was a snowfall beginning, at others I wondered what might happen if a really large lump or a stone came. We had stayed roped up just in case and tied the middle of it round a spike of rock close to the tent. I prayed for fine weather tomorrow, otherwise we would not stand a chance. The others had done their utmost to get us as high as possible, so we must not let them down. An awful responsibility lay upon our shoulders. I cursed myself for working with my bare fingers just a moment too long that morning for now they were slightly frostbitten; the tips all blistered. I hoped they wouldn't handicap me next day.

The God of Kangchenjunga was kind to us, for May 25 dawned fine. We woke automatically when the oxygen was exhausted at five o'clock. We breakfasted on a couple of pints of tea and a biscuit or two and made off up the Gangway at 8.15, swerving out left to meet the sunshine. Near the top of the Gangway we had planned to turn off right at a string of snow patches and climb across the face, because we had seen earlier through binoculars that the West ridge itself was extremely broken and difficult.

Unfortunately, we had very little idea as to how far up the Gangway we really were and we turned off too early at the wrong snow patch. By the time we had realized our mistake and turned back, an hour and a half of precious time was lost. So we hurried on up the Gangway as fast as possible to try and make up time. Apart from the snow of the Gangway, most of the climbing would be on rock, so we had left our canvas overboots behind, and now, when we reached the first rocks, we took our crampons off.

We were aiming for a little subsidiary snow-ridge which would lead us back to the main West ridge beyond its worst difficulties. The approach to this snow-ridge was steep and we had to climb pitch by pitch for about three hundred feet. There was one tricky section where you had to swing round a corner on your hands. It might have ranked as 'difficult' at sea-level, and Joe safeguarded it with a piton since I had a poor belay. Just above was an impressive ice-slope, sixty degrees in places, which required two pitches. There was a sensational rocky eyrie half-way; one seemed to be poised in mid-air thousands of feet above the Shelf and the glacier below.

Because of the time we were taking, every breath of oxygen was vital, so we cut down our supply to the minimum rate of two litres per minute, only increasing the flow when wrestling with some difficulty. This low rate seemed hardly sufficient for a person of my size and weight, and may have accounted partly for the fact that Joe was now definitely going better than I was. I had led at first, then we had a period leading through, and now Joe was in front. He offered to stay in the lead, and I was happy to agree.

We came out on to the crest of the snow-ridge and the summit pyramid was at last visible, culminating about 400 feet above. We had been climbing for over five hours without a rest, such was our feeling of urgency, so after cutting up the snow-ridge, we joined the West ridge and sank down in a little hollow behind and above the cluster of pinnacles. My throat was parched. We took off our oxygen masks and had a quick snack of lemonade, toffee and mint cake.

A strong breeze was blowing up the North-west face, carrying flurries of snow over our heads. I looked over at the North ridge and then photographed our route ahead. The ridge was easier at first, and by keeping a little down on the right we would avoid the wind. But at the last a nose of rock reared up, sheer and smooth. We could have no idea what it held in store for us. It was 2 P.M. We only had a couple of hours' oxygen left.

'We ought to turn back by three o'clock, Joe,' I said, 'or we may have to spend the night out.'

'We've just got to reach the top before then,' he replied.

We carried on. The West and South peaks of Kangchenjunga were now well below us. We skirted below the rock nose, round a corner, and up a little gully. There above us the wall was broken by several vertical cracks about twenty feet high, with a slight overhang to finish. Joe was keen to try one. As he said later: 'I knew that at sea-level I could climb it quite easily, but at that height you don't know just how long your strength's going to last you if you hang by your arms for any length of time. You might just fall off in sheer exhaustion.' Turning his oxygen to the full six litres a minute and safeguarding his lead with a couple of running belays, he struggled and forced his way up. It was the hardest part of the whole climb; perhaps 'very difficult' had it been at normal altitudes. From the top, I remember him shouting, 'George, we're there!'

I joined him, with no more than a tight rope I'm glad to say, and there before us, some twenty feet away and five feet higher than the ground on which we stood, was the very top, formed by a gently sloping cone of snow. It was a quarter to three. We had come as far as we were allowed.

We took photographs of each other and of the view round about. There was a great sea of cloud at 20,000 feet, so only the highest mountains stood out like rocky islands with the waves lapping round about them. To the west, beyond the sharp ridge of Kangbachem, were the giants, Makalu, Lhotse and Everest, eighty miles away, silhouetted deep blue against the faint horizon. Sikkim was hidden by both cloud and the concealing curve of the summit, but over to the north were the snow-streaked, drumlin-like hills of Tibet. Close at hand, we could just see the summit of the Bavarians' north-east spur and, through rents in the cloud, the grey snake of the Kangchenjunga Glacier beneath us, where Dyhrenfurth's party had tried in vain.

We turned to descend. After an hour, the oxygen finished and we discarded the sets and carried on down, feeling very weary. Once, when crossing a patch of unstable snow, a foothold suddenly broke. I slipped, rolled over on to my stomach and dug my axe-point into the snow to arrest myself. In a split second it was all over, but I had to lie there panting while Joe said: 'It makes me breathless just to watch you do that.'

Guided by shouts, we reached our tent as darkness fell. As planned, Hardie and Streather had arrived there ready for a second attempt in case we had failed. They had been waiting anxiously, as we should really have gone on down to sleep at Camp V, but now, in the dark, it was too dangerous. So the four of us squeezed into that tiny two-man tent, overlapping the narrow ledge, and they plied us generously with tea and soup, and more tea and more soup. I'd never felt so thirsty in my life before. There was no tossing up for the outside position this time; they reckoned I knew all about it, so there I went. The sewing of the canvas would creak beneath me, and each time I thought: 'Supposing the stitching goes?'

Somehow we managed to pass the night. We insisted that Hardie and

Streather used the two sleeping-bags and some oxygen because they still wanted to have a crack at the top. Joe was in agony through snow-blindness – again caused by removing fogged-up goggles – but fortunately we were still able to see ourselves down early next day while the other two repeated our ascent. It was May 26, the day of the General Election at home.

Hardie and Streather had brought plenty of oxygen, as they felt that shortage of it would be the first reason for failure on our part. So when they left Camp VI at 8.30 A.M., they carried a yellow (1,600 litres) and a blue (800 litres) cylinder each. They followed our route and, being able to use traces of our old steps in places, they made good speed. Incidentally, unlike us, they wore their crampons the whole time. But, as Streather says, they didn't have everything their own way:

'Hardie was leading and I shouted to him to stop, for I noticed that the windproof jacket on his frame was loose. He stopped, and swung the frame off his back. As he did so, his large oxygen cylinder slid out of its straps and went sliding down the mountain. The valve was knocked open, and I can still remember the cylinder hissing as it rushed down the face and out of sight.' So they had to share the remaining oxygen, Hardie carrying the yellow cylinder and leading, and Streather the two blue cylinders on a special one litre per minute flow rate.

At last they came to our vertical crack near the top. Joe and I had left a sling halfway up for them and were wondering how they would like it. They didn't, so they went on a few yards round the wall and there was a perfect little snow-ridge running easily up to the summit! They arrived at 12.15 P.M. and spent an hour there. Streather changed his cylinders round and left the exhausted one behind. Unfortunately, a misconnection rendered the second one useless, so he had to make the whole of the descent without oxygen, and they, too, ended by spending the night at Camp VI.

Charles and Dawa Tensing were waiting at Camp V when they came down. When Charles shouted, 'Have you been to the top?' there was no answer. It seemed a silly question; where else could they have been all that time? A little closer, Norman shouted back, 'Who won the Election?' Charles didn't think that one worth answering either.

By May 28 everyone was off the mountain. But our great jubilation over the double success of our Kangchenjunga Reconnaissance was marred by some very sad news on our return to Base Camp. One Sherpa, Pemi Dorje, had returned exhausted from the high carry. Three days later he seemed recovered, but suddenly developed the symptoms of cerebral thrombosis and, despite all that John Clegg could do, he had died on May 26 – within the very hour that Hardie and Streather had reached the near-summit. So, to the Sherpas, it seemed that, after all, the God of Kangchenjunga had demanded the sacrifice of one of the keenest and most likeable of their number. We buried him near the site of Pache's grave, under a rock carved by the other Sherpas with his name and the eternal Buddhist prayer, *Om mane padme hum* – 'Hail to the Jewel in the Lotus.'

❋ (From 'Kangchenjunga Climbed' by George Band. Vol. LX.)

Ian Clough

28 ❄ A Storm on the Badile

Geoff and I were at the tail end of our party of three pairs. Cassin's famous route on the North-east face of the Piz Badile was almost ours but it was getting late and the weather looked ominous. A few flakes of snow fell as Geoff rounded the arête and set out on the traverse. The others had disappeared into the mist. Then, as if someone had torn open a thousand pillow-cases, the snow began to pour down. All was whiteness. I shouted, urging Geoff to hurry on to the next stance where the first of the two abseils into the easy final couloir began. After agonizing minutes he gave the order to 'Come on'. I saw then the position my companion had been in; the holds on the smooth slab were completely masked by the deathly white coverlet and the protecting pitons had vanished. It was impossible for me to continue by normal means but, by dint of patient scratching and scraping, I discovered pitons enough to tension traverse to the stance, using both ropes and leaving several karabiners and slings in my wake. The distant rumblings had grown steadily nearer and it was obvious that we were about to experience an electric storm. Also, due to the heavy cloud, it was becoming prematurely dark. We were compelled to bivouac where we were, on a small ledge below a big flake belay. But what of the others? A rope was fixed to the flake, indicating that they had already completed the first abseil. A difficult conversation was carried out above the booming of the thunder and the constant hiss of the snow as it swept its way downwards in countless little avalanches. Sid had been caught alone at the top of the second abseil and Nev, who had followed the others down this 70-ft. pitch, was still holding on to the end of the ropes, unable to join the leading pair on their cramped stance. His position was extremely precarious as the block on which he was standing had already moved almost a foot under his weight, and the ice-axe point, sticking up above his rucksack like a lightning conductor, was a mass of blue-green fire! In desperation he swarmed back up the rope, hand-over-hand and unprotected. With great difficulty we pulled these two up to our stance which, though small, offered more protection than the snow-swept couloir below. All the while lightning cracked and spat about us. We were in the very centre of the inferno. The peaks of our caps were lit by St. Elmo's fire, the hair rose on the back of our necks and even the flecks in the perlon ropes began to glow with an eerie phosphorescence. It was now too dark and the others were too far away for us to do anything to help them. They would have to sit it out on their own. We put on all our bivouac equipment and sat huddled together for warmth. The snow eased and finally stopped, but everything was well plastered by now. After about two hours the storm moved on and the mists thinned and occasionally blew clear. Without the prospect of sudden incineration hanging over us our morale improved and, to pass the cold weary hours until dawn, we began to sing. It was significant perhaps that hymns enjoyed great popularity! Our previously gay little party would be engaged in a grim struggle in the morning.

It had started well. After leaving the Dolomites we had driven through Italy into eastern Switzerland, past St. Moritz and down into the deep pine-clad valley dominated by the jagged rock spires of the Bregaglia. From the little village of Promontogno we had made our way up to the Sciora Hut which is surrounded by fine granite peaks. As we were five (Mike James, Nev Crowther, Sid Clarke, Geoff and myself) we had added a sixth member to our team to enable us to climb in pairs; an Italian guide who had asked to join us. In conversation with him, we had discovered that he was none other than Claudio Corti, the only survivor of the Eigerwand tragedy of 1957. As a result of Harrer's book, *The White Spider*, Corti had a notorious reputation; we considered him sane enough, however. As he had already completed the Cassin route once, and had added a new route on the face with the unfortunate Longhi, we thought he would be a valuable asset. We had started from the hut very early and, after a long, monotonous tramp across scree, had reached the foot of the wall by dawn. The day promised to be fine as we climbed steadily upwards by delightful pitches of slabs and grooves. There was never any pitch which could be classed as really hard but the climb maintained a constant level of difficulty, between Severe and mild Very Severe by British standards. But our progress was not as rapid as we would have wished. Corti and Mike were at the head of our caravan and Claudio insisted on taking tension on every peg, even inserting some of his own though the existing ones gave adequate protection. The incessant cries of '*Tirra la bianca*' became monotonously irritating. Despite this however we made fairly steady progress and before noon we were all reassembled at a large snow patch halfway up the 3,000-ft. face, at the foot of the major difficulties. Here we sat down to wait. Above us was a party of three Italians, moving very slowly, who told us they had already spent one day and night on the wall. They had bivouacked near the snow patch and the third man was still only one pitch above us! It was some time before we were able to move off and although our speed was now determined by the slow threesome ahead, we still hoped to reach the summit by nightfall. However, this was not to be. The weather had slowly deteriorated until finally the storm had brought us to a sudden stop. The Italians were bivouacked in the final couloir, a few yards from Corti and James.

The morning dawned fair, although a few dark clouds over the snow-caps of the Bernina added an element of uncertainty. We were soon on the move. The great grey slabs of yesterday were now transformed into a sweep of sparkling whiteness as the thin sprinkling of snow which had adhered to them shone in the early morning sunshine. The ropes were frozen as stiff as steel cables and, before we had made them flexible enough to abseil down, Corti was climbing. The mood this morning was one of grim determination. Corti proceeded slowly up the bed of the gully, a formidable-looking ice pitch. While waiting below, Mike told us of their ordeal. They had spent a miserable night as their stance had been insufficient even to sit down and it had been directly in the line of the snow which had poured down the gully. As a result of being cold and wet for so long, they were both suffering from frost-bite. Mike quoted his companion as saying, 'This is worse than the Eiger!' During the night Mike had climbed above the stance, with its single belaying piton, to find a better perch. Here he had dozed off. Startled from his sleep, he had found himself bouncing down the slab for 20 ft. until jerked to a halt as the rope came tight on the piton, much to Corti's consternation. For the first few pitches this morning we climbed as two ropes, James and the Italians (who had decided to join up with us) with Corti, while I, wearing crampons, led the remaining three. Despite its fierce appearance, the first pitch of the couloir only compared with a Scottish 'V. Diff.' but, without crampons, it represented a good effort on Corti's part. After these few rope lengths in the normally easy but now ice-bound couloir, we came to the foot of a big groove which swept steeply up to the North ridge. This was not the normal route but as it was clear of snow we decided to follow it and, some hours later, we arrived at the summit. After a short rest we began the descent, reaching the foot of the mountain on the Italian side by late afternoon. But our little epic was not yet over.

The Italian hut was said to be expensive, so we agreed to return to the Sciora Hut with Claudio, who had left a client there. We reached the col at sunset after a long weary plod. We understood that Claudio knew the way back so we placed ourselves in his hands. We tied ourselves on to a single rope and set off down the glacier on the far side at break-neck speed. It was dark by the time we reached a steep rounded ridge which disappeared into the gloom. We had only two ice-axes between us (which Geoff and I had brought despite Corti's assurance that such aids were unnecessary) and I had my crampons. I was stationed at the rear to safeguard, while Corti led the way, using the second axe. The ridge soon steepened and someone slipped, starting a chain reaction which I was only able to hold with difficulty. But this was only the beginning; the ridge continued endlessly, down, down, down into the blackness. The snow became harder until finally I was only able to use the pick of my axe to safeguard the others. Corti never hesitated but kept straight on, apparently unaware of the tense situation. I would belay the rest of the party until the rope came tight, then move rapidly down on the front points of my crampons to secure the others once more. But what if someone should slip while I was moving down? What chance was there of holding five people on one ice-pick belay anyway? There was no need to speak as the others were all aware of the position; no one must slip. They clawed at the ice with their hands and crashed their toes hard into the slope to gain what purchase they could on the tough, slippery surface. There were daubs of blood on the ice where torn fingers had been scratching for a hold. Claudio seemed oblivious to all this, pressing on relentlessly. Indeed, it was only the use of some abusive language which induced him to slow down occasionally. Our nerves were now almost at breaking point and our calf muscles screamed out from weariness. Yet a mistake by any one of us could mean disaster for all. After what seemed an eternity we arrived at the base of the ridge only to be confronted by towering séracs and great yawning crevasses, a veritable chaos of tormented ice. Here, though the small circle of light cast by his torch only penetrated the blackness for a few feet, Corti demonstrated a remarkable piece of route-finding and, by balancing precariously over narrow ribbons of ice and leaping across bottomless black voids, we found our way out on to the gentle lower slopes. Now that the tension was gone it was only by a great effort that we forced ourselves to continue but eventually, after more hours of purgatory, we found the hut, ate our first meal in forty-eight hours and fell into a deep sleep. We learned, next day, the reason for the difficulties of our descent – the crossing is normally made by the Passo Bondo but we had unwittingly come over the Falso Passo which our guidebook stated 'must on no account be taken'!

❊ (From 'A Season of Plenty' by Ian Clough. Vol. LXVII.)

Ian Clough

29 ❄ *Eigerwand, 1962*

We arrived, panting and sweating, at a low, shallow cave with a sandy floor. It would be dark in an hour and we could both lie here comfortably so we settled ourselves in to bivouac below the Difficult Crack. The sudden decision, the rushing round trying to borrow money for the fare, the early morning train drawing out of Chamonix Station, all seemed a long way away now. The wall had looked black and dry as the train had rounded the last bend to Grindelwald and we had known that the journey had been worth while; conditions were very favourable. I remembered the girl in the bookshop, where we had copied the description from the back of Heinrich Harrer's book, trying to dissuade us with stories of the most recent fatalities, the look in the blacksmith's eyes as he had sharpened our claws, the bloodstains on the lower rocks where the fall of a solitary Austrian climber had been halted, the moments of doubt and indecision. But we were here now, on the Eiger's North Wall, happy and confident, with four days of fine weather ahead if the Zürich forecasters were correct.

Two small figures had been scurrying up the wall behind us. Like ourselves they wore crash helmets and carried bulging rucksacks on their backs. Now the first climbed the old fixed rope to the ledge near us. He introduced himself as an Austrian – Moderegger. Then his companion arrived: 'Hello' – we were surprised to hear English – 'I'm Tom Carruthers.' We talked for a while. Tom's Scottish friends hadn't wanted to come on the wall and he had met the Austrian at Alpiglen, the little mountain hotel at the foot of the wall. 'What has he done?' we asked cautiously. 'He's been in the Caucasus,' Tom replied. I pictured Moderegger on a Caucasian coach tour. We didn't like it: a chance companion, experience doubtful, barely able to make themselves understood! It seemed foolhardy in the extreme. Still, they weren't our responsibility. We agreed that, should we all move at the same speed, it would be pleasant to have company, it would be a mutual morale booster against the frightening, cruel vastness of this notorious wall. The other pair went to bivouac round the corner. We cooked and ate a huge meal. Our sacks were too heavy, they must have weighed forty pounds but felt like eighty as we had staggered up the thousand feet of scree and broken walls that evening, but now they were much lighter. We dressed in our down clothing and were soon asleep on our little sandy ledge, reassured that we were well nailed on. It was already a long way down.

Chris was shaking me. He was impatient to get away for it was late – 5 A.M.! A hasty breakfast, then away. Carruthers and the Austrian were just behind us as we scurried up the Difficult Crack but they didn't keep up with us. We moved quickly together, along a fault of ledges and easy pitches below a great yellow overhanging wall, to the Hinterstoisser. There were several ropes across this rubicon of the old days and we were soon over the traverse, past the overhang of the Swallow's Nest bivouac, and climbing up what should have been the First Ice-field. But the ice had receded and we were able to climb the rock beside it. We reached a steep step, the Ice Hose. Now we really began to appreciate just how good conditions were, for the Hose was a straightforward rock climb. Above us, bands of rock were showing bare beneath the Second Ice-field. Using these, connecting them by little verglassed ribs sticking up out of the ice, we trended leftwards until we were under the great, glassy, smooth sweep of the main part of the Second Ice-field. 'Whatever happens here, don't look up,' Chris called, drawing on the experience of his previous attempts on the wall with Don Whillans. Over a thousand feet above us, above a great vertical wall, was the mouth of the White Spider which usually belches forth debris from the upper part of the face. We were now entering the most dangerous area on the face; the zone of heaviest bombardment. I tried to make myself as small a target as possible, receding into my crash helmet as a frightened tortoise does into his shell. But the Ogre was frozen into stillness this morning. Not a stone fell.

There was no snow overlying the ice and crampons tended to scart off the tough surface. We decided to go directly up the ice-field to its upper lip. If we went diagonally across, as one normally does, we would have to cut countless steps in the hard blue ice. It would take hours and the mountain's artillery might have opened up before we were clear. By going straight up we could use our crampons to better advantage. We moved off; crampons crashing, pick and dagger thrashing, only a quarter of an inch into the ice; teetering in precarious balance until a great bucket was beaten out and a security spike hammered in. We kept pitches short because our straining calves tired quickly and also because it was safer. One couldn't hope to hold a long fall. Using ice-pegs and screws for belays, cutting small nicks to rest on between quick staccato crampon moves, leading alternately, we proceeded rapidly and in comparative safety. But security on ice is only make-believe, and nerves as well as muscles were taut as we stabbed our way upwards. The angle wasn't that steep, about the same as a house roof, but the way the smooth giant of the slope plunged away beneath us to the meadows was awe-inspiring. It was a relief to be nearing the upper rim.

As I stood in the bucket step, protecting Chris's advance, I was able to look around me for the first time that day. From the foot of the wall a great dark pyramid, the shadow of the Eiger, reached out across the meadows to the tourist hotel of Kleine Scheidegg. The rubbernecks and pressmen would be enjoying their breakfasts. Later they would come to peer through the telescopes, to enjoy the free entertainment. Were we actors in some drama, gladiators in the arena? A long, low, plaintive note rang clear over the meadows and echoed across the wall. An alpenhorn. The old man whose daily task it was to play it for the benefit of the tourists was in position on his hillock. At first the sound was comforting, but as the day wore on, its repetitiveness became wearisome and irritating.

The upper rim went easily, sometimes providing a gangway to walk along, at other times giving a sharp edge for the hands. We tried to leave the ice-field too early but, quickly realizing our error, abseiled back and continued the long traverse. A steep little rock buttress took us up onto the flank of the Flatiron, the ridge which separates the Second and Third Ice-fields. We were high on the face now, going well. It wouldn't be long before we were clear of stonefall danger, before we reached the safety of the Ramp.

Down below us was a ledge cut from the ice, scattered with equipment. It was a grim reminder that the Eiger was not always in such a benevolent mood as it was this morning. For Chris particularly, it conjured up bitter memories . . . memories of the tragedy of the previous month when the Ogre had claimed his first British victim: the sickening sight of a body falling; the hours of cutting across an ice-field which, with a hail of stones falling, seemed more like a battleground; the weary, semi-delirious fellow countryman they had nursed back down the wall as the stones fell and the storm broke. It was an experience that he and Don Whillans would never forget.

Morbid thoughts were quickly dismissed; one's whole being had to be concentrated on the present. We reached the crest of the Flatiron and scrambled up to the overhang of the Death Bivouac. Glancing back over the Second Ice-field we saw two black dots, Tom Carruthers and Mode-regger, hardly moving, at the foot of the ice-field and inching their way *diagonally* across it. We were worried by their mistake but they were too far away for us to shout advice and we had yet to get ourselves out of the danger zone.

The Third Ice-field is the steepest and has to be crossed more or less horizontally to the start of the Ramp, a steep gangway which provides the only break in a 500-ft. leaning yellow wall. We slashed big steps and at one point saved time by making a long tension traverse from an ice-peg. The Ramp itself gave steep climbing reminiscent of the Dolomites. The rock was comparatively sound. We were glad, for this was technically the most difficult part of the climb. We enjoyed being on rock again. This didn't seem at all like the ferocious Eigerwand we had read about, it was just another great climb. But, on some of the stances were tattered remnants of polythene, occasionally a rusty can; some of our predecessors had had a hard time.

Wispy clouds, which had slowly been forming down at the base of the wall, drifted up over the face like a shroud, hiding us from the prying telescopes and baffling the sound of the alpenhorn.

We arrived at the Waterfall Pitch where the Ramp steepens to a shallow corner chimney. This is often, as its name implies, the most unpleasant pitch on the climb – icy water gushing down one's neck and sleeves makes a poor prelude to a bivouac. Today there was no water pouring down the corner, but a thin veneer of verglas covered all the holds. It gave one of the hardest pitches on the climb; inch upwards, scratch the ice from the next tiny hold; inch, balance, scratch, reach carefully and clip into a rusty old peg. Once or twice a foot would skid off its slippery wrinkle giving a tense moment for the second man but the leader was too absorbed in the next move to worry. After another section of clean, dry rock we came to the Ice Bulge. It was a short chimney with verglas on one wall and thick, bulging, blue ice on the other. We climbed it back-and-foot. Now we were in a funnel of ice which led up to an amphitheatre of steep buttresses which lost themselves in the mist. It was cold. Another rope move from an ice-peg saved time and laborious step-cutting and landed us on a gentle rock rib beside the ice-funnel. We climbed upwards, wondering where the start of the Traverse of the Gods was. We must be near it now. Then we heard muffled voices. The mists thinned for an instant and we saw, on the precipitous skyline on our right, a horizontal step. On it we could distinguish two small figures. We cut steps across the upper edge of the amphitheatre, traversed a crumbling ledge and by a steep crack gained the ledge on the arête.

Sitting there were two grinning Swiss. They introduced themselves as Jenny and Hauser. Although it was now only five o'clock they were going to bivouack as one of them had been hit by a stone, but they didn't need any assistance. They were going slowly; they had spent the previous night, their second bivouac, in the Ramp. We decided to press on since we still felt quite fresh and there were a few hours of daylight remaining. With luck we might even make the summit that night.

The Traverse of the Gods, a series of broad but outward-sloping scree-covered ledges, was almost clear of snow and we followed it easily towards the centre of the face, towards the White Spider. As we moved along, the veil of mists fell away from the face and the huge walls rearing up around us, plunging away below, glowed pink in the late afternoon sun. We looked out over the billowing clouds which still filled the valleys. We felt elated standing on that splendid belvedere, isolated from the world; it was truly a situation worthy of the Gods.

At the end of the ledge system we were confronted with a broad ice-gully leading up into another huge overhung rock amphitheatre. Chris had begun to cut the first steps towards the little ice-rib in the middle of the Spider when, suddenly, there was a tremendous crashing and roaring and an avalanche of rocks came thundering down the gully and screamed out into the void below. The sunshine which we were enjoying was loosening rocks from their icy clasps. Chris came back quickly and we looked at each other, shaken: 'It'll probably freeze tonight. Let's bivvy here.'

We sat on our ledge and watched the sun slowly sink below the cloud horizon. It was a cold night. We slept for a few hours, then sat talking and brewing hot beverages until it became light. Stiff and clumsy at first, but soon warming up with the strenuous work of cutting steps, we climbed the Spider. Jenny and Hauser, following up our steps, were just behind us as we reached the top of the ice-basin. The entrance to the Exit Cracks was a narrow gully of frozen rubble. The gully continued upwards until it became lost in a forest of overhangs. We consulted our description and decided that we had to climb a steep ice-filled chimney on the left. Chris climbed it slowly. It was vertical and fearfully loose, only the ice keeping the holds in place. It was by far the hardest pitch we had encountered. I followed with a struggle and we pulled the leading Swiss up to the stance to join us. I had run out half the rope again before I realized that we were directly above the Spider. Surely we should be going over to the left? There now seemed to be a way round the overhangs at the top of the gully line. We were annoyed at losing so much time as we abseiled back into the gully. It didn't help much when we had to teach one of the Swiss how to abseil and we weren't particularly sympathetic when he excused himself by saying he had only been climbing a year! But later, at Kleine Scheidegg, we were amused when we were told of the sensation we had created at the telescopes. Apparently there was tremendous excitement when it was announced, by an 'authority' on the climb, that the British party were attempting a new Direct Finish!

The gully line, the Exit Cracks, became easier and easier as we climbed upwards. Soon there was no snow or ice. We marvelled that these were the same Cracks that had presented such great difficulties to men like Hermann Buhl. But, on the Eiger, conditions can mean everything. We were lucky to have it so easy. We took off the ropes and soloed up to the final ice-field. Hard ice again; on with the ropes. We were on the summit in the early afternoon and our happiness was so complete that we ran most of the way down the easy West flank. In less than two hours we were at Kleine Scheidegg. Jenny and Hauser reached the summit at about the same time as we entered the hotel.

In the hotel the joy of our success was taken from us. We were told that two bodies had been sighted near the foot of the wall that morning. Did we know who they were? It came like a vicious blow. We felt shattered, sick with pity. Tom Carruthers and his Austrian partner were dead.

❊ (From 'Eigerwand, 1962' by Ian Clough. Vol. LXVIII.)

B. M. Annette

30 ❄ Solo

Desperate situations are not necessarily our proudest moments, and are difficult to describe truthfully; afterwards you wish that you had responded differently. Yet I do not analyse or try to explain why; I only write how I felt and what happened.

To be brief, when I arrived in Chamonix I was depressed, for my climbing partner had deserted me in Paris and I was now solo. His excuses had been long, explicit and, worst of all, reasonable. Sometimes a good row clears the air, but this time there was no occasion for one.

Looking for a partner in the Alps is not one of the greater joys of mountaineering. I had had it before; you are regarded with suspicion by everyone you approach, and it feels like begging. So I decided if I found no one I knew quickly, I would return home to climb in Wales.

But plans change. When alone, you are affected by atmosphere and mood more than when you are in company. And the dusty, typically lethargic continental platforms stilled my impatience. Apathy breeds apathy: what was one day, two days? After all, I would be in the mountains; perhaps I could go for a walk. When depressed I become cynical and, as I strolled the streets, I even found the guides in their white caps stupid. I did not care which way I headed; time was no object, and I mixed with the people seething round – the tourists, townspeople, climbers. I did not scorn the tourists; in fact I looked like one myself, sun glasses, tan, check-shirt. It was the town's cheap atmosphere that sickened me, the sense of one community preying on another. You almost felt that the mountains all around were unreal also. I stared endlessly at the river, rolling, boiling white with glacier particles, then settled over a bottle of wine in the Café National.

That night I camped behind the Biollay, as everybody else does. Some friends of mine had been there just previously, but they had all left, either for England or for other parts of the Alps, so that was no good. I joined a party of German climbers camped near by and, as you could detect immediately from the serious gloom over their tent, they were hard men, out to do hard climbs. When I helped myself to coffee, politely asking if they didn't mind, one just looked up and nodded. Presently someone else spoke, asked me if I had just arrived, and the ice broke. Then someone inquired if I was alone, but at my answer the old suspicious silence returned. What did I want? Would I get in their way? After establishing that there was no likely partner among them I told them to enjoy themselves and returned to my tent.

In the night it rained and I lay awake, not tired, yet unthinking. When time lies heavily, sleep merges into consciousness, and in this semi-trance hours passed almost deliciously, and my mood changed. The drops drummed on the canvas, persistently, all through the night, and you could hear the wind in the pines. Down here it was warm, but higher it was wild and, inevitably, someone, somewhere in the mountains, was spending the night out. I imagined the summits in the storm and felt the same wind round me, penetrating my lungs. Why worry about a partner? The mountains were there waiting; just a few thousand feet to be among them. I could walk up to one of the huts or do an easy climb, the Moine or the Plan, or even traverse across to Courmayeur to look for a partner there, at the same time getting myself fit. This last idea, at first ridiculous, gradually crystallized until I knew I had to go. Then I felt like a guilty schoolboy plotting some escapade, for I already saw myself breaking all my good resolutions. Temptation always beats me. Some people have 'good sense', but on the whole I do not envy them.

Next day the peaks were plastered with ice, and the Germans were even less sociable, grouped like vultures when nothing has died recently. That night the sky cleared, and next morning the first light warmed the tent quickly; birds sang, and even inside the sleeping bag there was a sense of the life of a new day. Today I could climb – but now my mood had changed and there seemed no hurry. If I never reached Courmayeur it did not matter; tomorrow would do. So I lay there putting off the start. Presently, though, I heard voices and, later, sounds of cooking, and I looked out to see the time. Mist rose from the saturated forest, the sun was not yet over the Dru, and all but one of the tents were still quiet: about seven. Perched on a stone with a primus beside me I cooked and watched the day awaken, and almost mechanically I was ready to move. Then, pushing through the forest, I glanced back just once to see my tent steaming in the new warmth.

The path led upward steadily and soon, through the trees, I caught my first vista of the valley, the square new buildings of Chamonix, white and efficient, the scattered chalets of Les Praz. Then I turned to my long grind again, enjoying the steady effort, the pull of the rucksack straps as I got my second wind. Each turn revealed new views, but I did not stop again. Several times I crossed the Montenvers railway, which was zig-zagging a similar course to mine up the mountain side; once a train passed and the tourists stared down at me like strangers from another world. Later, the Dru appeared, a cold, grey shaft into the sky, and from then on it was a

constant companion. The path wound into the sun, and splashes of light
and shadow danced about the stones in front of me.

But, strangely, I viewed all this like a prisoner, the physical sensation of
the exercise being no antidote to my solitude; and, although I was free to
go anywhere, do what I liked, it seemed pointless. If some guardian angel
had promised to protect me up any climb I wished to do, I doubt if I would
have been interested. A thin film of cirrus cloud, twisting itself into a knot,
showed some disturbance in the stratosphere which might well be the fore-
runner of a storm. Yet I was going on, getting higher, and eventually the
Montenvers appeared above me, first on my right, then on my left, then on
my right again as I zig-zagged upward.

At the Montenvers camp site I met a party I had seen before somewhere.
They had just started breakfast, and gave me coffee in a corned-beef tin;
there was no milk, but the corned-beef fat gave it a taste. We talked for an
hour, but they knew no one I could climb with. So I told them I was going
over to Courmayeur.

'How?'

'By the Torino.'

'Solo? You must be mad. Best of luck.' I thanked them.

The sun was now high and I had to hurry if I was to get firm snow. But
I did not hurry. No point: this was a holiday. Tomorrow morning would do
for the ice-fall, and this afternoon I could bask at the Requin; possibly find
someone to climb with there.

It was going to be hot, so I bought a lemon to suck. It prevents thirst.
Then I threaded down through the tourists on to the Mer de Glace. Once
on the ice I soon left them behind. It was like sailing away from a crowded
beach; now there was silence. When climbers appeared from the distance,
they soon disappeared like ships on a lonely sea; and the thrill that
precedes all climbs returned. Peaks now surrounded me: the Verte,
Jorasses, Rochefort, Charmoz, Grépon; mountains huge, bare, unrealistic,
against which I was just a tiny dot. Their size made my climbing ambitions
seem ridiculous.

But, steadily, I progressed, sometimes stopping to rest and sometimes
to consider the weather. Now clouds were massing over the summit of
Mont Blanc, and mist was boiling up against the face of the Jorasses, thin
vapours appearing from nothing, writhing and twisting, knitting themselves into a thick blanket. Then the summit of the Jorasses was hidden
too. A warm gust hit me: the Föhn – that was never a good sign.

Where the two glaciers meet, the Leschaux and the Géant, the ice
steepens, and the route through the crevasses is chaotic. Sometimes I have
been through quickly, but today I became hopelessly lost, traversing one
ice-ridge after another that led nowhere, or just to a black, gaping hole in

the bowels of the glacier. The extra walking seemed no trouble: walking here was no different to walking elsewhere. And what would I do with the time if I arrived sooner?

Still in this mood, I eventually surmounted the steep path up to the Requin hut. I bought a chocolate drink and went outside to watch the helicopter dropping supplies. They came down in a net, which was left behind. The machine was overhead for several minutes, so that you became accustomed to the noise, and when it swooped away silence returned unexpectedly. Just a net full of provisions and a distant dot in the sky remained of the episode, and the mountains closed in again oppressively, so that you could be conscious of nothing else.

But, after sitting for about an hour, I was bored with inactivity; the mountains made me restless and I wondered about going on. It was not unusual for the cloud to build up in the afternoon and come to nothing; perhaps it would be all right. This was just wasting time. A party coming through the ice-fall seemed to have no difficulty with the snow, so I went down to the glacier to feel it for myself. Could the snow bridges be trusted? To a certain extent the snow was wet. No, I decided; without a rope I would have no second chances. But as I sat there, growing increasingly restless, the danger diminished in my mind and the Torino came nearer. A three-hour trek, perhaps, maybe less. I studied the map and the tracks as far as I could see them, and formed a clear picture of the route in my mind, for if the weather continued deteriorating I would soon be in mist. Then I put my crampons on and started off.

At first it was deceptively easy; the snow bridges were big, solid; and the route was well marked with the tracks of others. I passed two parties of French coming down, then a party of British. We greeted each other briefly in English, then passed. But one of them stopped. 'Hey, you British?' It had taken him a long time to realize. 'What you doing here?' Now the others had stopped too.

'Going over to Courmayeur.'

'Why don't you join somebody's rope?'

'Nobody's going up.' On the whole mountain side I was the only one. 'Everybody's coming down.'

'On your own?' You could have regarded this as a stupid question, but it was natural. I explained that I had no partner and there was no one to climb with in Chamonix. 'That's why I'm going over to Courmayeur.'

'The snow's bad higher up.'

'I thought it would be.'

'Come down with us and join a party going up tomorrow morning.'

'I'll go on.'

'Watch the weather. Where Fred fell into a crevasse there's a hole. You'll see.'

I left them standing there; mad, I expect they thought, but how could you communicate, the way I felt?

After the ice-fall, on the upper reaches of the glacier, I grew more confident. You shouldn't fall into a crevasse in this flat place, and I had tracks to follow. But, almost before I knew it, the mist swallowed me up. One minute I had a huge view of many peaks, and the next my world had shrunk to a few square feet. The wind sprang up, and I donned my anorak. Now, without the view, it was impossible to judge time or distance; one step was like another. But it was halfway, I think, when it first began to snow.

At first it was imperceptible, light flakes floating in the mist, and it was no trouble; then it became thick, muffling everything, even the noise of the wind. I passed a hole down which was a black, bottomless gulf: Fred's hole, perhaps. I gave it a wide berth. Then I passed another – they had not been exaggerating. Underfoot it was becoming soft, and the thick flakes in the air and the gathering darkness made it difficult to watch the shadows, hollows and lines in the surface that revealed weaknesses. But I went on; that now was the only way – returning through the ice-fall alone would be suicidal in this weather. Gradually the steps I was following filled with snow until I had lost them. Frequent zig-zags to avoid crevasses made my compass useless, and my only clue to direction was the plane of the slope around me. Tacking diagonally up leftwards to avoid a section which I suspected from the twist of the glacier to be dangerously crevassed, I made regular estimates of the time, my speed and my position.

Then the slope steepened and the first effects of altitude and unfitness overcame me. Already I had climbed 6,000 ft. or more that day and ahead was a further 2,000 ft. Once, after stopping to rest, it was a struggle to force myself on again. A hundred steps before I stop again, I resolved; if I keep going like that, it will not be long. But I felt sick, and no sooner did I realize it than I wanted to vomit. I stopped again. I thought it would leave me weak and managed fifty more steps; leaned on my axe, panted and managed another fifty. Then I changed my mind; I was slowing down, getting nowhere, and vomiting could do no harm. Afterwards I took glucose and felt better temporarily.

But it was only temporary, and the storm developed rapidly. Now you had to brace against the wind. Visibility was three yards, leaving no distinction between air and glacier; every direction, up, down, in front, behind, it was the same blinding white. Every step was a battle; I panted, gasped, thrust up, kicked my foot home, moved my axe forward, then I panted again and the cycle repeated itself. When I slipped, wasting all the effort of a step, I despaired and slid down in the snow.

It was delicious to give up. And justifiable. Crevasses were now difficult, if not impossible, to detect, and I had no doubt I could outlive the storm. But, as I lay there, the wind cut through my clothes, and I unconsciously rose to my feet again. The rhythm of placing one foot in front of another carried me on. Now it was three steps between each rest. My stomach was empty, and hurt when I retched. The dark shadows of crevasses were blurred and danced about. Frequently I crossed one without realizing it, and I gritted, 'Concentrate, concentrate,' only to discover on glancing behind that I had automatically taken a safe way. This instinct surprised me at first, then, as I grew weaker, I trusted it; when my foot retreated from the snow and planted itself elsewhere I no longer questioned its judgement. Darkness would come, if not sooner, later; then I could sleep, and in the morning perhaps my sickness would be gone and I would be acclimatized.

At intervals I turned further right, towards a depression which led to the frontier ridge; but I ran into dangerous ground. Was I too high or too low? In my condition I was more likely to be too low, so I returned left and tried higher up. This time I got through. Now to find the depression. I peered into the grey murk, but nothing was recognizable in the general steepening of the slope. So I imagined the shape of the mountain, judged my position, then turned directly upwards, hoping my line was correct.

The steepness almost beat me. I slipped continuously and sank in to the knees. Snow clung to my boots; it was like walking through a thick morass. Exhausted, I took more glucose, and had strength for half an hour; then I needed it again, then again. I lost track of time, and gradually lapsed into a trance. You did not think about things any more. You moved when you could; otherwise you rested.

This may have lasted an hour, two hours, or more. Then the note of the wind changed. While it had been steady, I had been unconscious of it, but now, above the general roar, was a different, higher note. Then a wavering, grey, indefinable line appeared in the universal blur above me. It became clear quickly, for it was so near – the ridge.

I should have been overjoyed, but I was too exhausted. In any case my problems were not over. Now how did I locate myself? As I approached the ridge – carefully, for fear of a cornice; I did not wish to descend yet – the blast hit me. It was not going to be easy.

I studied my compass. Strange. I shook it and stared again; then checked the line of the ridge. Something wrong. But what? That black, howling void in front was Italy; it couldn't be anything else. Yet I was facing north-west. Impossible. The compass was wrong; it had to be. I strode several yards, leaving my axe behind, and tried again. Same result. And the wind, which I had last noticed coming from the south-west, was on my left cheek. *Could* I be facing north-west? I fought with the map against the wind, stared at it, but I could see nothing; the map was tearing apart, and I was too spent to focus on the contours. The fruitless effort made me sick again. So what was the answer?

There was none. Two incompatible facts faced me. Somewhere I had gone wrong. I had traversed at the right level, otherwise I would have run into difficulties. The error must have come later. Had I worked too far right? I knew from experience that I had that tendency. If so, the correction was to follow the ridge leftwards. Easy, if you looked at it that way and forgot every other factor. For instance, why was it a snow ridge? To the right of my route I had expected rocks. So many questions posed themselves that there was no hope of solution, and I rejected them all. My impulse was to go left and I followed that, shielding my face against the blast on the open ridge. It was a fight, a dangerous one, but it needed no psychologist to deduce that this was precisely what I had been looking for. Yet I do not remember thinking once, 'this is great'; I was too tired. Instead, I thought, 'I might make it, or I might not.' You had to take what the mountains gave you. It was strange that there was no one near; you felt the presence of someone behind, then when you turned they were not there.

By now I could not think, and instinct was my only guide. Through the blizzard and the wind, over there, was the Torino. Why over there, I did not know. If I was wrong, it meant a night out – too bad; I could only keep moving. And I thought, so this is what I've always climbed for, the ultimate freedom. Here it was howling round me, grey now, not white, and deathly. Was I glad that I had found it?

The ridge led down, so I must have climbed too high. Then I reached a row of sticks – for skiers, I thought; they must lead to the Torino; but after a short way, they turned abruptly down to Italy. I became suspicious but followed them. Then they turned back into the wind, and I was heading in the direction from which I had come. Perhaps they marked crevasses. Staring into the murk, I thought I could see dark shadows in the slope above me, but I could not be sure – not until they turned uphill again, leading back to my old footprints.

This was no joke: half an hour wasted, and I had got nowhere, just gone round in a circle. And time was getting short. You could not see it getting dark, but you could feel it. There was not much daylight left, but, as I lost height, not only did I gain confidence but also strength; and soon I reached a plateau. This was more like it. The compass was sensible now. The Torino could not be far, and I took the opportunity of a last rest.

Back into the wind I looked to where France was. That morning I had been down in the pines, striding up the path in the sun, speaking to friends, watching the helicopter. How things happened. It was strange to remember how I had stared at the crevasses. I wondered, what was fear? All there had been was pointlessness. Recalling the emotion of my first climb, a ridge walk in Skye, I wondered: why was the thrill (not perhaps the enjoyment) today not proportionately greater? Why did company, somebody at the other end of the rope, make so much difference?

The compass told me to beat against the wind, and I renewed my effort. But presently I met rocks. They barred my way. What now? Was I lost after all? Confidence had so run away with me that now I was shocked. But, I thought, no, the hut will be on the rocks. So I walked along their foot looking for a path. Yes! Here it was. The relief! I climbed a short way, then, not fifty feet away, was a dark shadow. A building. The hut? No, the *téléférique*.

But it was all right. I was now safe; five minutes, and the hut was in view. Inside was music. Of course: Saturday night, an ordinary Saturday night dance. After the unreal, the real seemed strange; it was even strange, my boots striking a solid, level floor. Ah, well! This strangeness would not last. Tomorrow I would descend to Courmayeur. There I might meet someone. Then perhaps we might do some real climbs.

❋ (Vol. LXIX.)

John Harlin

31 ❋ The West Face
of the Petit Dru Direct

I started mixed climbing of an alpine standard at an early age and found it much to my personal taste. I had never been very interested in pure rock climbing, despite its challenge; but a few years ago looking at the Drus, I became intrigued with their 1,000 m of sheer granite. It seemed to me that there should be a route directly up the diamond of the West face. There was none. That big diamond on a mountain which has become an alpine symbol has an attraction. So over a relatively long period of time, the desire and plan to do the Drus' *direttissima* took form.

Although I understand that the late Scottish climber, Robin Smith, had contemplated the route years ago, I was quite unaware of anyone's interest in this as a possible route. In fact, I was not sure that the 'direct' was valid. The nature of the route was not revealed until further study and an actual attempt had thoroughly acquainted me with the intricacies of the face. Once I stood on the top of the grey ledges themselves and looked up at that soaring face with its great barriers of overhangs, some of which were the biggest I had seen in granite, I realized the magnitude of the problem and was challenged.

Contrary to most route possibilities where one has the option of turning large overhangs, this route forces them to be tackled each in turn. Another rather negative aspect was the two great white scars of recent rock-fall which are inhospitable areas of loose, fractured blocks and detachable flakes. Nature has not had the opportunity to wash clean her sculpturing.

In the summer of 1964, the Drus' *direttissima* became a project. Royal Robbins, with whom I was in correspondence, advised me of a fellow coming from the States that summer. His name was Lito Flores. Royal recommended him highly both as a fine climbing partner and, what is more important, as a fine person. So when I met Lito in the Biollay camp ground, he was already known to me. Thus, Lito and I joined forces for this climb in July.

We put up a high camp on the *rognon*, a rock spur below the face, with the help of another American climber, Court Richards. Nick Estcourt,

President of the Cambridge University Mountaineering Club, joined us as well, for we were thinking in terms of a party of three with one man always prusiking with the loads. On granite, where secure anchors can be placed quickly, this is a good method. It allows the team to move rapidly and relatively unencumbered and with good photographic possibilities.

We had been talking earlier to Gary Hemming, who had convinced us that the best way to start the route was via the *socle* (divorced lower section of face) instead of the couloir. This creates an extremely long route (over 1,000 m). My disagreement was and still is, that this completely goes against the grain of the rock, thereby forcing the route a little too much. Anyone who has studied the face will see what I mean although, like Gary, he may still disagree. The rock of the two lower sections of the face has a grain, or crack and chimney system, that leans far to the left and is completely separate from the main or upper part of the true West face. Forcing a direct line in order later to continue on the upper face is to swim against a current. So, swim we did that summer.

One cold morning in July under clear skies, the three of us left our tents behind and embarked on our adventure. The *socle* went fast via the Robbins–Hemming route, and soon we were tackling new ground, heading slightly diagonally towards the top of the grey ledges, a system of platforms and scree just below the monolithic portion of the face. The going got rough, particularly the changing from one crack system to another in order to bear right to the start of the upper face. Flaring cracks and difficult climbing brought us very late and very tired to the desired spot at the top of the grey ledges. We had done more than fifteen rope lengths of highly technical climbing, both free and artificial, and we were satisfied. However, looking up, we were certainly intimidated by the fantastic problem that lay before us. It is very similar to the overwhelming impression the Eiger 'direct' gives from the top of the second ice-field – small man, damn big mountain!

The next day, we started up just at the left border of the first rock scar, and sure enough, the rotten nature of the rock caused some gripping moments. Higher up, small overhangs that we hardly counted as overhangs, being so dwarfed by their big brothers, suddenly became overhangs of 10 and 15 ft. Around and up one of these I bade Lito to take the lead to give me a rest. I was anchored just on top of the lip of the overhang on a small ledge to the side of my anchor pins. A little above me, Lito and a flake disagreed as to relative security, the pin popped out and down came Lito. I was pulled from my stance. The anchor held, while I in turn held Lito from falling an additional 150 ft. by the rope around my back. While our hearts were beginning to beat again, we watched the pack with our radios and down equipment bounce 1,500 ft. towards the couloir. Nick looked up from a ledge below and asked us what the hell kind of a climbing manoeuvre we were trying to perform. Luckily, a piton was left in the lip of the overhang, and we got a step sling on it. Then our eyes widened as the piton shifted several degrees with our weight. It held, though, and we got back to the belay ledge, needless to say shaken and minus some equipment.

We left fixed rope and retreated. That evening, during our descent, a storm came on. As we crossed a couloir near the bottom, we found the down equipment. Lightning flashes betrayed their colour in the stream bed. At least some luck was with us.

Disgusted, we went to the Dolomites. Even more disgusted, we returned later to Chamonix. It was evidently another one of those seasons!

Another attempt with Lito, Pierre Mazeaud and Roberto Sorgato ended with bad weather and high winds dampening our spirits just above our last high point. Finished with the Drus that summer, we packed up our high camp and left. The climb had long ago ceased to be fun.

Summer, 1965 – a new season – comes, but what a season! It would have been better if it had stayed winter, for one would at least have been able to ski.

We began the long-talked-about International School of Mountaineering and, despite the weather, it went well. I mentioned to Royal that of all the possible new routes this year, the *direttissima* on the Drus would be one of the most feasible because its verticality would not hold the snow long. Royal was particularly interested, this being his brand of climbing. So throughout the summer, we instructed in the climbing school with an eye to the weather and plans to try the Drus.

On one occasion, in July, we started on our approach across the Mer de Glace hoping that the rain would stop, and that we could take advantage of the beginning of a good weather cycle. However, on the second day, the deluge only increased.

On still another occasion, we got as high as the top of the grey ledges by climbing directly from the second couloir intersection. This route makes a straight line with the upper part of the route that we later did from bottom to top. We climbed to the grey ledges, after a long series of difficult free-climbing pitches quoted as 5·8 and 5·9, interrupted by one artificial pitch using the large pitons called 'bongs'. Here we received our weather report. Of course, it was bad, which meant another retreat, although the temptation was to throw reason to the wind and to blunder on. These many frustrations were hard to take.

But the dawn of a new day always brings more hope. It is amazing how this commodity is continually re-born. So on August 9, two thoroughly determined figures go over the check list of equipment as it is packed away.

Then comes the long plod up the moraine – hours of back-bending toil, the scenery never changing. There are tracks in the trail; moving specks are visible up the moraine, and others on the *rognon.* 'Good Lord, there's an army ahead.' At dusk we bivouac among Germans, Czechs, Japs, French, Austrians, British, Poles. These numbers may mean an accident or death in the couloir; everyone resolves to be first up. As we make our morning preparations, there are already ants mounting the avalanche-cone by head lamp. I have put two socks on one foot and one on the other, but we move off anyway; time is more important than symmetry. We do not rope up. The rocks whirl down the couloir barrel; already there are some close calls.

Despite the weight on our backs, we catch up with those in the couloir above. A large rock is dislodged by the lead, a German. There is a crunch near by as a leg is broken in the second rope party, another German. We climb by on the verglas-covered rock and ask to help – refused, for there are five to help the one. Sympathy is given to the groaning one, and off we go to our own brand of misery and joy. Royal's watch comes apart. Miraculously, we find all the pieces, and it still functions.

A huge rock-fall is started by a party above, on the grey ledges; ten minutes lower, and this would have meant death. Shouts and angry recriminations follow; then silence. Everyone, the whole international lot, contemplates the consequences of mistakes.

We catch up with a Scottish party on the hard part of the grey terraces, and then – onward to the start of the route. Royal asks to lead the first few pitches to my previous high point as I have already had the pleasure. He can have the pleasure. We gain altitude, and finally, yes finally, pass last year's high point. This seems like a gateway to success, as the Hinterstoisser had seemed on the Eiger.

We use a method of hauling our gear developed by Royal which, in my opinion, is revolutionary on this type of climb. Using jumars, carabiners and a sling, the packs are hauled all at once by an efficiency method using the leader's leg power. The second climbs simultaneously using jumars on the anchored climbing rope, taking out the pitons with no belay.

I lead up to the base of our second large barrier of overhangs. Royal takes over on 40 m of continuous overhanging climbing, somewhere between that which is called roof-like, and that which is called very overhanging. We dub this lead the '40 m overhang', lacking further imagination.

Dusk comes while I de-piton. Royal prepares some grade IV with a delicate traverse. Then by head lamp, I lead up to what joyously is a really spacious ledge. We bivouac.

Morning comes, and shouts are exchanged with parties on the original Magnone route; their down jackets make splashes of colour. We make a late, cold start.

Our route is 50 ft. left of our ledge, and I must climb down and across to start up. I climb down taking out the pitons. When I start up, I push the free climbing hard, so as not to put in a piton until well above the bivouac ledge. This makes it easier on the second man. Above the ledge is rotten rock in an overhanging crack with guillotine flakes.

The climbing is tense and dangerous, perhaps one of the most danger-ous rope's lengths of my career. It is delicate work. I have to make a succession of sky-hook moves to avoid putting in pitons which would dislodge huge blocks and flakes. A foolish free move leaves me nowhere. I use a sky-hook, a little chrome molly-hook that cannot possibly hold – but it does! And, finally, success and a belay ledge. Happiness is a belay ledge after a pitch like that.

The route looks easier above, but Royal finds it deceptively hard, and then, in this of all places, comes the ordeal.

Royal hears a whirr and shouts a warning. For me a sound, an impact, and white-hot pain. Incredible pain that overwhelms, that seems to go to the core of one's being. My leg is paralysed, and I'm certain that it is broken. A rock of unknown size having evidently fallen a very long distance, perhaps 1,000 ft. or more, has struck me on the thigh.

Royal waits on a piton while I try to drive order into the trauma of my mind and body. Luckily, I have muscular thighs, and this muscle has protected the bone; however, the stone has delivered a blow like a dum-dum bullet. (I later found out that the muscle and sciatic nerve had been extensively injured, for the interior of the leg bled and drained into the knee for nearly three months afterwards.)

Not being able to fathom defeat after so much frustration on the face and needing time to think, I advise Royal to finish the lead. I still think the leg is broken, even when the time comes to prusik up and take out the pitons. In order to prusik, no matter how gingerly you treat an injured leg, some straightening movements are necessary. In my weakness to the pain, I several times emotionally break down while going up those 40 m. And never in all the injuries of a long athletic and military career, do I force myself so much. (I later learned from a neurosurgeon that it was the trauma of such a blow to the trunk nerve that contributed to the general shock which I was having to fight.)

On the belay ledge, the top of several large, rotten flakes, Royal and I discuss the pros and cons of going on. Here is where, if Royal were not so eminently qualified for this kind of climbing, there would be but one decision – to go down. Leading for me for the remainder of the day and probably the next is out of the question. We decide to go on. Advising Elizabeth, Royal's wife, by radio, of our predicament and decision, we further suggest that someone come to the summit to help us down the back side. We predict a tough time getting down. Walking or easy climbing seem particularly difficult with this injury; for less vertical rock means more reliance on leg strength. This commodity is decidedly absent.

The next lead goes around the corner to avoid a bad roof overhead. Royal is soon encountering the same trouble that I had, for huge sections of the rock move that ordinarily should be stable. There is no security. Royal rappels from half way to take out some traverse pitons. This cuts down the distance that I will eventually pendulum, and I am grateful. He complains that this is probably his most dangerous lead in his career to date. Will it ease off? Hours go by with mutterings from above about loose blocks and flakes weighing many tons. As daylight fades, a small ledge is found, and the journey of pain is about to begin. First, the packs are to be hauled. When the hauling rope comes taut, I let the packs go, and out they swing, nearly 20 ft.

When one has deliberately to torture oneself by continuous and regular movement of an injury, there develops a curious sensuousness to the pain. One tends to analyse its dimensions in different terms, from colour to form. So up I move, trying different ways of contracting and extending the torn muscle. About the only relief is the change in the quality of the pain, varying from sharp spikes of accent to round deep rendering. White to red – Bach to Wagner – cry to groan. The 40 m pitch becomes a never-ending journey into infinite variations on a single theme, punctuated by the concentration of taking out pitons. Even the blows of the hammer and the feel of the rock take on sensuous qualities, unpleasant except in academic reflection.

The ledge is reached and bivouac prepared, while just above us looms a spectre. The largest overhang on the wall spreads its wings of shelter. A great roof, which for us humans looking up for our escape is a barrier of formidable proportions.

The night brings apprehension, while those ballerinas, hope and confidence, dance in the shadow of a stone roof. Our legs hang over the side, a bivouac position that never lets one doubt the spatial relationship of the situation. We are careful not to lose equipment to the void, and this takes concentration. Despite the tenuousness, there is satisfaction; and despite the leg, there is peace. The night is not unpleasant, and we do in fact feel the reward of our profession.

With dawn, our two ballerinas take centre stage, and our great overhang betrays its weaknesses.

In fact, getting to the barrier is more of a problem, but knife-blades and sky-hooks provide the answers until a gracefully curving jam-crack leads Royal strenuously to the roof. The roof is split by a crack large enough to chimney through. Royal removes his helmet. Finally, our lion is tamed.

Thirst becomes an added discomfort, so the icicles that now appear are very welcome. Two pitches higher, we come to the second rock scar, which produces another friable section of the mountain. The usual afternoon mist has closed in, but we climb out of it into the sunshine that seldom warmed us below. This penetration from monocolour to brilliance is joy. From below, we hear a helicopter working its way up the wall for a look at the two lunatics. But, when nearly at our level, the pilot gives up and heads away for the security of space.

Several rope lengths higher, we leave the rock scar by means of two illusive cracks around an airy corner. Then, at our closest point to date to the Magnone route, we pounce on some more ice. We even take time out and on our small stance use the stove to make water.

Like two gargoyles, we watch an oddly, if not shabbily, clad figure work his way out of the depths parallel to us on the Magnone route. Oblivious to our presence, he climbs in his own inner sanctum. How amusing it is to observe from our remote position. A man on a lead out of sight of everyone is incredibly private. I was never so aware of this until we watched this man as stone carvings must watch their counterparts. Finally, it is too much of a trespass, and we call to him.

Hearing voices from such an unlikely place, his surprise is pleasant to see. He speaks to his mate in a slavic tongue. So they are Poles. Greetings are exchanged, and we watch as a pack is hauled up. An ice-axe works its way out and hangs by a thread. We gesticulate wildly, but to no avail, as the pack is hauled on. Miraculously it stays, and we turn our attention to our own work.

We've had enough climbing for that day, so we leave a fixed rope and rappel down to a ledge below for the night. Our ledge needs improvement, so the master engineers get to work with the loose blocks. Some snow is found and all that is necessary to make the mountaineer happy is provided: a mountain, a good ledge, snow for water and clear skies.

I am particularly happy, because my leg has improved so much during the day. I have hopes that with my massaging it tonight, I can lead tomorrow.

The importance of leading may seem odd to the layman, for obviously my leg will not be up to par, and therefore inefficient. However, there is an element of enjoyment and pride in leading that is of great personal importance. Many of the factors that make up the climber's *raison d'être* are found most strongly when he is in the lead.

In the morning, after an excellent night, we are ready to go for the summit. Thunder in the distance, though the weather report is good, gives us added motivation.

I do in fact share leads, having great fun on several, despite the impairment. The leg makes steady improvement.

The helicopter shows up, and Royal takes pictures of the helicopter taking pictures. Later we find out that the journalist is annoyed, for picture after picture appears in the developer with climber taking picture of journalist. Despite this annoyance, a suitable photograph is run on the front page of the newspaper, while we are still on the mountain. The journalistic feat survives despite our apparent efforts of sabotage.

Finally, the West face ends, and from our perch on the Bonatti Pillar, we see our friends coming up to meet us on the normal route.

The packs weigh us down, and we feel the lethargy of relaxed tension. We still must climb several rope lengths of the Bonatti route before we reach the quartz ledge where we can traverse to the descent. As I lead a short bit of artificial, my step sling breaks, but I catch myself on the lower piton.

We reach the ledge, traverse and start down. The mist closes in, and it begins to rain. Obviously, we won't make it down today. We intercept two Swiss descending, but take a different line for reasons of safety. Rappel after rappel brings us closer to the voices of our friends, Bev Clark and Lito Flores. We and the Swiss reach them simultaneously, just as the storm breaks in earnest, and the light fails.

I apologize for their wild goose chase, since my leg has improved so much. However, we are all happy that I shall not be a burden on the descent.

The electrical display begins with the rain turning to snow. Two French friends can be seen opposite on the Bonatti Pillar in a very unhappy position. We cram in, three to a bivouac sack. Lightning hits near by, giving those of us leaning on the rock arm-numbing shocks. We soon realize that tomorrow our world will be transformed. The descent to safety will be very difficult. Royal has left his camera on the quartz ledge and is particularly depressed. Offers are made to go up tomorrow but are graciously turned down, because of the obvious jeopardy to life. When the lightning stops for good, I turn on the transistor radio and music warms the air both by its nature and by its incongruity with the situation. We all dread the descent.

The next day, it is still snowing furiously, and our mountain has a white, sliding, cold skin. The descent is slow and treacherous. I feel exhilaration and enjoy climbing down except for the drenching rappels. Finally, on the glacier, I feel like a dog tugging at a leash. I think to myself that it is wrong to feel so energetic.

Eventually, with shouts and laughter, we do sitting glissades down the last slope to the hut, after an exceptionally dangerous descent.

Much to the consternation of loved ones, friends, television crews and journalists, we hole up in our new shelter for half that day, the night, and half the next day. Finally, a helicopter routs us out to the unfortunate world of rebukes, congratulations and misunderstandings.

What remains of these efforts? A line on a mountain? An adventure recalled? Photographs? They are all empty of life; no, there's nothing left, for even memory will fade. Today puts an end to yesterday, but tomorrow can only create from efforts of the past. That is what truly remains.

✤ (Vol. LXXI.)

Mick Burke

32 ❄ The Good Guys v. The Mountain

After practising at failing on the Nollen route on the Mönch, and at succeeding on the Gervasutti Couloir on Mont Blanc du Tacul, Dougal Haston and I decided we would *have ourselves* the Matterhorn.

The North face fell a few winters back to a mass onslaught of Swiss, Austrians and Germans; and just afterwards Bonatti removed any chances of glory for anyone else when he walked all over it by himself one weekend. Just before our ascent three Japanese gentlemen succeeded in placing the rising sun on the summit in the early evening of their fifth day. For the mountain's credit it had nearly claimed Huber and Nally, the toes and odd digit of members of the first ascent, and had repulsed such famous men as Hiebler and Mazeaud. The time was ripe for another round.

Early on February 12, we left our Scottish friends in their beds at the Hörnli and ploughed out into the frightening night. First round fell to the good guys when we found the Japs' footsteps leading through the séracs. No obvious excuse was forthcoming so we had to continue. Easy walking across a genuinely un-crevassed glacier and the preliminaries were over. No luck on the ice slope in the way of Japanese footsteps so we started to cut. I'm certain now that we could have front-pointed that slope. I was just as certain on the day that we couldn't. Arriving at the rock we awarded ten points to the mountain. The cold was nearly as bad as the rock itself was. I had the feeling that there would be news comments the next day, of hell freezing over. The good guys pressed on regardless and eventually found the first Japanese bivouac. It wasn't the best overnight stop I'd ever had by quite a lot of stops. However, home is where you make it and anyway it was nearly dark. The day's climbing had been disappointing, at least from the point of view of speed: also the rock was very bad and some of the ice pitches seemed very dangerous, especially when I was on the sharp end. We gave ourselves five points for finding somewhere to sit down.

The problems of winter bivouacs are ten times greater than summer ones and another thing is that it's a lot colder. We were working office hours so we started at nine. If anything, it was colder than the previous day. We were hoping to get to the top that night but it didn't take very long to realize that we wouldn't make it. The climbing was very much the same as the day before, difficulty being caused where the loose rock steepened up. We reached the famous couloir, crossed over to the right and then went back left. We were still within 50 ft. of the couloir itself but we weren't too bothered because there were no stones falling, apart from those knocked down by leaders prospecting for better rock. Contrary to popular opinion it was very easy to get good piton belays. I don't know what they would be like in summer when there isn't the ice to secure the blocks but they seemed good to us. Still, we didn't have much choice.

Some time during the afternoon we reached the top of the couloir. This was our only route-finding mistake. We went right too soon and as a result never found the easy staircase which, rumour has it, goes to the summit from this point. After the proper number of rope lengths rightwards we reached the only feasible way upwards. We were still following the guide book despite our mistake. It was Dougal who told me that it was the only feasible way upwards and by coincidence it was also my turn to lead. The problem was a 60–70 ft. cliff composed of dry stone walling, but it was all leaning towards me. It looked dangerous just to stand underneath, let alone climb on it. Still, who is afraid of these slight problems? (Anyone who is, please get in contact – I'm forming a club.) For a short while the cold weather disappeared and was followed by a very hot spell. I was really sweating. I think I managed to get one or two pitons in. I was so frightened I can't remember that passage very well. Dougal came up and traversed across to the next belay. It was five o'clock so we knocked 40 pitons in and prepared for the night. We then threw away our bivouac sheet, just so that we wouldn't be too warm during the night. We had our two ounces of water and our cold bacon. The cold harsh night was at our doss.

A clear night. Lots of cigarettes and a clever Scottish trick with an anorak and a piece of string hurried the night through. Today if we don't fall over should see our finest hours (this year's). We traversed across to the Zmutt ridge, said hello to the sun, quickly said goodbye and hurried towards the summit. What a nice way to do the Totterhorn. Two-thirty saw us back in contact with the sun on the summit. We sat on Honourable Japanese bivouac site at the notch between the two summits and ate a few nuts.

So far, with the points it had won from last night's fiasco, the mountain was still way ahead. We scorched off in the direction of the Solvay hut. There were ten bonus points if we reached it before nightfall. That's saying nothing about the good sleep we would get. Despite myself trying to go head first down the East face and Dougal being stuck halfway down an abseil rope, we arrived at the Solvay hut just as the light went out. Our brave, faithful Scottish friends were there on their way to the summit via the Hörnli ridge. They refused to spoil us and allowed us to make brews for ourselves.

The next day saw us arrive despite ourselves at the Hörnli hut. We then awarded ourselves a hundred bonus points for cheating the mountain and therefore won the game. The prizes were awarded in Zermatt the next day.

❄ (*The fourth ascent of the North face of the Matterhorn in winter, February 12–14, 1967,* Vol. LXXIII.)

Allen Fyffe

33 ❄ From Zero to Astronomy

In recent years one of the most significant advances in climbing style has been the change in ice-climbing equipment and technique. The old step-cutting method has given way to climbing on front points and curved or inclined picks. Steep ice, if solid, begins to lose its terrors, and the old hard ice-climbs become classics. Luckily, at the same time that much of the sense of commitment and seriousness was going out of straight snow and ice routes, there was a move on to steeper, more open faces. With less ice and generally harder technical climbing, these routes are now the ones with the Alpine style commitment. Summer VS routes climbed in winter conditions as opposed to the gullies full of ice.

In past winters you laboriously cut steps and Grade 5 gullies were usually minor epics. One day in February 1967 Jim McArtney and I left the CIC hut below Ben Nevis in early half-light full of a greasy breakfast and trepidation, and headed towards the foot of Zero Gully. The climb looked impressive and conditions good but hard. About 60 ft. up, an 80° thinly-iced, trough-shaped groove ran upwards to peter out below some roofs: to the right of this was a solid pillar of vertical ice, on the left steep rocks swept out towards the Orion Face. Above this lower 200 ft. we could see nothing, but knew it was more steep ice. We put on our crampons, Grivels in those days, and holstered our blunt sawn-off ice-axes and peg hammers. I led up to below the trough and belayed on my axe and one of our two ice screws. Jim came through, left me with the pack and moved into the groove. An hour later and 150 ft. up he was below the roofs after some wild bridging on flattened-off ice bumps. The sole protection was a baby nylon sling which poked out through the ice and a poor ice peg 10 ft. below the two-step stance. Another hour later and a belay had been arranged, an angle in a V groove and an axe in the snow where it curled out into a shelf below the roof. The plea to climb carefully as the belay could not hold a fall inspired no confidence. The pitch dragged out in a hazy teeter broken by the shock of the snow shelf collapsing when Jim tried to give me some tension. Eventually I stood below the belay clutching Jim's ankles while he dropped the gear round my neck. The way was right then – a short vertical section of awkward cutting leading on to the front of the ice where it filled the whole gully. One hundred and fifty ft. later after two rock pegs dropped from a frozen karabiner, a broken ice screw, no protection, and continuous steep cutting on hard ice, I dug out a vague spike belay. Jim came up the steps, which decreased in size, shape and spacing as the pitch progressed, and led through. Steep but fairly straightforward ice eventually led to our first solid rock peg in 500 ft. At least when seconding, a pitch with steps was a fairly mechanical process except for the spindrift and powder avalanches filling up steps and cutting off sight and generally making life less than pleasant. Life for the second was none too good either though, with the continuous rain of ice chips from above.

What should then have been the last major ice pitch loomed before me, steep and bulging, green hard ice with rock walls splaying out on either side. Zero is not so much a gully as a groove between two huge buttresses. Step cutting was the scene, as small and well-shaped as possible, spaced for most efficient use, but allowing retreat. The only snag was the jelly-like arms and aching calf muscles. The pitch must have dragged in the cold for Jim but was eternity for me. Hanging on, cutting, getting nearer and nearer the limit, I came to the last bulge. A blunt arête of ice led on to a slab of ice, followed by awkward cutting round corners and over the lip. On the last move a step breaks; I hang and slip with iced-up gloves until a desperate last-ditch lunge gets me over, calves and arms quivering with strain, to a belay.

From then on it was easier. Short ice pitches at reasonable angles led to the final snow slopes, then the plateau in the evening glow, eight hours from the foot. We went rapidly down No. 5 Gully in the near dark, full of the joys of a good route near our limit, one we had done and had no desire to do again.

Then, four years later came a climb further left. It was a Monday morning, not early admittedly, but weather and conditions were good. MacInnes, Spence and I stood about mumbling about who was to lead off. It had only taken us since early Saturday morning to get here – more than two days from Glencoe to the Orion Face on Ben Nevis. First it had been the pre-dawn drive to Creag Meaghaidh, then retreat in the face of bad weather outside the van, then on the way back the Ben showed its face and looked better. We returned to Glencoe, went on to Fort William, then walked to the CIC Hut that evening. The morning thaw drove us down but Sunday night frost sent us back up again. So there we were, under the first pitch of our route in a state of semi-organization. The line we hoped to follow was that of Astronomy, a 900-ft. VS which took a line of corners and grooves and slabs. Because of the time of day and the length of the climb we took bivouac gear, since after the route finished, there was another 600 ft. of N.E. Buttress before the top.

With three climbers the system adopted was that each person led four pitches before the lead changed, the middle climber belayed the first man normally, and the last man through a jumar. The last man hauled the gear and used jumars to hasten things when possible. The climb was in hard but good conditions. The ice was good but thin in the lines of weakness and steep bare rock elsewhere, the type of climb where you looked up and saw little snow, looked down and saw little rock.

Anyway I was pushed out into the unknown by way of a short desperate crack in the toe of the buttress. This eventually yielded to a peg and suggestions from below and I reached a ramp of reasonable snow. Linked patches of snow and ice led me in two pitches up left, then back right to below a large left-facing corner. The climbing was good, technical rock and ice to a halfway bulge where the gloves had to come off to fix a thread. Bridge and layback lead up until the last move when an unhealed cut on my hand tears open, blood drips into the snow and a flap of skin dangles from my knuckles. A grey-coloured handkerchief turns red but the rest of the pitch is easy using the then fairly newly-developed Terrodactyls and Salewa crampons. My last pitch is a shallow flake chimney which is great – technical climbing on front-points up steep solid rock and ice to emerge right from our corner into a snow bowl and belay.

Kenny then takes over and disappears from sight to emerge 50 ft. higher – profiled on a steep rib, to belay eventually on a thin ledge directly above. The stance is small and the wall above forces you out and, as there is only room for one, I rest on my jumars while Kenny leads the next pitch, a hard descending traverse into a groove. In my suspended state I watch, as Hamish belays on his tiny ledge, Kenny works slowly up the groove on front-points and Terrodactyls hooked into occasional cracks, until he is up and the impending wall above forces him left to a ramp overlooking Minus One Gully. Hamish joins him and I organize the ledge to follow. The descent and traverse into the groove looks hard but the haul sack makes it easy for me. It is attached to the end of the rope that my prusik is on, so when it falls off the ledge I go with it and we both describe a graceless arc across the face and into the groove. By the time I rejoin the party they are moving off and it is almost dark. Hamish is in the lead now and working well until eventually a tricky torch-light section is reached, a traverse and descent into a steep chimney cutting the final headwall. His torch disappears; he eventually appears on the ridge. I help Kenny with a back rope and then pendulum in myself and shuffle to the top, impressed by the late-night lead.

On the top a bivouac ledge is prepared – a small shelf below an overhanging wall. Hamish has dug the ledge so gets the best position. Kenny and I huddle together with the gear tied on above our heads. A long night drags out to a misty morning. Everything is wet with a thaw well set in as we trudge up N.E. Buttress. We must go to the summit and all that! In the white-out we reach the abseil posts, and on down to the CIC Hut to scrounge a brew, then on valleywards.

Front-pointing up bulges of perfect green ice under cloudless blue sky is a Scottish myth. However, what can be scratched from the weather can compensate. We were lucky to manage that route at all.

❋ (Vol. LXXX.)

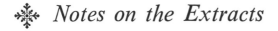 *Notes on the Extracts*

1. Edward Whymper – The Ascent of Mont Pelvoux

Edward Whymper (1840–1911) was without doubt the dominating figure in mountaineering during the early 1860s, the climactic years of the Golden Age of alpinism. He stormed through the Alps like a whirlwind: youthful, thrusting, ambitious. Between 1861 and 1865 he made fifteen important first ascents, culminating in the dramatic and tragic ascent of the Matterhorn. His great book *Scrambles Amongst The Alps* became one of the classics of mountain literature. After 1865 his interests turned to mountains further afield: Greenland, the Andes and the Canadian Rockies.

The expedition described in this story was his first, and the first ascent of Pelvoux by an Englishman. The mountain had been climbed in 1848 by V. Puiseux, and possibly even earlier by Captain A. A. Durand who certainly reached a secondary summit in 1828.

2. A. C. Ramsay – Llyn Llydaw

Any climber of today will immediately recognize the simple yet detailed description of this famous lake. Sir Andrew Crombie Ramsay (1814–91) was an eminent geologist who was instrumental in solving the geological structure of Snowdonia. He was an active mountaineer, taking part in the first ascent of Lyskamm in 1861.

3. Philip C. Gosset – The Death of Bennen

J. J. Bennen (1824–64) had a brief but notable career as a guide, including the first ascent of the Weisshorn with Professor Tyndall in 1861. He also led Tyndall on three attempts to climb the then unconquered Matterhorn, but he was a moody, inconsistent character, and it was this as much as anything which robbed Tyndall of the great prize. As the story shows, it was inconsistency which led to his death, on the Haut de Cry.

Gosset was an Anglo-Swiss artist and engineer who made a number of minor first ascents. He later joined the Swiss Federal Topographical

Bureau and was responsible for the first detailed survey of the Rhone glacier.

4. In the Cause of Science

A common justification for mountain climbing during the pioneering days was that it contributed to the great Victorian god of Physical Science. After sometimes hair-raising adventures, the pioneer climbers would solemnly measure the air temperature and pressure at the summit. When Leslie Stephen poked gentle fun at this pseudo-scientific activity, Professor Tyndall resigned from the Alpine Club in a rage.

The selections here show some of the more bizarre observations. Holland did little real climbing, but Barrett was a keen rock climber with some minor Alpine new climbs to his credit.

5. Edward Whymper – The Fatal Accident on the Matterhorn

The dramatic story of the first ascent of the Matterhorn and its fatal aftermath has been told countless times, not least by Whymper himself in his classic *Scrambles*. However, the piece reproduced here is his first account, written initially for *The Times* shortly after the event, and in response to the tremendous furore the accident raised.

Readers familiar with the story will notice at once that, despite Whymper's avowed intention to make 'a plain statement of the accident itself, and of the events that preceded and followed it', he does not once mention the rival attempt which the Italian guide J. J. Carrel was making at the same time on the opposite side of the mountain – and which caused Whymper to join with the others in a hastily arranged attempt from Zermatt.

6. Clinton Dent – The First Ascent of the Dru

The Aiguille du Dru is one of the most impressive peaks in the Alps. It rises as a great obelisk of rock above the Mer de Glace, near Chamonix: startling in outline and seemingly impregnable. A modern climber finds it incomprehensible that peaks like the Dru and the other rocky aiguilles around Chamonix were disregarded by the pioneers, who preferred the bigger mountains, where the climbing was on snow or ice. It was the second generation of climbers who showed that the smaller peaks were just as difficult, if not more so, than their bigger counterparts. Amongst these pioneers was Clinton Thomas Dent (1850–1912), a London surgeon who climbed with the great guide, Alexander Burgener. Dent made nineteen attempts on the Dru before he was finally successful in 1878.

7. W. Penhall – The Matterhorn from the Zmutt Glacier

The Matterhorn has four ridges, set at right angles one with another to form a rough cross. The N.E. or Hörnli ridge was Whymper's route of 1865, and the S.W. or Italian ridge was climbed by the Italian guide J. J. Carrel in the same year; but such was the reputation of the mountain that the other two ridges remained unclimbed for many years. 'It goes, Melchior,' said a client to the famous guide, Melchior Anderegg, examining the Zmutt ridge of the Matterhorn through a telescope. 'Yes, it goes,' replied Anderegg, '– but I'm not going.' (See Selection 10 below.)

Then, quite suddenly, in 1879 two parties set out to climb the Zmutt ridge simultaneously, and something of a race developed. One was led by Mummery and the other by William Penhall (1858–82), a strong and daring medical student. Both succeeded: but Mummery climbed the true ridge whilst Penhall made the dangerous ascent of the West Face related here. It is a climb rarely repeated even today. Penhall was killed on the Wetterhorn three years later.

The fourth ridge of the Matterhorn – the Furggen – was not climbed until 1911.

8. W. W. Graham – The Dent du Géant

The Aiguille du Géant, as it is now called, is one of the highest and most spectacular of the rocky pinnacles in the Mont Blanc area. It has two summits 85 feet apart, and the lower of these was attained by an Italian party barely a month before the climb described here.

William Woodman Graham (b. 1859) is something of a controversial and mysterious character. In the year following his ascent of the Géant he visited the Himalaya – the first climber to do so for purely sporting reasons – and claimed ascents of a number of impressive peaks, including Changabang and Kabru. His account of these climbs was vague and largely discounted. Graham's later life is equally mysterious. He is believed to have lost his money and died in obscurity as an American cowboy.

9. A. F. Mummery – The Aiguilles des Charmoz and de Grépon

Albert Frederick Mummery (1855–95) dominated the Alpine scene from 1879 until his tragic death on Nanga Parbat in the Himalaya sixteen years later. He stands beside Whymper as the most important figure in nineteenth-century mountaineering. Like Whymper, Mummery wrote a classic account of his adventures, *My Climbs in the Alps and Caucasus,* which in its final chapter revealed his philosophy of mountaineering and had a great effect on future climbing, perhaps more immediately on the Continent than in Britain. Something of this philosophy is revealed in the piece reproduced here.

Though he climbed with the great guide Alexander Burgener for the first part of his career, he later turned to guideless climbing and quickly gathered around him a company of brilliant climbers: Slingsby, Collie, Hastings and others.

10.   C. E. Mathews – The Alpine Obituary

The Alpine season of 1882 was a particularly bad one for accidents. W. E. Gabbett was killed on the Dent Blanche, along with his guide J. M. Loch-matter, and Lochmatter's son. On the Wetterhorn, W. Penhall and the guide Andreas Maurer were killed, whilst on the unclimbed Aiguille Blanche de Peuteret, the brilliant young scientist F. M. Balfour and his guide, Johann Petrus, died in mysterious circumstances.

These were skilful climbers with experienced guides, and their deaths caused almost as much of a furore as the Matterhorn accident seventeen years earlier. Queen Victoria was so incensed she asked Gladstone whether she should speak out against mountain climbing as a foolishly dangerous pastime – but he advised against it.

C. E. Mathews was a former President of the Club. To him fell the task of defending the faith whilst admonishing the faithful. His advice was regarded as gospel by British climbers for years to come, including the oft-quoted 'Whatever number is right, two is unquestionably wrong.'

11.   Ellis Carr – Two Days on an Ice Slope

An attempt by Mummery, Carr and Slingsby on the icy North Face of the Aiguille du Plan: a daring and difficult climb years ahead of its time. The climb failed – but resulted in one of the greatest climbing stories ever written.

12.   What the Climber Eats . . . and Wears

A *Which?* type of report published in 1893 as a supplement to the *Journal.* The full report is very detailed and includes the names and addresses of recommended suppliers throughout Europe.

13. J. N. Collie – Early Days in the Cuillins

Professor John Norman Collie (1859–1942), a scientist, aesthete and a man with an impish sense of humour, was one of the pioneers of rock climbing in Britain. He was particularly fond of the Isle of Skye and the jagged Cuillin ridge. It was here that he began his climbing career, and it was here that he came to die and be buried alongside his old friend John Mackenzie.

Collie climbed in many parts of Britain, in Norway and in the Canadian Rockies. In the Alps he was one of that élite band who accompanied Mummery, and was a member of the ill-fated Nanga Parbat expedition of 1895, during which Mummery was killed.

14. G. W. Young – Mountain Prophets

A wide-sweeping and perceptive analysis of the men who dominated the mountain world during the nineteenth century by one who was their natural successor. Geoffrey Winthrop Young (1876–1958) made a series of brilliant new ascents in the years immediately preceding the First World War. During that conflict he was wounded and lost a leg, which curtailed but did not finish his climbing career – he was active until 1935. In 1920 he wrote a climbing textbook, *Mountain Craft,* which remained the would-be climber's Bible for the next quarter-century, and he also wrote of his own adventures in a series of fine books. He was, perhaps, the most polished of mountain writers, and a considerable poet.

15. T. S. Blakeney – Whymper and Mummery

An alpine historian comments upon Whymper's copy of Mummery's autobiography with its acid marginalia, and Whymper's review of the book.

16. R. L. G. Irving – Five Years With Recruits

Nowadays, when adventure education is an accepted part of the curriculum and school expeditions to distant parts of the globe are commonplace, it is difficult to understand the stir caused by R. L. G. Irving, a young Winchester schoolmaster, with this lecture to the Alpine Club. The idea that pupils (albeit senior pupils) should actually be taken on real and quite difficult climbs without guides was frowned upon.

17. Condemnation

The feelings of the Club about Irving's audacity and his reply to the same. Some of the names on the 'Disclaimer' are rather surprising – one might not have expected Young or Longstaff to be against adventure in education. The Ice Club at Winchester was really just a few friends who climbed together, and their star performer was the young George Leigh Mallory.

18.   G. L. Mallory – Pages from a Journal

Mallory wrote relatively little, but this memory of a climb on Mont Blanc, recalled whilst he was serving as a soldier in France, has long been regarded as a minor masterpiece. In the years after the War, Mallory was the golden boy of British climbing, though in fact his actual achievements were quite small. It was the Everest expeditions of 1921 and 1922 which brought his name to a wider public, and his disappearance on Everest in 1924 caused a shock to the nation.

19.   Frank Smythe – A Bad Day on the Schreckhorn

In the years preceding the Second World War, no climber was better known to the general public than Frank Smythe. Smythe was a strong and competent mountaineer and, though he was trained to be an engineer, he soon discovered that he had talents with pen and camera that could earn him a pleasanter livelihood. He produced a series of books about his mountain adventures which became widely popular.

He was with Brown on the Sentinelle Route and Route Major (see Selection 20 below). In 1931 he led a successful expedition to Kamet in the Himalaya – the first peak over 25,000 feet ever climbed, and in 1933 he equalled the height record set nine years previously by Norton on Everest, 28,126 feet. He died in 1949.

20.   T. Graham Brown – Route Major

The three routes made by Graham Brown on the south side of Mont Blanc – the Brenva Face – were the most important new routes made by British climbers in the Alps during the inter-war years. On the first two routes, the Sentinelle and the Major, Brown was partnered by Frank Smythe. It was an odd, fortuitous partnership. Neither man was noted for having an even temper and they didn't particularly like one another – in fact, each tried to find someone else to do the climbs with. Strangely enough, instead of bringing them closer together, their success drove them further apart, and they hardly ever spoke to one another afterwards.

21. Erwin Schneider – Disaster on Nanga Parbat

In the years between the Wars, only the British were allowed to attempt Mount Everest, but the same restriction did not apply to other Himalayan peaks. The Germans began a series of campaigns against Nanga Parbat in 1932. In 1934 the terrible tragedy described in this extract occurred: four Germans and six Sherpas died, including Willo Welzenbach, one of the greatest climbers of the period. In 1937, an even greater disaster overtook the Germans on the mountain when seven climbers and nine Sherpas were buried in an avalanche. They tried again in 1938 and 1939, and were eventually successful when in 1953 Hermann Buhl, climbing alone, reached the summit. Since then, the mountain has been climbed several times by various routes.

22. Angtsering – A Sherpa's Story

It is not often that a Sherpa's account of some famous event is published, but after the Nanga Parbat tragedy of 1934, George Wood-Johnson managed to take statements from three of the surviving Sherpas, including Angtsering.

23. E. L. Strutt – Peepshow for the Proletariat

Attacking the great faces of Alpine peaks instead of the safer, more traditional ridges was not altogether unknown before the inter-war years, but it was this period which brought such climbing to the public's attention, mainly due to the dramatic and often disastrous attempts on the Eiger-wand. Austro-German climbers were the principal participants in this new 'extreme' form of alpinism, following the example set by Welzen-bach. Many died, and the traditionalists, amongst whom the British and Swiss were foremost, castigated the new movement, no one more so than Colonel Strutt, then Editor of the *Journal*.

Some observers attributed the new wave to National Socialism and there is no doubt the Nazis encouraged it and latched on to it for propaganda purposes, but it had begun long before Hitler came to power and was in fact a logical (if somewhat premature) natural development of the sport. The Eigerwand was climbed in 1938 by an Austro-German party, and has been repeated many times since.

24. T. S. Blakeney – Two Editors

The Editor of the *Alpine Journal* has always been appointed from within the ranks of the Alpine Club. The choice has not always been a happy one;

in this extract, Blakeney looks at two strong characters and their influence on the *Journal*.

25. Kurt Diemberger – My Finest Route in the Alps

The ascent of the entire Peuterey Ridge of Mont Blanc is one of the longest, most arduous expeditions in the Alps: a seemingly interminable ridge, bristling with difficulties. Diemberger and his companion made the third ascent in 1958, taking five days over it in order to make a film. The first ascent was by Hechtel and Kittelmann in 1953.

Diemberger, an Austrian, is one of the great masters of post-war mountaineering. He has climbed throughout the world and his record of high Himalayan ascents is almost without equal. In 1978 he reached the summit of Mount Everest.

26. Sir Edmund Hillary – The Last Lap

In 1953 Ed Hillary, a New Zealander, and the Sherpa Tenzing were the first men to reach the summit of Mount Everest. In this extract, Hillary describes the final ridge. The mountain has been climbed many times since, and by several different routes, but at the time it was rightly hailed as an outstanding achievement.

27. George Band – Kangchenjunga Climbed

In 1953 Everest, the highest mountain in the world, was climbed by a British expedition, and in the following year an Italian expedition climbed K 2, the second highest. In 1955 another strong British party under the leadership of Charles Evans returned to the Himalaya to tackle Kangchen-junga, the third in height. The attempt was extremely successful, as the extract shows: on 25 May, George Band and Joe Brown reached the summit, and on the following day this achievement was repeated by Tony Streather and Norman Hardie.

The 1950s turned out to be the Golden Age of Himalayan ascents. One by one all the highest mountains in the world – those over 8,000 m – were climbed for the first time. Dhaulagiri held out until 1960 when the Swiss finally climbed it, which left only Gosainthan (Shisha Pangma), a peak inaccessible to Western mountaineers for political reasons. The Chinese climbed it in 1964.

28. Ian Clough – A Storm on the Badile

By the late 1950s and early 1960s more climbers were beginning to tackle the great Alpine face climbs. A favourite, because it was on the whole not as serious as most, was the N.E. face of Piz Badile in the Bregaglia Alps, first climbed by the great Italian mountaineer Ricardo Cassin in 1937.

Clough tells of an adventure with some of his Yorkshire climbing companions. The guide they encountered, Claudio Corti, had attempted the Eigerwand in 1957 with Longhi, who was killed in the attempt. Corti became the subject of one of the most dramatic rescue attempts ever seen in mountaineering.

29. Ian Clough – Eigerwand, 1962

Ian Clough and Chris Bonington were the first British climbers to succeed in overcoming the Eigerwand, recognized as the greatest and most dangerous face climb in the Alps. Both men were of the new, thrusting school of British climbers who were later to take their techniques to more distant mountain ranges with great effect. Sadly, it was at the conclusion of Bonington's successful expedition to the South Face of Annapurna in 1970 that Clough was caught by an ice avalanche and killed instantly.

Tom Carruthers, who was attempting the face at the same time, had made the first British ascent of the Matterhorn North Face the year before.

30. B. M. Annette – Solo

Despite all the solemn advice to the contrary which they liberally hand out to novices, leading climbers often climb alone, even on the hardest routes. The increased danger is weighed against the increased satisfaction of the challenge. In the extract given here, Barry Annette was not attempting any spectacular climb, but making his way alone across a difficult tract of mountains. Nevertheless, he brings home forcibly the tensions and fears of the solo climber.

31. John Harlin – The West Face of the Petit Dru Direct

A very hard modern rock climb described by a leading American climber of the 1960s. In 1966 he led an attempt on a new direct route up the Eigerwand using siege tactics, i.e. fixing ropes to the face so that climbers could go up and down over a long period. Unfortunately, one of the fixed ropes broke and Harlin fell to his death.

32. Mick Burke – The Good Guys *v.* The Mountain

A light-hearted account of the fourth ascent of the Matterhorn's North Face in winter. The underlying seriousness is unmistakable all the same, but one senses the immense technical competence which gives the climbers such an advantage over those of the 1930s. Burke and Haston were both members of that élite group whose activities centred round Bonington in the late 1960s and early 1970s. On the successful 1975 expedition to the S.W. Face of Everest, Burke disappeared whilst making a solo attempt on the summit. Haston died in a ski-ing accident in 1977.

33. Allan Fyffe – From Zero to Astronomy

Whilst great advances were being made in rock-climbing techniques after the war, ice climbing changed barely at all. Then, during the 1960s, new climbing tools were invented which took away much of the hard labour and time wasting which had been a feature of ice climbing. The old hard climbs could be done much more quickly and new climbs, previously unthinkable, attempted. In this extract a leading Scottish climber contrasts two winter climbs on Ben Nevis.

Charles Stanley

Walking In Wisdom

Vidio or Audio cassette

ATLANTA GA   In touch. org

IN Touch ministrie

PHone 1-800-323-3747
         In Touch
         Box 7700
                    30357

In Touch Rally 2000
         Aug. 4th
         CHarloote, N.C. 1-888-730-4211